Elizabeth Lee, J. J. (Jean Jules) Jusserand

The English Novel in the Time of Shakespeare

Elizabeth Lee, J. J. (Jean Jules) Jusserand

The English Novel in the Time of Shakespeare

ISBN/EAN: 9783337032432

Printed in Europe, USA, Canada, Australia, Japan

Cover: Foto ©Thomas Meinert / pixelio.de

More available books at **www.hansebooks.com**

THE
ENGLISH NOVEL

IN THE

TIME OF SHAKESPEARE

BY

J. J. JUSSERAND

TRANSLATED FROM THE FRENCH BY
ELIZABETH LEE

REVISED AND ENLARGED BY THE AUTHOR

NEW IMPRESSION

London
T. FISHER UNWIN
PATERNOSTER SQUARE
MDCCCXCIX

*T*HE work here presented to English readers was published in French three years ago in an abbreviated form. Worthy of attention as are the older novelists of Great Britain, it was not to be expected that details about Chettle, Munday, Ford, or Crowne, would prove very acceptable south of the Channel, especially when it is remembered that the history of French fiction, not an insignificant one, from "Aucassin" to "Jehan de Saintré," to "Gargantua," and to "Astrée," still remains to be written. A compressed account of the subject, amounting to scarcely more than a hundred pages of the present volume, was therefore deemed sufficient to satisfy such craving as there was for information concerning Nash, Greene, Lodge, and the more important among their peers. According to the publishers of the book this estimate was not fallacious, and there were no complaints of omission.

When the honour of a translation was proposed for the small volume, it appeared that a more thorough account of the distant forefathers of the novelists of to-day would perhaps be acceptable in England; for here the question was of countrymen and ancestors. The work was for this reason entirely remodelled and rewritten in order to furnish fuller particulars on our authors' lives and works, and to extract from their darksome place of retirement such forgotten heroes as Zelauto, Sorares, Parismus, who had, some of them, once upon a time, been known to fame, and had played their part in the toilsome task of bringing the modern English novel to shape.

In writing of Shakespeare's contemporaries, care has been taken to enable the reader to judge them on their own merits. With this view an effort has been made to illustrate their spirit by what was best in their books, and not necessarily what would recall the master-dramatist's works, and would expose them to the extreme danger of being dwarfed by him beyond desert, and of fading away in his light as moths in the sunshine. Considered from this standpoint, they will not, however, cease to offer some degree of interest to the Shakesperean student, for this process makes us aware not merely of what materials Shakespeare happened to use, but from what stores he chose them. On this account such works as Greene's tales of real life have been studied at some length, and a chapter has been devoted to Nash, who, high as he stands among the older novelists, has been allowed to pass unnoticed as a tale writer by all historians of fiction. If, therefore, a large use has been made of the publications of learned societies devoted to the study of Shakespeare, liberal recourse also has been had to the depositories of old *original pamphlets, to the Bodleian library especially, where, surprising as it may be in this age of reprints, single copies of early novels, not to be met anywhere else, are even now to be found. Some other writings of the same kind, even less known, such as " Zelinda," a very witty parody of a romantic tale by Voiture, the " Adventures of Covent Garden," illustrative of the novel and the drama in the seventeenth century, were found in the primitive and only issue nearer at hand, in that matchless granary of knowledge, whose name no student can pronounce without a feeling of awe, because it is so noble, and of gratitude, because it is so generously administered, the British Museum.*

Engravings have been added, for it seemed that scattered as the rare originals of our tales remain, it would be of assistance to gather together those curious characteristics. They give an idea of the kind of illustrations then in fashion, of the sort of appearance some of our authors wore; they show how in the course of centuries, Guy of Warwick was transformed from an armour-clad knight into a plain squire with a cane and a cocked hat; and they exemplify the way in which foreign artists were in several cases imitated with the burin, in the same books in which foreign literary models were imitated with the pen. Objection having been taken, in the very kindly criticisms passed upon this work, to the absence of the only known representation of Greene, this defect has been supplied in the present edition.

I need not say that the translator of the portions written originally in French took the trouble to overlook my additions, and to revise my revisions. I need say

*that my heartiest thanks are due also to the well-known
Elizabethan scholar, Mr. A. H. Bullen, who, putting
aside for a while much more important work, has shown
me the great kindness of reading the proofs of this
volume.*   *J.*

    Saint Haon-le-Chatel,
        Nov., 1890.

CONTENTS.

PAGE

TABLE OF CONTENTS 5
EXPLANATORY LIST OF ILLUSTRATIONS ... 11
INTRODUCTION 23

CHAPTER I.

BEFORE SHAKESPEARE 31

I. Remote origin of the novel—Old historical romances or epics—Beowulf.
The French conquest of England in the eleventh century—The mind and literature of the new-comers—Their romances, their short tales 31

II. Effects of the conquest on the minds of the English inhabitants—Slow awakening of the native writers—Awakening of the clerks, of the translators and imitators — The English inhabitants connected through a literary imposture with Troy and the classical nations of antiquity—Consequences of this imposture.
Chaucer—His lack of influence on later prose novelists—The short prose tales of the French never acclimatized in England before the Renaissance—More's Latin "Utopia" 37

III. Printing—Caxton's *rôle*—Part allotted to fiction in the list of his books—Morte Darthur.
Development of printing—Mediæval romances set in type in the sixteenth century 52

CONTENTS.

CHAPTER II.

TUDOR TIMES — THE FASHIONS AND THE NOVEL ... 69

I. The Renaissance and the awakening of a wider curiosity—Travelling in Italy—Ascham's censures ... 69

II. Italian invasion of England—Italian books translated, Boccaccio, Ariosto, Tasso, &c. English collections of short stories imitated from the French or Italian—Separate short stories—Lucrece of Sienna—A "travelling literature" ... 74

III. Learning—Erasmus' judgment and prophecies—The part played by women—They want books written for themselves—Queen Elizabeth, her talk, her tastes, her dress, her portraits—The "paper work" architecture of the time ... 87

CHAPTER III.

LYLY AND HIS "EUPHUES" ... 103

I. "Euphues," a book for women ... 103

II. "Euphuism," its foreign origin—How embellished and perfected by Lyly—Fanciful natural history of the time—The mediæval bestiaries—Topsell's scientific works ... 106

III. The plot of the novel—Moral tendencies of "Euphues"—Lyly's precepts concerning men, women and children ... 123

IV. Lyly's popularity—Courtly talk of the time—Translations and abbreviations of "Euphues" in the seventeenth and eighteenth centuries ... 135

CHAPTER IV.

LYLY'S LEGATEES ... 145

I. Lyly's influence—His principal heirs and successors, Riche, Dickenson, Melbancke, Munday, Warner, Greene, Lodge, &c. ... 145

CONTENTS.

II. Robert Greene's biography—His autobiographical tales—His life and repentance, characteristic of the times 150
III. His love stories and romantic tales—His extraordinary success—His tales of real life—His fame at home and abroad 167
IV. N. Breton, an imitator of Greene — Thomas Lodge, a legatee of Lyly—His life—His " Rosalynd " and other works—His relation to Shakespeare ... 192

CHAPTER V.

SIR PHILIP SIDNEY AND PASTORAL ROMANCE 217

Of shepherds.
I. Sidney's life—His travels and friendship with Languet—His court life and love—His death—The end of " Stella " 219
II. Sidney's works—Miscellaneous writings—The " Apologie "—Sidney's appreciation of the poetic and romantic novel.
The " Arcadia," why written — Sidney's various heroes: shepherds, knights, princesses, &c.—Eclogues and battles, fêtes, masques and tournaments—Anglo-arcadian architecture, gardens, dresses and furniture.
Sidney's object according to Fulke Greville, and according to himself—His lovers—Youthful love, unlawful love, foolish love, innocent love — Pamela's prayer—The final imbroglio.
Sidney's style as a novel writer—His wit and brightness—His eloquence—His bad taste—His fanciful ornaments 228
III. Sidney's reputation in England—Continuators, imitators, and admirers among dramatists, poets and novelists—Shakespeare, Jonson, Day, Shirley, Quarles —Lady Mary Wroth and her novel—Sidney's reputation in the eighteenth century, Addison, Young, Walpole, Cowper—Chap-books.

In France—He is twice translated, and gives rise to a literary quarrel—Charles Sorel's judgment in the "Berger extravagant," and Du Bartas' praise—Mareschal's drama out of the "Arcadia"—Niceron and Florian 260

CHAPTER VI.

THOMAS NASH; THE PICARESQUE AND REALISTIC NOVEL 287

I. Merry books as a preservative of health—Sidney's contempt for the comic.

Studies in real life—The picaresque tale; its Spanish origin—Its success in Europe—Lazarillo and Guzman... 287

II. Thomas Nash—His birth, education and life—His writings, his temperament—His equal fondness for mirth and for lyrical poetry—His literary theories on art and style—His vocabulary, his style.

His picaresque novel, "Jack Wilton"—Scenes and characters — Observation of nature — Dramatic and melodramatic parts — Historical personages — Nash's troubles on account of "Jack Wilton."

His other works—Scenes of light comedy in them—Portraits of the upstart, of the sectary, &c. 295

III. Nash's successors—H. Chettle—Chettle's combined imitation of Nash, Greene and Sidney.

Dekker—His dramatic and poetical faculty—His prose works—His literary connection with Nash—His pictures of real life—His humour and gaiety—Grobianism—A gallant at the play-house in the time of Shakespeare—Defoe and Swift as distant heirs ... 327

CHAPTER VII.

AFTER SHAKESPEARE 347

I. Heroical romances—Their origin mainly French—The new heroism à panache on the stage, in epics, in the novel, in real life—The heroic ideal—The Hôtel de Rambouillet 347

CONTENTS.

II. Heroes and heroism *à panache* migrate to England
—Their welcome in spite of the Puritans—Translations of French romances—Use of French engravings
—Imitation and appreciation of French manners—
Orinda, the Duchess of Newcastle, Dorothy Osborne,
Mrs. Pepys 362

III. Original English novels in the heroical style—
Roger Boyle, J. Crowne—Heroism on the stage ... 383

IV. Reaction in France—Sorel, Scarron, Furetière,
&c —Reaction in England—" Adventures of Covent
Garden," " Zelinda," &c. 397

V. Conclusion — The end of the period — Ingelo,
Harrington, Mrs. Behn ; how she anticipates Rousseau.
Connection between the master-novelists of the
eighteenth century and the prentice-novelists of the
sixteenth 411

INDEX 419

ARIES.

TAURUS.

EXPLANATORY LIST OF ILLUSTRATIONS.

PAGE

1.—Queen Elizabeth in State costume, with the royal insignia, after the engraving by William Rogers (born in London, about 1545) ... ... *Frontispiece*
2 to 13.—The signs of the Zodiac, after Robert Greene's "Francesco's Fortunes," 1590. Towards the end of this novel a palmer is asked by his host to leave a remembrance of his visit in his entertainer's house; the palmer engraves on an ivory arch verses and drawings illustrating at the same time, and in the same way as the signs of the Zodiac, both the course of the year and the course of human life *p. 9 et passim* [*tail-pieces to all the chapters*]
14.—An Elizabethan Shepherdess, from a wood-block illustrating a ballad (the inscription added) 23
15.—Beginning of the unique MS. of "Beowulf," preserved in the British Museum 31

16.—Chaucer's pilgrims seated round the table of the "Tabard" at Southwark, a reproduction of Caxton's engraving in his second edition of the "Canterbury Tales," 1484 45

17.—Robert the devil on horseback (*alias* Romulus), being the frontispiece of several romances in verse published by Wynkyn de Worde, London, 1510 (?), 8vo. The history of Robert is illustrated throughout ... 57

18.—The knight of the swan, from the frontispiece of the metrical romance : " The Knight of the Swanne. Here beginneth the history of ye noble Helyas knyght of the swanne, newly translated out of frensshe," London, Copland, 1550 (?), 4to 61

19.—"'Then went Guy to fayre Phelis." From the metrical romance " Guy of Warwick," London, 1550 (?), 4to, Sig. Cc. iij 65

20.—Drawing by Isaac Oliver (b. 1556) after an Italian model, from the original preserved in the British Museum ; illustrative of the cultivation of Italian art by Englishmen in Tudor times... 69

21.—Frontispiece to Harington's translation of Ariosto, London, 1591, fol. This engraving and the numerous copper-plates adorning this very fine book are usually said to be English. But these plates were in fact a product of Italian art, being the work of Girolamo

ILLUSTRATIONS.

Porro, of Padua; they are to be found, in the Italian edition of Ariosto published at Venice in 1588, and in various other editions. The English engraver, Thomas Coxon (or Cockson), whose signature is to be seen at the bottom of the frontispiece, only drew the portrait of Harington in the space filled in the original by a figure of Peace. Coxon, according to the "Dictionary of National Biography" and other authorities, is supposed to have flourished from about 1609 to 1630 or 1636. The date on this plate (1st August, 1591), shows that he began to work nearly twenty years earlier.

It must be added that this portrait of Harington has an Italian softness and elegance, and differs greatly in its style from the other portraits signed by Coxon (portrait of Samuel Daniel on the title-page of his Works, 1609; of John Taylor, "Workes," 1630, &c.). It is possible that Harington's portrait was merely drawn by Coxon, and engraved by an Italian 77

22.—How the knight Eurialus got secretly into his lady-love's chamber. From the German version of the history of the Lady Lucrece of Sienna, 1477, fol. (a copy in the British Museum) 82

23.—Queen Cleopatra as represented on the English stage in the eighteenth century: Mrs.

	PAGE
Hartley in "All for Love"; Page's engraving, dated 1776, for Bell's "Theatre"	97

24.—Sketches made by Inigo Jones in Italy, 1614; from his sketch-book reproduced in facsimile by the care of the Duke of Devonshire, London, 1832 100

25.—Persians standing as caryatides, from a drawing by Inigo Jones for the circular court projected at Whitehall, and reproduced by W. Kent: "The Drawings of Inigo Jones," London, 1835, 2 vols., fol. 101

26.—A dragon according to Topsell, "The historie of Serpents," London, 1608, fol., p. 153 ... 103

27.—The "Ægyptian or land crocodile," according to Topsell's "Historie of Serpents," London, 1608, fol., p. 140 109

28.—A Hippopotamus taking its food, according to Topsell's "Historie of foure footed beastes," London, 1607, fol., p. 328 ... 113

29.—"The true picture of the Lamia," *ibid.*, p. 453 117

30.—"The boas," from Topsell's "Serpents," 1608, frontispiece 121

31.—The Great Sea-serpent, *ibid.*, p. 236 ... 125

32.—Knightly pastimes; Hawking; illustrative of Gerismond's life in the forest of Arden as described in Lodge's "Rosalynd"; from

ILLUSTRATIONS.

PAGE

Turberville's "Booke of Faulconerie," London, 1575, 4to, frontispiece... 144

33.—Another dragon from Topsell's "Serpents," 1608, p. 153 145

33A.—Robert Greene in his shroud, from Dickenson's "Greene in conceipt," 1598 161

34.—Yet another dragon, from Topsell's "Serpents," p. 153 171

35.—Velvet breeches and cloth breeches, from Greene's "Quip," 1592, frontispiece ... 190

36.—Preparing for the Hunt, from Turberville's "Noble Arte of Venerie or Hunting," London, 1575, 4to, frontispiece 205

37.—Penshurst, Sidney's birthplace, from a drawing by M. G. du Thuit.

> "Thou art not, Penshurst, built to envious show
> Of touch or marble . . .
> Thou hast thy walks for health as well as sport . . .
> That taller tree which of a nut was set
> At his great birth, where all the Muses met."

(Ben Jonson, "The Forest") 217

38.—A shepherd of Arcady, as seen on the title-page of various editions of Sidney's "Arcadia," *e.g.*, the third, 1598 242

39.—A Princess of Arcady, *ibid.* 243

40.—Argalus and Parthenia reading a book in

their garden ; from Quarles' poem of
"Argalus and Parthenia," London, 1656,
4to, p. 135 265

41.—" The renowned Argalus and Parthenia " :

"See the fond youth ! he burns, he loves, he dies ;
He wishes as he pines and feeds his famish'd eyes."

From " The unfortunate Lovers, the History
of Argalus and Parthenia, in four books,"
London, 12mo, a chap-book of the
eighteenth century. Frontispiece 273

42.—" How the two princesses, Pamela and her
sister Philoclea, went to bath themselves in
the river Ladon, accompanied with Zelmane
and Niso : And how Zelmane combated
with Amphialus for the paper and glove of
the princess Philoclea, and what after
hapned." From " The famous history of
heroick acts . . . being an abstract of Pembroke's Arcadia," London, 1701, 12mo,
p. 31. Not without truth does the publisher
state that the book is illustrated with
" curious cuts, the like as yet not extant " ... 275

43.—" How the two illustrious princesses, Philoclea and Pamela, being Basilius's only
daughters, were married to the two invincible princes, Pyrocles of Macedon and
Musidorus of Thessalia : and of the glorious
entertainments that graced the happy nuptials," from the same chap-book, p. 139 ... 277

44.—An interior view of the Swan Theatre in the time of Shakespeare, from a drawing by John de Witt, 1596, recently discovered in the Utrecht library by M. K. T. Gaedertz, of Berlin. Reproduced as illustrative of Dekker's "Horne-booke," 1609 (*infra*, ch. vi. § 3). Spectators have not been represented. They must be supposed to fill the pit, " planities sive arena," where they remained standing in the open air, and the covered galleries. The more important people were seated on the stage. Actors, to perform their parts, came out of the two doors inscribed " mimorum ædes." The boxes above these doors, concerning which some doubts have been expressed, seem to be what was called "the Lords' room." " Let our gallant," says Dekker, "advance himself up to the throne of the stage. I meane not the Lords roome (which is now but stages suburbs) : no, those boxes, by the iniquity of custome, conspiracy of waiting women and gentlemen ushers, that there sweat together, and the covetousness of sharers are contemptibly thrust into the reare, and much new satten is there dambd by being smothrd to death in darknesse. But on the very rushes, where the comedy is to daunce, yea and under the state of Cambises himselfe must our fethered Estridge be planted valiantly, because impudently, beating downe the mewes and hisses of opposed rascality" (" Works," ed. Grosart, vol. ii. p. 247) ... 286

45.—Elizabethan gaieties. The actor Kemp's dance to Norwich, from the frontispiece of "Kemps nine daies wonder performed in a daunce from London to Norwich, containing the pleasure, paines and kind entertainment of William Kemp betweene London and that city . . . written by himselfe to satisfie his friends," London, 1600, reprinted by Dyce, Camden Society, 1840, 4to 287

46.—Portrait of Nash, from "Tom Nash his ghost . . . written by Thomas Nash his ghost" (no date). A copy in the British Museum 326

47.—Portrait of Dekker, from "Dekker his dreame," a poem by the same, London, 1620, frontispiece 333

48.—Heroical deeds in an heroical novel. "Pandion slayes Clausus," from "Pandion and Amphigenia," by J. Crowne, London, 1665, 8vo 347

49.—Sir Guy of Warwick addressing a skull, in a churchyard, from "The history of Guy, earl of Warwick," 1750? (a chap-book), p. 18 350

50.—Burial of Sir Guy of Warwick, from the same chap-book 351

51.—A map of the "tendre" country. The original map was inserted by Mdlle. de

Scudéry in her novel of "Clélie," Paris, 1654, *et seq.*, 10 vols., 8vo, vol. i. p. 399. It was a map drawn by Clelia and sent by her to Herminius, and which "showed how to go from New Friendship to Tender." It was reproduced in the English translations of "Clelie"; the plate we give is taken from the edition of 1678 359

52.—Endymion plunged into the river in the presence of Diana, after an engraving by C. de Pas, in "L' Endimion de Gombauld," Paris, 1624, 8vo, p. 223. The French plates were sent to England and used for the English version of this novel: "Endimion, an excellent fancy ... interpreted by Richard Hurst," London, 1639, 8vo 367

53.—Frontispiece to Part IV. of the translation of La Calprenède's "Cléopatre," by Robert Loveday: "Hymen's præludia or Loves master-piece," London, 1652, *et seq.*, 12mo. This frontispiece was drawn according to the instructions of Loveday himself, "Loveday's Letters," Letter lxxxiii. 371

54.—A fashionable conversation, from the frontispiece of "La fausse Clélie," by P. de Subligny, Amsterdam, 1671, 12mo. An enlarged plate was made after this one, to serve as frontispiece to the English version of the same work: "The mock Clelia, being a comical history of French gallantries ... in imitation of Don Quixote," London, 1678, 8vo 375

55.—Conversations and telling of stories at the house of the Duchess of Newcastle, from a drawing by Abr. a Diepenbeck, engraved for her book: "Natures pictures drawn by Fancies pencil to the life," London, 1656, fol. 379

56.—Moorish heroes, from an engraving in Settle's drama : " The Empress of Morocco," London, 1673, 4to 393

57.—A poet's dream realized, from the English version of Sorel's " Berger Extravagant," " The extravagant Shepherd," London, 1653, fol., translated by John Davies. The usual description of the heroine of a novel has been taken to the letter by the engraver, who represents Love sitting on her forehead, and lilies and roses on her cheeks. Two suns have taken the place of her eyes, her teeth are actual pearls, &c. 401

GEMINI.

AN ELIZABETHAN SHEPHERDESS.

The English Novel in the Time of Shakespeare.

INTRODUCTION.

THE London publishers annually issue statitsics of the works that have appeared in England during the year. Sometimes sermons and books on theology reach the highest figures; England is still the England of the Bible, the country that at the time of the Reformation produced three hundred and twenty-six editions of the Scriptures in less than a century, and whose religious literature is so abundant that to-day twenty-eight volumes of the British Museum catalogue treat of the single word Bible.

When theology does not obtain the first rank, it holds the second. The only writings that can compete with it, in the country of Shakespeare, of Bacon and of Newton, are neither dramas, nor books of philosophy nor scientific treatises; they are novels. Theology had the supremacy in 1885; novels obtained it in 1887, 1888, and 1889. Omitting stories written for children, nine hundred and twenty-nine novels were published in England in 1888, and one thousand and forty in 1889. Thus the conscientious critic who wished to acquaint himself with all of them would have to read more than two novels and a half, often in three volumes, every day all the year round, without stopping even on Sundays.

This passion for the novel which does not exist in the same degree in any other nation, only acquired its full strength in England in the eighteenth century. At that time English novels produced in Europe the effect of a revelation; they were praised extravagantly, they were copied, they were imitated, and the popularity hitherto enjoyed by the " Princesse de Clèves," " Marianne," and " Gil Blas," was obscured for a while. " I say that Anglicism is gaining on us," wrote d'Argenson; " after ' Gulliver ' and ' Pamela,' here comes ' Tom Jones,' and they are mad for him; who could have imagined eighty years ago that the English would write novels and better ones than ours? This nation pushes ahead by force of unrestricted freedom." [1]

Modern society had at length found the kind of

[1] " Mémoires et Journal inédit du Marquis d'Argenson," Paris, 1857, 5 vols.; vol. v., " Remarques en lisant."

literature which could be most suitably employed to depict it. Society had been presented on the English stage by the authors of domestic comedies; Steele and Addison had painted it in their essays. But in both forms the portrait was incomplete. The exigencies of the stage, the necessary brevity of the essay, made it impossible to give adequate expression to the infinite complexity of the subject. The novel created anew by Defoe, Fielding, and Richardson, made it an easy thing to introduce into the arena of literature those men and women of intelligence and feeling who, for long ages, had been pleased to see other people the chief subjects of books and inwardly desired that authors should at last deal more especially with themselves. The age of chivalry was gone ; the time of the Arthurs and the Tristans had passed away; such a society as the new one could not so well be sung in verse ; but it could extremely well be described in prose.

As Fielding remarked, the novel takes the place of the old epic. We think of the Harlowes when in the olden time we should have dreamed of the Atridæ. While man's attachment to science and demonstrated truth is growing year by year, so, simultaneously, the art of the historian and the art of the novelist, both essentially empirical, become more highly valued and more widely cultivated. As for the lengthy tales devoted to Tristan and to "l'Empereur magne," we know that their day is done, and we think of them with all the pensive tenderness we cannot help feeling for the dead, for the dim past, for a race without posterity, for childhood's cherished and fast-fading dreams. Thus in the same age when Clarissa

Harlowe and Tom Jones came to their kingdom, the poets Chatterton, Percy, Beattie, and others, turned back lovingly to the Middle Ages; and thus too the new taste for history, archæology, and the painting of real life, all put together and combined, ended by producing a particular school of novel, the *romantic* school, at whose head stands Sir Walter Scott.

Perhaps, however, something besides poetry is to be sought for in these bygone epochs. Movements of human thought have seldom that suddenness with which they are sometimes credited; if those literary innovations, apparently so spasmodic, are carefully and closely studied, it will be nearly always found that the way had been imperceptibly prepared for them through the ages. We are in the habit of beginning the history of the English novel with Defoe or Richardson; but was there no work of the kind in England before their time? had they to invent it all, matter and method? It is not enough to say that the gift of observation and analysis was inborn in the race, as shown already, long before the eighteenth century, in the work of the dramatists, moralists and philosophers. Had not the same gift already manifested itself in the novel?

The truth is that the novel shed its first splendour during the age of Elizabeth; but the glory of Shakespeare has overshadowed the multitude of the lesser authors of his time, a multitude which included the early novelists. While they lived, however, they played no insignificant part; now they are so entirely forgotten that it will perhaps be heard with some surprise that they were prolific, numerous, and very popular. So great was the demand for this kind of literature that some succeeded in making an income out of their novels. Their books went through many editions for that age, many more than the majority of Shakespeare's plays. They were translated into French at a time when even the name of the great dramatist was entirely unknown to the French people. Lyly's "Euphues," for example, went through five editions in five years; in the same period "Hamlet" passed through only three, and "Romeo and Juliet" through two editions. Not a line of Shakespeare was put into French before the eighteenth century, while prose fictions by Nash, Greene, and Sidney were translated more than a century earlier.

As in our own day, some of these novelists busied themselves chiefly with the analysis of passion and refined emotion; others chiefly concerned themselves with minute observation of real life, and strove to place before the reader the outward features of their characters in a fashion impressive enough to enable him to realize what lay below the surface. Many of these pictures of manners and of society were considered by contemporaries good likenesses, not the less so because embellished. Thus, having served as models to the novelists, the men and women of the day in their turn took as example the copies that had been made from them. They had had their portraits painted and then tried hard to resemble their counterfeit presentments. Lyly and Sidney embellished, according to the taste of the age, the people around them, whom they chose as patterns for the heroes of their novels; and as soon as their books were spread over the country, fashionable ladies distinguished themselves from the common sort by being "Arcadian" or "Euphuizd."[1]

Thus through these very efforts, a literature, chiefly intended for women, was arising in England, and this is one characteristic more that links these authors to our modern novelists. So that, perhaps, bonds, closer than we imagine, unite those old writers lost in a far-off past with the novelists whose books rep·inted a hundred times are to be found to-day on every reading-table and in everybody's hands.

We make no pretence of covering in the present volume this vast and little trodden field. To keep within reasonable bounds we shall have to leave altogether, or barely mention, the collections of tales translated by Paynter, Whetstone and others from the Italian or French, although they were well known to Shakespeare, and provided him with several of his plots. In spite of their charm, we shall in like manner pass by the simple popular prose tales, which were also very numerous, the stories of Robin Hood, of Tom-a-Lincoln, of Friar Bacon, however "merry and pleasant," they may be. "not altogether unprofitable, nor any way hurtfull, very fitte to passe away the tediousness of the long winters evenings."[2] We intend to deal here chiefly

---

[1] Dekker, "The Guls Horne-booke," 1609.
[2] "The Gentle Craft," 1598. "Early English Prose Romances," ed. W. J. Thoms, London, 2nd edition, 1858, 3 vols., 8vo, contents: "Robert the Devyll," "Thomas of Reading," by Thomas Deloney, "Fryer Bacon," "Frier Rush," "George a Green," "Tom-a-Lincoln," by Richard Johnson, "Doctor Faustus," &c. Nearly all the stories in this collection bear the date of Shakespeare's time.

with those writers from whom our modern novelists are legitimately descended. These descendants, improving upon the early examples of their art left by the Elizabethan novelists, have won for themselves a lasting place in literature, and their works are among the undisputed pleasures of our lives. Our gratitude may rightly be extended from them to their progenitors. We must be permitted, therefore, to go far back in history, nearly as far as the Flood. The journey is long, but we shall travel rapidly. It was, moreover, the customary method of many novelists of long ago to begin with the beginning of created things. Let their example serve as our excuse.

CANCER.

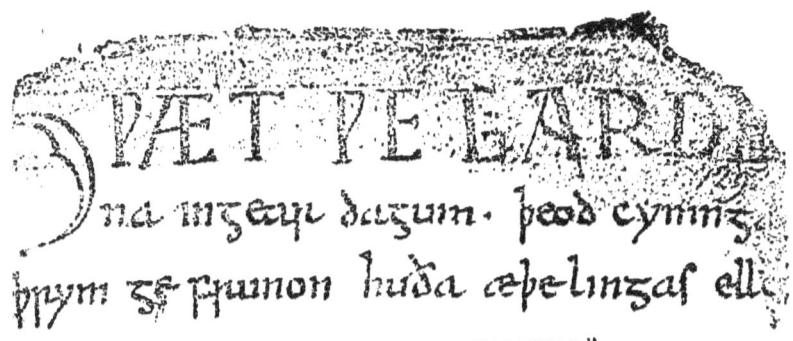

BEGINNING OF THE UNIQUE MS. OF "BEOWULF."

CHAPTER I.

BEFORE SHAKESPEARE.

I.

MINUTE research has been made, in every country, into the origin of the drama. The origin of the novel has rarely tempted the literary archæologist. For a long time the novel was regarded as literature of a lower order ; down almost to our time, critics scrupled to speak of it. When M. Villemain in his course of lectures on the eighteenth century came to Richardson, he experienced some embarrassment, and it was not without oratorical qualifications and certain bashful doubts that he dared to announce lectures on "Clarissa Harlowe" and "Sir Charles Grandison." He sought to justify himself on the ground that it was necessary to track out a special influence derived from England, " the influence of imagination united to moral sentiment in eloquent prose." But this neglect can be explained still better.

We can at need fix the exact period of the origin of the drama. It is not the same with the novel. We may go as far back as we please, yet we find the thin ramifications of the novel, and we may say literally that it is as old as the world itself. Like man himself, was not the world rocked in the cradle of its childhood to the accompaniment of stories and tales? Some were boldly marvellous; others have been called historical; but very often, in spite of the dignity of the name, the "histories" were nothing but collections of traditions, of legends, of fictions: a kind of novel. This noble antiquity might doubtless have been invoked as a further justification by M. Villemain and have confirmed the reasons drawn from the "moral sentiment and eloquence" of novels, reasons which were such as to rather curtail the scope of his lectures.

In England as much and even more than with any other modern nation, novelists can pride themselves upon a long line of ancestors. They can, without abusing the license permitted to genealogists, go back to the time when the English did not inhabit England, when London, like Paris, was peopled by latinised Celts, and when the ancestors of the puritans sacrificed to the god Thor. The novelists indeed can show that the beginning of their history is lost in the abysm of time. They can recall the fact that the Anglo-Saxons, when they came to dwell in the island of Britain, brought with them songs and legends, whence was evolved the strange poem of "Beowulf,"[1] the first epic,

---

[1] "Beowulf, a heroic poem," ed. T. Arnold, London, 1876, 8vo. The unique MS. of this poem, discovered in the last century, is

the most ancient history, and the oldest English romance. In it, truth is mingled with fiction ; besides the wonders performed by the hero, a destroyer of monsters, we find a great battle mentioned by Gregory of Tours, where the Frenchmen, that were to be, cut to pieces the Englishmen that were to be ; the first act of that bloody tragedy continued afterwards at Hastings, Crécy, Agincourt, Fontenoy, and Waterloo.

The battle of Hastings which made England subject to men from France resulted in a complete transformation of the literature of the Teutonic inhabitants of the island. Anglo-Saxon literature had had moments of brilliance at the time of Alfred, and afterwards at that of Saint Dunstan ; then it had fallen into decay. By careful search, accents of joy, though of strange character, may be discovered in the texts which now represent that ancient literature. Taking it as a whole, however, this literature was sad ; a cloud of melancholy enveloped it, like those penetrating mists, observed by Pytheas and the oldest travellers, which rose from the marshes of the island and concealed the outlines of its impenetrable forests. But the conquerors who came from Normandy, from Brittany, from Anjou, from all the provinces of France, were of a cheerful temperament ; they were happy : everything went well with them. They brought with them the gaiety, the wit, the sunshine of the south, uniting the spirit of the Gascon with the tenacity of the Norman. Noisy and great talkers, when once they became masters of the

preserved at the British Museum ; it has been reproduced in facsimile by the Early English Text Society (Ed. J. Zupitza, 1882, 8vo). We give in fac-simile the first few lines of the MS.

country, they straightway put an end to the already dying literature of the conquered race and substituted their own. God forbid that they should listen to the lamentations of the Anglo-Saxon mariner or traveller ! They had no concern with their miserable dirges. "Long live Christ who loves the French !"[1] Even in the laws and religion of the French there now and then appeared marks of their irrepressible *entrain*. Shall we not, then, find it in their stories?

The new-comers liked tales of two kinds. First, they delighted in stories of chivalry, where they found marvellous exploits differing little from their own. They had seen the son of Herleva, a tanner's daughter of Falaise, win a kingdom in a battle, in course of which the cares of a conqueror had not prevented him from making jokes. When, therefore, they wrote a romance, they might well attribute extraordinary adventures and rare courage to Roland, Arthur and Lancelot : in face of the behaviour of the bastard of Normandy, it would be difficult to tax the exploits attributed to those heroes with improbability. The numberless epic romances in which they delighted had no resemblance with the "Beowulf" of old. These stories were no longer filled with mere deeds of valour, but also with acts of courtesy ; they were full of love and tenderness. Even in the more Germanic of their poems, in "Roland," the hero is shaken by his emotions, and is to be seen shedding tears. Far greater is the part allotted to the gentler feelings in the epics of a subsequent date, in those written for the English Queen Eleanor, by Benoit

[1] " Vivat qui Francos diligit Christus ! " ("Prologue of the Salic Law," Pardessus, 1843, p. 345.)

de Sainte More in the twelfth century, which tell for the first time of the loves of Troilus and Cressida; in those dedicated to Arthur and his knights, where the favour of the mortal deities of whom the heroes are enamoured, is responsible for more feats of chivalry than is the search after the mysterious Grail.

They can take Constantinople, or destroy the Roman armies ; they can fight green giants and strange monsters, besiege castles of steel, put traitors to death, and escape even the evil practices of enchanters ; but they cannot conquer their passions. All the enemies they have in common with Beowulf, be they men or armies, monsters or sorcerers, they can fight and subdue; but enemies unknown to the Gothic warrior oppose them now more effectually than giants, stormy seas, or armed battalions; enemies that are always present, that are not to be destroyed in battle nor left behind in flight : their own indomitable loves and desires. What would the conqueror of Grendel have thought of such descendants ? One word in his story answers the question : " Better it is," says he, " for every man, that he avenge his friend than that he mourn much." This is the nearest approach to tenderness discoverable in the whole epic of " Beowulf."

In this contest between heroes differing so greatly in their notion of the duties and possibilities of life with whom do we side, we of to-day? With Beowulf or with Lancelot ? Which of the two has survived ? Which of them is nearest of kin to us ? Under various names and under very different conditions, Lancelot still continues to live in our thoughts and to play his part in our stories. We shall find him in the pages of Walter Scott; he is present in the novels of George Eliot. For better or for worse, the literature begun in England by the conquerors at the battle of Hastings still reigns paramount.

Moreover, the new possessors of the English country were fond of tales and short stories, either moving or amusing, in which a word would make the reader laugh or make him thoughtful; but where there was no tirade, no declamation, no loud emphasis, no vague speculation, a style of writing quite unknown to the islanders and contrary to their genius. When they returned of an evening to their huge and impregnable castles, in perfect security and in good humour, they liked to hear recited stories in prose, some of which are still extant and will never be read without pleasure: the story of Floire and Blanchefleur, for instance, or perhaps, also that of Aucassin, who preferred "his gentle love" to paradise even more unconcernedly than the lover in the old song rejected the gift of "Paris la grand ville;" of Aucassin, in whose adventures the Almighty interposes, not in the manner of the Jehovah of the Bible, but as "God who loveth lovers;"[1] and where Nicolete is so very beautiful that the touch of her fair hands is enough to heal sick people. According to the author the same wonder is performed by the tale itself; it heals sorrow:

---

[1] "Nouvelles Françaises en prose," ed. Moland and d'Héricault, Paris, 1856. Four English versions of the story of Floire and Blanchefleur are extant. The story of Amis and Amile was also very popular. "Amis and Amiloun," ed. Kölbing (Heilbronn, 1884). The cantefable of Aucassin is of the twelfth century (G. Paris, "Littérature française au moyen âge," 1888, § 51).

> "Sweet the song, the story sweet,
> There is no man hearkens it,
> No man living 'neath the sun,
> So outwearied, so foredone,
> Sick and woful, worn and sad,
> But is healed, but is glad
>   'Tis so sweet."[1]

So speaks the author, and since his time the performance of the same miracle has been the aim of the many tale-writers of all countries; they have not all of them failed.

The fusion of these two sorts of stories, the epic-romance and the tale, produced long afterwards in every country of Europe the novel as we know it now. To the former, the novel owes more especially its width of subject, its wealth of incident, its occasionally dignified gait; to the second, its delicacy of observation, its skill in expression of detail, its naturalness, its realism. If we care to examine them closely, we shall find in the greater number of those familiar tragi-comedies, which are the novels of our own day, discernible traces of their twofold and far-off origin.

II.

The first result of the diffusion in England, after the Conquest, of a new literature full of southern inventions and gaieties, and loves, and follies, was the silencing of the native singers. This silence lasted for a hundred

---

[1] Mr. Andrew Lang's translation, "Aucassin and Nicolete" (London, 1887, 16mo.).

years; the very language seemed doomed to disappear. What was the good of writing in English, when there was hardly any one who cared to read it, and even those few were learning French, and coming by degrees to enjoy the new literature? But it turned out that the native English writers had not been swept away for ever. Their race, though silenced, was not extinct; they were not dead, but only asleep.

The first to awake were the scholars, the men who had studied in Paris. It was quite natural that they should be less deeply impressed with nationalism than the rest of their compatriots; learning had made them cosmopolitan; they belonged less to England than to the Latin country, and the Latin country had not suffered from the Conquest. Numerous scholars of English origin shone forth as authors from the twelfth century onwards; among them Geoffrey of Monmouth, of Arthurian fame, Joseph of Exeter, John of Salisbury, Walter Map, Nigel Wireker, and many others of European reputation.

In the thirteenth century another awakening takes place in the palace which the Norman enchanter had doomed to a temporary sleep. Translators and imitators set to work; the English language is again employed; the storm has abated, and it has become evident that there still remain people of English blood and language for whom it is worth while to write. Innumerable books are composed for them, that they may learn, ignorant as they are of French or Latin, what is the thought of the day. Robert Manning de Brunne states, in the beginning of the fourteenth century, that he writes:

> "Not for the lerid bot for the lewed,
> Ffor tho that in this land wone,
> That the Latyn no Frankys cone,
> Ffor to haf solace and gamen
> In felawschip when thay sitt samen '

They are to enjoy this new literature in common, be it religious, be it imaginative or historical ; they will discuss it and it will improve their minds ; it will teach them to pass judgments even on kings :

> " And gude it is for many thynges
> For to here the dedis of kynges
> Whilk were foles and whilk were wyse." [1]

In their turn the English poets sang of Arthur ; in all good faith they adopted his glory as that of an ancestor of their own. Among them a man like Layamon accepted the French poet Wace for his model, and in the beginning of the thirteenth century, devoted thirty-two thousand lines to the Celtic hero ; nor was he ever disturbed by the thought that Arthur's British victories might have possibly been English defeats.[2] Then came innumerable poems, translated or imitated from French romances, on Charlemagne and Roland, Gawain and the Green Knight, Bovon of Hanstone, Percival, Havelock the Dane, King Horn, Guy of Warwick, Alexander, Octavian, and the Trojan War.[3]

[1] "The Story of England," A.D. 1338, ed. F. J. Furnivall, London, 1887, two vols. 8vo, vol. i. p. 1.

[2] " Layamon's Brut," ed. Madden, London, 1847, three vols. 8vo.

[3] See, among others, the publications of the Early English Text Society, the Camden Society, he Percy Society, the Roxburghe Club, the Bannatyne Club, the Altenglische Bibliothek of E

Hundreds of manuscripts, some of them splendidly illuminated, testify at the present day to the immense popularity of these imitations of French originals, and provide endless labour for the many learned societies that in our century have undertaken to print them.

Layamon's indifference to the price paid by his compatriots for Arthur's glory was not peculiar to himself. It is characteristic of a policy of amalgamation deliberately followed from the beginning by the Normans. As soon as they were settled in the country they desired to unify the traditions of the various races inhabiting the great island, in the belief that this was a first and necessary step towards uniting the races themselves. Rarely was literature used for political purposes with more cleverness and with more important results. The conquerors set the example themselves, and from the first adopted and treated all the heroic beings who had won glory in or for England, and whose fame lingered in ballads and popular songs, as if they had been personal ancestors of their own. At the same time they

Kölbing (Heilbronn); the "Metrical Romances of the XIIIth, XIVth, and XVth Centuries," of H. W. Weber (Edinburgh, 1810, three vols. 8vo); the "Catalogue of MS. Romances in the British Museum," by H. L. D. Ward (London, 1887); "Bishop Percy's Folio MS. ; Ballads and Romances," ed. J. W. Hales and F. J. Furnivall, London, Ballad Society, 1867, &c.

The publications of the Early English Text Society include, among others, the romances of "Ferumbras," "Otuel," "Huon of Burdeux," "Charles the Grete," "Four Sons of Aymon," "Sir Bevis of Hanston," "King Horn," with fragments of "Floriz and Blauncheflur," "Havelok the Dane," "Guy of Warwick," "William of Palerne," "Generides," "Morte Arthure," Lonelich's "History of the Holy Grail," "Joseph of Arimathie," "Sir Gawaine and the Green Knight," &c. Others are in preparation.

induced the conquered race to adopt the theory that mythic Trojans were their progenitors, a theory already discovered and applied by the French to their own early history, and about which fables were already current among the Welsh people : both races were thus connected together as lineal descendants, the one of Brutus, the other of Francus ; and an indissoluble link united them to the classic nations of antiquity.[1] So it

[1] The adoption by Geoffrey of Monmouth, in the twelfth century, of Brutus the Trojan as father of the British race, as Nennius had done two centuries earlier, did much for the spreading of this belief; the popularity and authority of Geoffrey's fabulous history was so great that for several centuries the gravest English historians accepted his statements concerning Brutus without hesitation. Matthew Paris, the most accurate and trustworthy historian of the thirteenth century, gives an account of his coming to the island of Albion, "that was then inhabited by nobody but a few giants": "Erat tunc nomen insulæ Albion, quæ a nemine, exceptis paucis gigantibus habitabatur." Brutus proceeds to the banks of the Thames, and there founds his capital, which he calls the New Troy, Trojam novam, "quæ postea, per corruptionem vocabuli Trinovantum dicta fuerit" ("Chronica Majora," Rolls Series, I. pp. 21–22). In the fourteenth century Ralph, in his famous "Polychronicon," gives exactly the same account of the deeds of the Trojan prince, and they continued in the time of Shakespeare to be *history*. Here is the learned account Holinshed gives of these events in his "Chronicles":

"Hitherto have we spoken of the inhabitants of this Ile before the coming of Brute, although some will needs have it that he was the first which inhabited the same with his people descended of the Troians, some few giants onelie excepted whom he utterlie destroied, and left not one of them alive through the whole ile. But as we shall not doubt of Brutes coming hither . . ." &c.

' This Brutus or Brytus (for this letter Y hath of ancient times had the sounds both of V and I) . . . was the sonne of Silvius, the

happened that in mediæval England French singers were to be heard extolling the glory of Saxon kings, while English singers told the deeds of Arthur, the arch-enemy of their race. Nothing gives a better idea of this extraordinary amalgamation of races and traditions than a certain poem of the thirteenth century written in French by a Norman monk of Westminster, and dedicated to Eleanor of Provence, wife of Henry III., in which we read :

"In the world, I may confidently say, there never was country, kingdom or empire, where so many good kings, and holy too, were found, as in the English island. . . . Saints they were, martyrs and confessors, of whom several died for God ; others most strong and hardy, as were Arthur, Edmund, and Knut."[1]

Rarely was the like seen in any literature ; here is a poem dedicated to a Frenchwoman by a Norman of England, which begins with the praise of a Briton, a Saxon, and a Dane. The same phenomenon is to be noticed, after the Conquest in romances, chronicles and histories.

---

sonne of Ascanius, the sonne of Aeneas the Trojan, begotten of his wife Creusa, and borne in Troie, before the citie was destroied" (book ii. chap. i.).

[1] "En mund ne est (ben vus l'os dire)
Pais, reaume, ne empire
U tant unt esté bons rois
E seinz, cum en isle d'Englois . . .
Seinz, martirs e confessurs
Ki pur Deu mururent plursurs ;
Li autre forz e hardiz mutz,
Cum fu Arthurs, Aedmunz, e Knudz."

("Lives of Edward the Confessor," ed. H. R. Luard, London, Rolls, 1858, 8vo.)

Whoever the author may be, whether of French or English blood, the unity of origin of the two races receives almost invariably the fullest acknowledgment; the inhabitants of the great island cease to look towards Germany, Denmark and Scandinavia, for their ancestors or for the sources of their inspiration; they look rather, like their new French companions, to Rome, Greece and Troy. This policy produced not only momentous social results, but also very important literary consequences; the intellectual connection with the north being cut off, the Anglo-French allowed themselves to be drilled with the Latin discipline; the ancient models ceased to appear to them heterogeneous; they studied them in all good faith as the works of distant relations, with such result that they, unlike the Germanic and Scandinavian peoples, were ready, when the time of the Renaissance came, to benefit by the great intellectual movement set on foot by southern neo-classic nations; and while Italy produced Ariosto and Tasso, while Spain possessed Cervantes, and France Montaigne, Ronsard and Rabelais, they were ready to give birth to the unparalleled trio of Spenser, Bacon and Shakespeare.

From the fourteenth century this conclusion was easy to foresee; for, even at that period, England took part in a tentative Renaissance that preceded the great one of the sixteenth century. At the time when Italy produced Petrarca and Boccaccio, and France had Froissart, England produced Chaucer, the greatest of the four.

Famous as Chaucer was as a story-teller, it is strange that he was to have almost no influence on the development of the novel in England. When we read of Harry

Bailly and the Wife of Bath, of the modest Oxford clerk and the good parson ; when we turn the pages of the inimitable story of Troilus and the fickle, tender, charming Cressida, it seems as if nothing was lacking to the production of perfect novels. All the elements of the art are there complete : the delicate analysis of passions, the stirring plot, the natural play of various characters, the very human mixture of grossness and tenderness, of love songs and rough jokes, the portraits of actual beings belonging to real life and not to dreamland. It was only necessary to break the cadence of the verse and to write such stories in prose. No one did it ; no one tried to do it.

The fact is the stranger if we remember that Chaucer's popularity never flagged. It was at its height in the fifteenth and sixteenth centuries ; in the following period the kings of literature, Dryden and Pope, did homage to him. His works had been amongst the first to be printed. Caxton's original edition was quickly followed by a second.[1] The latter was adorned with illustrations, and this rapid publication of a second and amended text testifies to the great reverence in which the author was held. Nevertheless it is the fact that Chaucer stands alone ; authors of prose novels who wrote nearly two centuries after his time, instead of trying to follow in his footsteps, sought their models either in the old epic literature or in French and Italian story-books. This is exactly what

---

[1] Both editions are undated ; the first one seems to have been published in 1478, the second in 1484 (W. Blades, "Life and Typography of William Caxton," 1861, two vols. 4to).

CAXTON'S REPRESENTATION OF CHAUCER'S PILGRIMS, 1484.

Chaucer had done himself; but they did it with very different success, and entirely missed the benefits of the great advance made by him. By another strange caprice of fate it was these sixteenth-century writers, and not Chaucer, who were to be the ancestors of the world-famous novelists of a later age, of the Richardsons and Fieldings of the eighteenth century.

In one thing, then, the French conquerors entirely failed; they never succeeded in acclimatizing during the Middle Ages those shorter prose stories which were so popular in their own country, in which they themselves delighted and of which charming and sometimes exquisite models have come to us from the twelfth century downwards. When this art so thoroughly French began, as we shall see, to be cultivated in England, it was the outcome of the Renaissance, not of the Conquest. Hundreds of volumes of mediæval English manuscripts preserve plenty of sermons, theological treatises, epic-romances, poems of all sorts; but the student will not discover one single original prose story to set by the side of the many examples extant in French literature; nothing resembling the French stories of the thirteenth century, so delightful in their frank language, their brisk style and simple grace, in which we find a foretaste of the prose of Le Sage and Voltaire; nothing to be compared, even at a distance, in the following century, with the narratives of Froissart, who, it is true, applied to history his genius for pure romance; nothing like the anecdotes so well told by the Knight of La Tour Landry for the instruction of his daughters; nothing that at all approaches "Petit Jehan de Saintré" or the "Cent nouvelles" in the fifteenth century. To find English prose tales of the Middle Ages we should be forced to look through the religious manuscripts where they figure under the guise of examples for the reader's edification. A very troublesome search it is, but not always a vain one; some of these stories deserve to be included among the most memorable legends of the Middle Ages. To give an idea of them I will quote the story of a scholar of Paris, after Caesarius, but told in far better style by the holy hermit Rolle de Hampole, in the fourteenth century. It is short and little known :

"A scolere at Pares had done many full synnys the whylke he had schame to schryfe hym of. At the last gret sorowe of herte ouercome his schame, & when he was redy to schryfe till (to) the priore of the abbay of Saynte Victor, swa mekill contricione was in his herte, syghynge in his breste, sobbynge in his throtte, that he moghte noghte brynge a worde furthe. Thane the prioure said till hym : Gaa & wrytte thy synnes. He dyd swa, & come a-gayne to the prioure and gafe hym that he hade wretyn, ffor yitt he myghte noghte schryfe hym with mouthe. The prioure saghe the synnys swa grette that thurghe leve of the scolere he schewede theyme to the abbotte to hafe conceyle. The abbotte tuke that byll that ware wrettyn in & lukede thare one. He fande na thynge wretyn & sayd to the priour : What may here be redde thare noghte es wretyne? That saghe the priour & wondyrd gretly & saide : Wyet ye that his synns here warre wretyn & I redde thaym, but now I see that God has sene hys contryeyone & forgyfes hym all his synnes. This the abbot & the prioure tolde the scolere, & he, with gret joy thanked God."[1]

But instances of this kind of story lack those features of gaiety and satirical observation of which French stories are full, and which are an important element of the novel. Some are mystical; others, in which the devil figures on whom the saints play rude tricks, are intended to raise a loud laugh; in both cases real life is equally distant. A keen faculty of observation however existed in the nation; foibles of human nature did not escape the English writer's eye any more than its higher aspirations. This is illustrated not only by Chaucer, who chose to write poetry, but by such men as Nigel Wireker[2] and Walter Map who chose to write Latin.[3] But not

[1] "English Prose Treatises of Richard Rolle de Hampole," ed. G. G. Perry, London, Early English Text Society, 1866, 8vo. p. 7. Rolle de Hampole died in 1349. Cæsarius' tale (Cæsarius Heisterbacensis, d. 1240) begins thus: "Erat ibi juvenis quidam in studio, qui, suggerente humani generis inimico, talia quædam peccata commiserat, quæ, obstante erubescentia, nulli hominum confiteri potuit : cogitans tamen quæ malis præparata sunt tormenta gehennæ, & quæ bonis abscondita sunt gaudia perennis vitæ, timens etiam quotidie judicium Dei super se, intus torquebatur morsu conscientiæ & foris tabescebat in copore . . . ." ("Illustrium miraculorum . . . libri xii.," bk. ii. ch. 10).

[2] "Speculum Stultorum," in "Anglo-Latin Satirical Poets . . . of the Twelfth Century" ed. Th. Wright, London, 1872, 2 vols. 8vo.

[3] "Gualteri Mapes De nugis curialium distinctiones quinque," ed. Th. Wright, Camden Society, 1850, 4to. Part IV. of this work contains the celebrated "Disuasio Valerii ad Rufinum de ducenda uxore," long attributed to St. Jerome, and one of the principal text-books of the authors of satires against women during the Middle Ages. It was well known to the Wife of Bath, who held it in special abomination.

one English author before the Renaissance employed such gifts in writing prose studies of real life in his native tongue. Owing to the Conquest a certain discredit seemed to rest for generations on England's original language. Long after an English nation, rich in every sort of glory had come into being, writers are to be found hesitating to use the national idiom. This circumstance is chiefly noticeable in prose where the use of a foreign tongue offers less difficulties than in poetry. Prose was less cultivated in England even so late as the commencement of the sixteenth century than in France during the thirteenth. At the time of the Renaissance, Sir Thomas More, the wittiest Englishman of his day, whose English style was admirable and who moreover loved the language of his native land, wishing to publish a romance of social satire, the "Utopia,"[1] wrote it in Latin. It is one of the oldest examples in modern literature of that species of book which includes at a later date the story of Gargantua and Pantagruel, Bacon's "New Atlantis," Cyrano de Bergerac's "Etats et empires de la lune et du soleil," Fenelon's "Télémaque," "Gulliver's

---

[1] The "Utopia" was composed in 1515-1516, and was published anonymously at Louvain, under the title: "Libellus vere aureus, nec minus salutaris quam festivus de optimo reipublicæ statu ... cura P. Ægidii ... nunc primum ... editus." Louvain 1516, 4to. It was translated into English by Ralph Robinson in 1551, and this translation has been reprinted by Arber, London, 1869. Another famous novel of the same class was written in the following century also in Latin by another Englishman, or rather Scotchman, the celebrated "Argenis" of John Barclay (1582-1621). It was translated into English by Sir Robert Le Grys, 1629, 4to. Queen Elizabeth appears in it under the name of Hyanisbe.

Travels," Voltaire's tales, &c. More's use of Latin is to be the more regretted since his romance exhibits infinite resources of spirit and animation ; of all his writings it is the one that best justifies his great reputation for wit and enlightenment. His characters are living men and their conversation undoubtedly resembles that which delighted him in the society of his friend Erasmus.

The subject of the book is the quest for the best possible government. More and his companions meet at Antwerp one of the fellow voyagers of Amerigo Vespucci the famous godfather of America, and they question him concerning the civilizations he has seen. " He likewise very willingly tolde us of the same. But as for monsters, by cause they be no newes, of them we were nothyng inquisitive. For nothyng is more easye to bee founde, then bee barkynge Scyllaes, ravenyng Celenes, & Lestrigones devourers of people, & suche lyke great, & incredible monsters. But to find citisens ruled by good & holsome lawes, that is an exceding rare, & harde thyng."[1] By good luck Amerigo's companion had discovered an empire which presented this admirable quality : the island of Utopia, or the country of " Nowhere." This country became immediately famous all over Europe, so much so that Pantagruel would not look to any other place for immigrants to people his newly conquered kingdom of Dispodie. There he transported " Utopians to the number of 9,876,543,210 men," says Rabelais, with his usual care for exact numbers, " without speaking of women and little children." He did so to " refresh, people, and adorn the said country otherwise

[1] Ralph Robinson's translation (*ut supra*).

badly enough inhabited and desert in many places."[1] His acting in this manner was only natural, for, as is well known, connections existed between his family and the Utopians, his own mother Badebec, the wife of Gargantua, being "daughter to the king of the Amaurotes in Utopia."[2]

A hundred years later, something of this want of confidence in the future of English prose still lingered. Bacon, after having employed it in his essays and treatises, was seized with anxiety and kept in his pay secretaries with whose help he meant to translate all his works into Latin, in order to assure himself of their permanence.

III.

Some years before Sir Thomas More wrote his "Utopia," an Englishman, who had long lived abroad and had there learnt a new industry, unknown in his own land, returned to England and settled in Westminster. He and his trade were destined to exercise a very important influence on the diffusion of literature, and especially on the development of romances. His art was printing, and his name was Caxton. We can judge of the amazement he produced among his countrymen by his new art, from his own wonder;

---

[1] "Pantagruel, après avoir entièrement conquesté le pays de Dispodie, en icelluy transporta une colonie des Utopiens, en nombre de 9,876,543,210 hommes, sans les femmes et petitz enfans, artisans de tous mestiers et professeurs de toutes sciences liberales, pour ledict pays refraischir, peupler et aorner, mal aultrement habité et désert en grande partie" ("Pantagruel," bk. iii. ch. 1).

[2] "Pantagruel," bk. ii. ch. 2.

one of his prefaces shows clearly enough how extraordinary his performance seemed to himself: "And for as moche, says he, as in the wrytyng of the same my penne is worn, myn hande wery & not stedfast, myn eyen dimed with overmoche lokyng on the whit paper & my corage not so prone & redy to laboure as hit hath ben & that age crepeth on me dayly & febleth all the bodye, & also be cause I have promysid to diverse gentilmen & to my frendes to addresse to hem as hastely as I myght this sayd book, therfore I have practysed & lerned at my grete charge & dispense to ordeyne this said book in prynte after the maner & forme as ye may here see, & is not wreton with penne & ynke as other bokes ben, to thende that every man may have them attones, ffor all the bookes of this storye named the recule of the historyes of troyes thus enpryntid as ye here see were begonne in oon day & also fynysshid in oon day."[1]

The list of his books shows that he was no less intent upon diverting his customers than upon improving their knowledge and morals. The part allotted to fiction was extremely large, not perhaps quite so extensive as that occupied by the novel proper in the publishers' lists of to-day; but regarding it as merely a beginning, it must be admitted to be very promising. Not only did he print the tales of Chaucer, the confessions of Gower, with their numerous stories, several poems of Lydgate, a number of mediæval epic romances in verse, but he also issued

[1] "Recueyll of the historyes of Troye," Bruges, 1474? Epilogue to Book iii.

from his press the prose story of "Reynard the Fox," which contains so much excellent dialogue and so many fine scenes of comedy ; and, besides, the most remarkable prose romance that had yet been written in the English language, the famous "Morte d'Arthur" of Sir Thomas Malory. Its appearance marks an epoch in the history of English romance literature.

Why, among so many famous works, should this publication have obtained the preference and the attention of the printer? Caxton states his reasons very clearly : firstly, for him as for Layamon, Arthur is a national hero, and Englishmen should be proud of him : then again he is one of the nine worthies of the world. These nine dignitaries were, as is well known, three pagans, Hector, Alexander and Cæsar ; three Jews, Joshua, David and Judas Maccabæus; three Christians, Arthur, Charlemagne and Godfrey of Bouillon. And lastly, Caxton considered his undertaking justified by the great lessons that were to be drawn from Arthur's example : "And I accordyng to my copye have doon sette it in enprynte to the entente that noble men may see & lerne the noble actes chyvalrye the jentyl & vertuous dedes that somme knyghtes used in tho dayes by whyche they came to honour & how they that were vycious were punysshed & ofte put to shame & rebuke, humbly byseching al noble lordes & ladyes wyth al other estates of what estate or degree they been of, that shal see & rede in this sayd book & werke, that they take the good & honest actes in their remembraunce & to folowe the same. Wherein they shalle fynde many joyous & playsaunt hystoryes & noble & renomed actes of humanyte gentylnesse &

chyualryes. For herein may be seen noble chyvalrye, curtosye, humanyte, frendlynesse, hardynesse, love, frendshyp, cowardyse, murdre, hate, vertue & synne. Doo after the good & leve the evyl & it shal brynge you to good fame & renommee."[1]

Everything, in fact, is to be found in Malory's book; everything, except those marks of character which transform traditional types into living personalities; everything except those analyses of feeling which are for us the primary *raison d'être* of the modern novel and its chief attraction. The old knight's book is a vast compilation in which he has melted down and mixed together a large number of tales about Arthur, Lancelot, Gawain, Galahad, Percival, and all the Knights of the Round Table. An infinite number of short chapters, written in a clear and quiet style, possessing no other charm than its simplicity, tell of the loves and of the fights of these famous men; "of theyr marvaylous enquestes and adventures," as Caxton has it, "thachyevyng of the Sangraal, and in thende the dolorous deth and departyng out of thys world of

[1] "Le Morte Darthur by Syr Thomas Malory," ed. O. Sommer and Andrew Lang, London, 1889, 2 vol. 8vo. Caxton's Preface, p. 3. The book was originally published at Westminster, in 1485, under the title: "The noble and ioyous book entytled Le Morte Darthur notwythstondyng it treateth of the byrth, lyf and actes of the sayd kyng Arthur of his noble knyghtes of the rounde table, theyr marvayllous enquestes and adventures, thachyevyng of the Sangraal, and in thende the dolorous deth and departyng out of thys world of them al, whiche book was reduced into englysshe by Syr Thomas Malory knyght."

It ends with the statement that it was printed and "fynysshed in thabbey of Westmestre the last day of Juyl the yere of our lord M cccc lxxxv. Caxton me fieri fecit."

them al." Malory never made the slightest effort to reach a grand style; he did not think that there could be any other method of writing than that of putting on paper, without preparation, what first came into his mind. Since he possessed neither a passionate temperament nor a wandering imagination, he tells, without any apparent emotion, the most important of his stories, even the last battle of his hero [1] and his final disappearance, when he is borne by fairies into the Vale of Avilion. It is for sensitive hearts to weep over these misfortunes, if they choose. As for him, he goes on his way, telling tale after tale, in the same clear and even voice; but very rarely giving us his confidence or opening to us his heart.

Once in the whole length of this immense work he does impart to us his personal opinion on a question of importance: in the twenty-fifth chapter of his eighteenth book, Malory confesses what he thinks of love, and lays aside his usual reserve: and thus furnishes the first attempt at analysis of feeling to be found in the English prose romance. Malory declares that every man should love God first and his mistress afterwards; and so long as a man does love his God

---

[1] "And then kyng Arthur smote syr mordred under the shelde wyth a foyne of his spere thoroughoute the body more than a fadom. And when syr mordred felte that he had hys dethes wounde, he thryst hymself wyth the myght that he had up to the bur of kyng Arthurs spere. And right so he smote his fader Arthur wyth his swerde holden in bothe his handes, on the syde of the heed, that the swerde persyd the helmet & the brayne panne, & therwythall syr Mordred fyl starke deed to the erthe, & the nobyl Arthur fyl in a swoune to the erthe & there swouned ofte times" (*Ut supra*, book xxi. ch iv. p. 847).

ROBERT THE DEVIL, ABOUT 1510.   [p. 57.

first, the other love seems to him to be not only permissible but even commendable; it is a virtue. "Therfore, as may moneth floreth & floryssheth in many gardyns, soo in lyke wyse, lete every man of worship florysshe his herte in this world, fyrst unto God & next unto the joye of them that he promysed his feythe unto : for there was never worshypful man or worshipfull woman but they loved one better than another . . . & 'suche love, I calle vertuous love." But now-a-days, continues the old knight, little suspecting that his grievance is one of all ages, men cannot love seven-night but they must have all their desires. The old love was not so. Men and women could love together seven years, and no wanton lusts were between them, and then was love truth and faithfulness. "And loo," Malory adds forgetting that his Lancelot and his Tristan waited much less than seven years, "in lyke wyse was used love in Kynge Arthurs dayes."[1]

Very strikingly does this view of love contrast with the southern irrepressible impetuosities of young Aucassin, who, considering, three centuries earlier, this same question of holy and profane love, of earth and paradise, in the above-mentioned exquisite prose tale which bears his name, simply alters the order of precedence afterwards adopted by good Sir Thomas: "Tell me," says he, "where is the place so high in all the world that Nicolete, my sweet lady and love, would not grace it well? If she were Empress of Constantinople or of Germany, or Queen of France or

[1] "Le Morte Darthur," ed. Sommer and Lang, London, 1889, 8vo., book xviii. ch. 25, p. 771.

England, it were little enough for her. . . . In Paradise what have I to win? Therein I seek not to enter, but only to have Nicolete my sweet lady that I love so well. . . . For in Paradise go none but . . . these same old priests, and halt old men and maimed, who all day and night cower continually before the altars, and in the crypts. . . . These be they that go into Paradise; with them have I naught to make. But into Hell would I fain go; for into Hell fare the goodly clerks and goodly knights that fall in tourneys and great wars. . . . And thither pass the sweet ladies. . . . Thither goes the gold and the silver and cloth of vair, and cloth of gris, and harpers and makers, and the prince of this world. With these I would gladly go, let me but have with me Nicolete my sweetest lady." [1]

No one perceived the coldness of Malory's stories. He wrote for a youthful and enthusiastic people; it was a period of new birth throughout Europe, the period of the spring-time of modern literature, the epoch of the Renaissance. There was no need to depict in realistic fashion the passions and stirrings of the heart in order to excite the emotion of the reader; a relation of events sufficed for him; his own imagination did the rest, and enlivened the dull-painted canvas with visions of every colour. The book had as much success as Caxton could have expected; it was constantly reprinted during the sixteenth century, and enchanted the contemporaries of Surrey, of Elizabeth, and of Shakespeare. It was in vain that the serious-

[1] "Aucassin and Nicolete," done into English by Andrew Lang, London, 1887, pp. 6, 11, and 12.

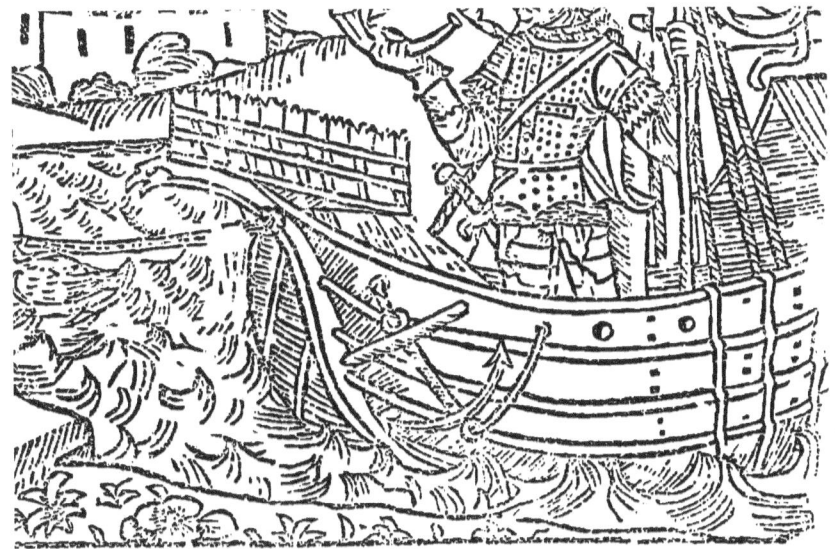

NOBLE HELYAS KNYGHTE OF THE SWANNE," ABOUT 1550. [*p.* 61.

minded Ascham condemned it; it survived his condemnation as the popularity of Robin Hood survived the sermons of Latimer. Vainly did Ascham denounce "Certaine bookes of Chevalrie. . . . as one for example, *Morte Arthure:* the whole pleasure of whiche booke standeth in two speciall poyntes, in open mans slaughter, & bold bawdrye. In which booke those be counted the noblest knightes, that do kill most men without any quarell, & commit fowlest aduoulteres by sutlest shiftes."[1]

When the people became more thoughtful or more exacting in the matter of analysis, they neglected the old book. After 1634, two hundred years passed without a reprint of it. In our time it has met with an aftermath of success, not only among the curious, but among a class of readers who are not more exacting than Caxton's clients, and who are far more interested in fact than in feeling. Children form this class of readers; in the present century Malory's book has been many times re-edited for them, and it is to Sir Thomas Malory, rather than to Tennyson, Swinburne or Morris, that many English men and women of to-day owe their earliest acquaintance with King Arthur and his Knights.

Caxton's example was followed by many; printing presses multiplied, and with most of them fiction kept its ground. A new life was infused into old legendary heroes, and they began again, impelled not by the genius of new writers, but simply by the printer's skill, their never ending journeys over the world. Their stories were published in England in small

[1] "The Scholemaster," London, 1570, 4to.

handy volumes, often of a very good appearance, and embellished with woodcuts. There were prose stories of "Robert the devyll," and there were verse stories of "Sir Guy of Warwick" and of "Syr Eglamoure of Artoys." Many of the cuts are extremely picturesque and excellently suited to the general tone of the story. On the title-page the hero of the tale usually sits on his horse, and indomitable he looks with his sword drawn, his plume full spread, his mien defiant. A faithful squire sometimes follows him, sometimes only his dog; between the feet of the horse fabulous plants spread their unlikely leaves, and give the sole and very doubtful clue to the country in which the knight is travelling, certainly a very desolate and unpleasant one. In this fashion does Duke Robert of Normandy travel, and so does Eglamoure, and Tryamoure, and Bevis, and Isumbras. In the same series too is to be seen "Y^e noble Helyas, Knyght of the Swanne," drawn by the said swan, a somewhat wooden bird, not very different from his successor of a later age whom we are accustomed to see swimming across the stage to the accompaniment of Wagner's famous music.[1]

The means by which English printers supplied themselves with these engravings, is a mystery that they

---

[1] "Robert the deuyll," London, Wynkyn de Worde, 1510? 8vo. "Syr Tryamoure," "Syr Beuys of Hampton," "Syr Isumbras," "Syr Degore," "The Knight of the Swanne," "Virgilius," and many others were published by W. Copland about 1550. "Guy of Warwick" was printed in the same style about 1560, "Syr Eglamoure of Artoys," about 1570. Many others were at this period printed in the same way with engravings from the same wood blocks.

"Then went Guy to fayre Phelis."
"SIR GUY OF WARWICK," ABOUT 1560.

have kept to themselves. Many of the blocks were very probably, purchased in the Low Countries. A very few are almost certainly of English manufacture, and among them are Caxton's illustrations of the Canterbury Tales : on this account we have given a fac-simile of the most important of them, representing the pilgrims seated round the table at the "Tabard" prior to starting on their immortal journey. What is certain is that many of these wood-block portraits of knights, supplied to the printers by English or Dutch artists, underwent many successive christenings. The same knight, with the same squire, the same dog and the same fabulous little wooden plants between the legs of the horse was sometimes Romulus and sometimes Robert of Normandy. In one book a rather fine engraving of a lord and a lady in a garden, represents Guy of Warwick courting "fayre Phelis,"[1] but in another book the same engraving does duty for "La bel Pucell" and the knight "Graund Amoure."[2] It may be observed, in passing, that these romances might be soundly criticized without much study of their contents by simply inspecting their illustrations. Full as they are of extraordinary inventions and adventures, unrestricted as their authors were by considerations of what was possible or real, some dozen well-chosen engravings seem enough to illustrate any number of them. For, alas, there is nothing more stale and more

[1] London, 1560 ? 4to.
[2] "The history of Graund Amoure and la bel Pucell, called the Pastime of pleasure," by Stephen Hawes, London, Tottell, 1555, 4to. The same engraving embellishes also "The Squyr of Lowe Degre," published by W. Copland, &c.

subject to repetitions than these series of extraordinary adventures; all their heroes are the same hero, and whether he was following the philosophical turn of his mind, or merely the thrifty orders of his printer, the engraver was well justified in leaving as he did in most of his drawings an empty scroll over the head of his knights, for the publisher to label them at will, Robert the Devil or Romulus.

We are thus fairly advanced into the sixteenth century; the Renaissance has come; before long Spenser will sing of the Fairy Queen and Shakespeare will leave his native Stratford to present to a London audience the loves of Juliet and Romeo. Scarcely any sign of improvement appears yet in the art of novel-writing; nothing but mediæval romances continue to issue from the press; it is even difficult to foresee an epoch in which something analogous to the actual novel might be produced in England. Contrary to what was taking place in France at the same time, that period seemed far off. In reality, however, it was near at hand; the great age of English literature, the age of Elizabeth and of Shakespeare, was about to furnish, at least in the rough draft, the first specimens of the true novel.

LEO.

DRAWING BY ISAAC OLIVER, AFTER AN ITALIAN MODEL.

CHAPTER II.

TUDOR TIMES, THE FASHIONS AND THE NOVEL.

I.

ONE of the most remarkable effects of the Renaissance was the awakening of a slumbering curiosity. The *régime* of the Middle Ages was just ended; its springs were exhausted, its mysteries unveiled, its terrors ridiculed. Armour was beginning to be thought troublesome; the towers of the strong castles, dark and too much confined for the pleasures of life; the reasonings of the schoolmen had grown old:

blind faith was out of fashion ; a world was ending, and all that was sinking with it appeared in the eyes of the young generation, out of season and "tedious as a twice-told tale." The rupture between the Middle Ages and modern times was complete in certain countries, partial in others, and consequently the Renaissance had very different results among the various peoples of Europe. But the same characteristic symptoms of an eager, newly awakened curiosity manifested itself in all. There was no longer question of continuing, but of comparing and of discovering. What did the ancient Greeks and the old Romans say? What do our neighbours think? What are their forms of style, their recent inventions? England competed with France in her youthful curiosity, and English poets and travellers following the example of their rivals beyond the seas, "plundered" (in the words of Joachim du Bellay's famous manifesto [1]), not only Athens and Rome, but Florence, Paris, Venice, and all the enlightened towns of France, Italy, and Spain.

This curiosity spurred on the English in the different paths of human knowledge and activity with an audacity worthy of the Scandinavian Vikings. After having destroyed the Armada, they were going to burn the Spanish fleet at Cadiz, to discover new lands in America and to give them the name of "Virginia" in

[1] "Là doncques, Françoys, marchez couraigeusement vers ceste superbe cité romaine ; & des serves dépouilles d'elle, comme vous avez fait plus d'une fois, ornez vos temples & autelz. . . . Pillez moi sans conscience les sacrez thésors de ce temple Delphique . . . Vous souvienne de vostre ancienne Marseille, secondes Athènes!" ("La Deffense et illustration de la langue Françoyse," 1549).

honour of their queen, and to attempt the impossible task of discovering a way to China through the icy regions of the North Pole. The fine gentlemen and the fine wits, even the lack-dinner, lack-penny Bohemians of literature crossed the Channel, the Alps, and the Pyrenees, seeking, they too, for gold mines to work, gathering ideas, listening to stories, noting down recent discoveries, and often appropriating the elegant vices and the light morals of the southern nations. " An italianized Englishman is a devil incarnate " is a popular proverb which quiet home-keeping men were never tired of repeating.

Kindly Ascham who had personally visited Italy, had come back as much horrified with the sights he had seen as Luther had been when he returned from Rome. Of the masterpieces of art, of madonnas and palaces he has little to say ; but he has much to note concerning the loose morals of the inhabitants. He beseeches his compatriots not to continue to visit this dangerous country : they will meet " Circe " there, and will certainly greatly enjoy themselves ; but, behold, they will come back to their native land with an ass's head and a swine's belly. In Italy, according to his experience, a man may sin to his heart's content and no one will in any way interfere. He is free to do so, " as it is free in the citie of London to chose without all blame, whether a man lust to weare shoo or pantocle." Yet he speaks of what he has seen with his own eyes : " I was once in Italie my selfe ; but I thanke God my abode there was but ix dayes. And yet I sawe in that little tyme in one citie more libertie to sinne than ever I heard tell of in our noble citie of London in ix yeare... The lord maior of London, being but a civill officer, is commonlie for his tyme more diligent in punishing sinne ... than all the bloodie inquisitors in Italie be in seaven yeare."

When Englishmen come back from Italy they are full of smiles; they have a ready wit, and delight in vain talk. They give up all idea of getting married; love and no marriage is their only wish; they arrange assignations; they behave most improperly. "They be the greatest makers of love, the daylie daliers, with such pleasant wordes, with such smilyng & secret countenances, with such signes, tokens, wagers, purposed to be lost before they were purposed to be made, with bargaines of wearing colours, floures & herbes, to breede occasion of often meeting of him & her & bolder talking of this & that, &c."[1]

According to some, travelling increased, in a certain number of Englishmen, the tendency we have already noticed, to feel contempt towards their mother tongue. There are persons, wrote George Pettie in 1581, "who will set light by my labours, because I write in English: and those are some nice travailours who retourne home with such queasie stomachs that nothing will downe with them but French, Italian or Spanish ... They count [our tongue] barren: they count it barbarous: they count it unworthy to be accounted of." The more reason, thinks Pettie, to try to polish it; if it is barren it can be enriched by borrowing from other languages, especially the Latin: " It is indeed the readie

---

[1] "The Scholemaster," London, 1570, 4to, p. 26; Arber's reprint, 1870, 4to, pp. 83, *et seq.* Ascham had died in 1568; this work was published by his widow.

waie to inrich our tongue and make it copious ; and it is the waie which all tongues have taken to inrich themselves." [1] Pettie, as we see, wished Du Bellay's advice to be followed, and Rome to be " plundered."

But Ascham's pleading, though many others spoke to the same effect,[2] had very little result. Learned and well informed as he was, his "conservatism" in all things was so intense that much might be laid to the account of this tendency of his mind. Had he not written that " his soul had such an horror of English or Latin books containing new doctrines that, except the psalter and the New Testament, this last, too, in the Greek text, he had never taken any book, ' either small or big,' to use Plato's words, concerning Christian religion " ? [3] Had he not recommended the bow as, even in those gunpowder times, the best weapon in war ? " If I were of authority, I would counsel all the gentlemen and yeomen of England not to change it with any other thing, how good soever it seems to

---

[1] Preface dated 1581 to "Civile Conversation," London, 1586, 4to.

[2] The novelist Greene, for example, and the novelist Lyly. The latter writes in his " Euphues," 1579 : " Let not your mindes be caryed away with vaine delights, as with travailing into farre & straunge countries, wher you shal see more wickednesse then learn vertue & wit " (Arber's reprint, 1868, p. 152). As for Greene, see *infra*, chap. iv. One of the most curious of these denunciations of travel was the "Quo vadis? a juste censure of travel," by Bishop Joseph Hall, 1617, 12mo. The author demonstrates that most of the vices of the English are of foreign importation, chiefly from France and Italy ; good qualities alone are native and national. The best thing to do, then, is to keep at home.

[3] Letter (in Latin) to the Archbishop of York, 1544. "Works," ed. Giles, London, 1865, 4 vol. 16mo, vol. i. p. 35.

be ; but that still, according to the old wont of England, youths should use it for the most honest pastime in peace, that men might handle it as a most sure weapon in war." [1] The other "strong weapons" must not lead men to forget this one : a thing they have nevertheless done.

Nothing dismayed by the threat of the dire consequences of Circe's wiles, travellers eager to see her crowded to the south. They continued not to "exchewe the way to Circes court, but go & ryde & runne & flie thether." [2] No education was complete without a sojourn on the continent. Surrey, Wyatt, Sidney, penniless Robert Greene, and hundreds if not thousands of others went there. There was an eagerness to see and to learn that no sight and no knowledge could satisfy, that no threat nor sermon could stop. Paris, Venice, Rome, Vienna, the Low Countries, received an ever-increasing flood of English visitors.

II.

England in her turn, not to mention the classics of antiquity that were being speedily translated, was flooded with French, Spanish, and Italian books, again to the great dismay of good Ascham. If "Morte d'Arthur" was bad, nothing worse could well be imagined than Italian books in general. " Ten ' Morte d'Arthures' do not the tenth part so much harme as one of these bookes made in Italie and translated in England." They are to be found "in

[1] "Toxophilus," 1545, in "Works," ed. Giles, vol. ii. p. 5.
[2] "Scholemaster," 1570, Arber's reprint, p. 77.

every shop in London," and each of them can do more mischief than ten sermons at St. Paul's Cross can do good. They introduce into the land such refinements in vice "as the single head of an Englishman is not hable to invent." [1]

But, if unable to invent, the English seemed at least determined to enjoy and imitate, for translating and adapting went on at a marvellous pace. Boccaccio's "Filocopo," [2] for instance, to speak only of the better known of these works, was translated in 1567, his

[1] "The Scholemaster," Arber's reprint, pp. 79, 80.

[2] "A pleasant disport of divers noble personages . . . intituled Philocopo . . . englished by H. G[ifford?]," London, 1567, 4to; "Amorous Fiametta, wherein is sette downe a catalogue of all & singular passions of love and jealosie incident to an enamoured yong gentlewoman . . . done into English by B. Giovano [*i.e.*, B. Young]," London, 1587; "The Decameron, containing an hundred pleasant novels," London, 1620, fol. (with woodcuts); "The Civile Conversation . . . translated . . . by G. Pettie . . . and B. Yong," London, 1586, 4to; "The lamentations of Amyntas . . . translated out of latine into english hexameters," by Abraham Fraunce, London, 1587, 4to; "Godfray of Bulloigne, or the recoverie of Hierusalem . . . translated by R. C[arew] . . . imprinted in both languages," London, 1594; "The courtier of Count Baldesar Castilio . . . done into English by Th. Hobby," London, 1588, 8vo (contains an Italian, English and French text); "Diana of George of Montemayor, translated by B. Yong," London, 1598, fol. Among other translations three of the most important were Lord Berners' "Froysshart," "translated out of Frenche into our maternall Englysshe tonge," 1522, North's translation of Plutarch after the French of Amyot (1579), and Florio's translation of Montaigne, 1603, fol., which were well known to the dramatists, and went through several editions. The British Museum possesses a copy of Florio's Montaigne, which was the property of Ben Jonson. A far more satisfactory translation of the same author was made by Cotton, 1685–6, 3 vol. 8vo.

"Amorous Fiametta, wherein is sette downe a catalogue of all and singuler passions of love," in 1587; his "Decameron" in 1620. Guazzo's "Civile Conversation" was translated in 1586; Tasso's "Amynta" in 1587, and his "Recoverie of Hierusalem" in 1594. Castiglione's "Courtier . . . very necessary and profitable for young gentlemen abiding in court, palace or place" was published in English in 1588. It was "profitable" in a rather different sense from the one Ascham would have given the word, for it contains lengthy precepts concerning assignations and lovemaking: "In my minde, the way which the courtier ought to take, to make his love knowne to the woman, me think should be to declare them in figures and tokens more than in wordes. For assuredly there is otherwhile a greater affection of love perceived in a sigh, in a respect, in a feare, than in a thousand wordes. Afterwarde, to make the eyes the trustie messengers that may carrie the Ambassades of the hart."[1] Many heroes in the English novels we shall have to study were apparently well read in Castiglione's "Courtier." Montemayor's Spanish "Diana," a tale of princes and shepherds, well known to Sidney, was published in 1598. Ariosto's "Orlando furioso" appeared in 1591, in a magnificently illustrated edition, and was dedicated to the Queen. The engravings, though sometimes said to be English, were in fact printed from the Italian plates of Girolamo Porro, of Padua, and had been used before in Italy.[2] Their circulation in England

---

[1] Sig. F. f. 1.
[2] "Orlando Furioso, in English heroical verse," by John Harington, London, 1591, fol. The plates were used in the

FRONTISPIECE TO HARINGTON'S TRANSLATION OF ARIOSTO, 1591, BY COXON AND GIROLAMO PORRO. [*p.* 77.

is none the less remarkable, and the influence such a publication may have had in the diffusing of Italian tastes in this country cannot be exaggerated. For those who had not been able to leave their native land, it was the best revelation yet placed before the public of the art of the Renaissance. That it was an important undertaking and a rather risky one, the translator, John Harington, was well aware ; for he prefaced his book not only with his dedication to the Queen, a sort of thing to which Ascham had had great objection,[1] but by a " briefe apologie of poetrie," especially of that of Ariosto. It must be confessed that his arguments are far from convincing, and it would have been much better to have left the thing alone than to have defended the moral purposes of his author by such observations as these : " It may be and is by some objected that, although he writes christianly in some places, yet in some other, he is too lascivious. . . . Alas if this be a fault pardon him this one fault ; though I doubt too many of you, gentle readers, wil be to exorable in this

Italian edition : "Orlando Furioso . . . novamente adornato di Figure di Rame da Girolamo Porro Padouano," Venice, 1588, 4to. There is, however, a difference in the frontispiece, where the allegorical figure of Peace is replaced in the English edition by a portrait of Harington, engraved by Thomas Coxon, who signed as if the whole frontispiece was by his hand. We give a reduced facsimile of this frontispiece.

[1] He had written in his " Scholemaster " : These "fond books" are " dedicated over boldlie to vertuous and honourable personages, the easelier to beguile simple and innocent wittes. It is pitie that those which have authority and charge to allow and dissallow bookes to be printed, be no more circumspect herein than they are " (Arber's reprint, p. 79).

point, yea me thinks I see some of you searching already for those places of the booke and you are halfe offended that I have not made some directions that you might finde out and reade them immediately. But I beseech you ... to read them as my author ment them, to breed detestation and not delectation," &c. And he then appends to his book a table, by means of which the gentle readers will have no trouble in finding the objectionable passages enumerated in the "Apologie" itself.

At the same time as translations proper, many imitations were published, especially imitations of those shorter prose stories which were so numerous on the continent, and which had never been properly acclimatized in England during the Middle Ages. Their introduction into this country had a great influence on the further development of the novel; their success showed that there was a public for such literature; hence the writing of original tales of this sort in English. Among collections of foreign tales translated or imitated may be quoted Paynter's "Palace of Pleasure," 1566,[1] containing histories from Boccaccio, Bandello, Ser Giovanni Fiorentino, Straparole, the Spaniard Guevara, the Queen of Navarre, "and other italian and french authours." One of them is the history of "Rhomeo and Iulietta," from which Shakespeare derived his immortal drama; another tale in the same collection supplied the plot of "All's Well," and another the main events of "Measure for Measure." Then came G. Fenton's "Tragicall Dis-

[1] Old Style. The dedication is dated: "Nere the Tower of London the first of Januarie 1566."

courses," 1567, finished at Paris and published by the author as the first-fruits of his travels; T. Fortescue's "Foreste or collection of histories . . . done out of French," 1571; George Pettie's "Pettie Pallace of Pettie his pleasure," 1576; Robert Smyth's "Straunge and tragicall histories translated out of french," 1577; Barnabe Rich's "Farewell to militarie profession," 1584, where Shakespeare found the plot of "Twelfth Night"; G. Whetstone's "Heptameron of civill discourses," 1582; Ed. Grimeston's translation of the "Admirable and memorable histories" of Goulart, 1607, and several others.

Besides such collections many stories were separately translated and widely circulated. A number have been lost, but some remain, such, for instance, as "The adventures passed by Master F. I.," adapted by Gascoigne from the Italian,[1] or a certain "Hystorie of Hamblet," 1608,[2] which was destined to have great importance in English literature, or the "Goodli history of the . . . Ladye Lucres of Scene in Tuskane and of her lover Eurialus," a translation from the Latin of Æneas Sylvius Piccolomini, and one of the most popular novels of the time. It went through twenty-three editions in the fifteenth century, and was eight times translated, one of the French translations being made "à la prière et requeste des dames." A German translation by

[1] First published in Gascoigne's "Hundreth sundrie flowres bound up in one small poesie," London, 1572, 4to.

[2] Translated from the French of Belleforest, who had himself translated it from Bandello. Though the date of the only known edition of the story in English is later than the production of "Hamlet," it seems to have been known before, and to have been used by Shakespeare. See Furnivall's "Leopold Shakspere," p. lxix.

Nicolaus von Wyle is embellished with coloured woodcuts of the most naïve and amusing description. Three English translations were published, one before 1550, another in 1669, and a third in 1741.[1]

It is a tale of unlawful love, and tells how Lucrece, a married lady of Sienna, fell in love with Eurialus,

THE KNIGHT EURIALUS GETTING SECRETLY INTO HIS LADY-LOVE'S CHAMBER, 1477.

a knight of the court of the Emperor Sigismond. It is, we are told, a story of real life under fictitious names. The dialogue is easy, vigorous, and passionate, and the translator has well succeeded in transmuting

[1] "The historie of . . . Plasidas and other rare pieces," ed. H. H. Gibbs, Roxburghe Club, London, 1873, 4to. One of these "pieces," prefaced with an important introduction, is the "Goodli history" of Lady Lucrece.

these qualities into his yet unbroken mother torgue. Here, for instance, Lucrece is discussing with the faithful Zosias the subject of her love.

"Houlde thy peace quod Lucrece, there is no feare at all. Nothynge he feareth that feareth not death. . .

"Oh! unhappie quod Zosias, thou shalt shame thy house, and onlye of all thy kynne thou shalte be adulteresse. Thinkest thou the deede can be secreate? A thousand eyne are about thee. Thy mother, if shee do accordinge, shall not suffer thy outrage to be prevye, not thy husbande, not thy cousyns, not thy maidens, ye, and thoughe thy servauntes woulde holde theyr peace, the bestes would speake it, ye dogges, the poostes and the marble stones, and thoughe thou hyde all, thou canste not hyde it from God that seeth all. . .

"I knowe quod she it is accordinge as thou sayest, but the rage maketh me folow the worse. My mynde knoweth howe I fall hedling, but furour ha'h overcom and reygneth, and over all my thought ruleth love. I am determined to folow the commandement of love. Overmuche alas have I wrestled in vaine; if thou have pytie on me, carye my mesage."[1]

If the German translation was adorned with woodcuts, the English text had an embellishment of a greater value; it consisted in the conclusion of the tale as altered by the English writer. In the Latin original of the future pope, Pius II., Lucrece dies, and Eurialus, having followed the Emperor back to Germany, mourns for her "till the time when Cæsar married him to a virgin of a ducal house not less beautiful than chaste and wise," a very common-place

[1] *Ut supra*, p. 119.

way of mourning for a dead mistress. This seemed insufferable to the English translator. Faithful as he is throughout, he would not take upon himself to alter actual facts, yet he thought right to give a different account of his hero's feelings: "But lyke as he folowed the Emperoure so dyd Lucres folow hym in hys sleep and suffred hym no nygtes rest, whom when he knew hys true lover to be deed, meaved by extreme dolour, clothed him in mournynge apparell, and utterly excluded all comforte, and yet though the Emperoure gave hym in mariage a ryghte noble and excellente Ladye, yet he never enjoyed after, but in conclusyon pitifully wasted his painful lyfe." [1]

The greater the display of feeling in such tales of Italian origin, the bitterer were the denunciations of moral censors, and the greater at the same time their popularity with the public. The quarrel did not abate for one minute during the whole of the century; the period is filled with condemnations of novels, dramas and poems, answered by no less numerous apologies for the same. The quarrel went on even beyond the century, the adverse parties meeting with various success as Cromwell ruled or Charles reigned; it can

---

[1] Here is Piccolomini's text: "Sed ut ipse Cæsarem, sic cum Lucretia sequebatur in somnis, nullamque noctem sibi quietam permittebat. Quam ut obiisse verus amator cognovit, magno dolore permotus, lugubrem vestem recepit; nec consolationem admisit, nisi postquam Cæsar ex ducalo sanguine virginem sibi cum formosam tum castissimam atque prudentem matrimonio junxit." The French translator did not alter this end. It will be remembered that the conclusion of Chaucer's "Troilus" compares in the same way with Boccaccio's and with the French translator's, Pierre de Beauveau.

scarcely be said to have ever been entirely dropped, and the very same arguments used by Ascham against the Italian books of his time are daily resorted to against the French books of our own age.

Be this as it may, the Italian novels had the better of it in Elizabethan times; they were found not only " in every shop," but in every house; translations of them were the daily reading of Shakespeare, and as they had an immense influence not only in emancipating the genius of the dramatists of the period, but, what was of equal importance, in preparing an audience for them, we may be permitted to look at them with a more indulgent eye than the pre-Shakespearean moralists.

A curious list of books, belonging during this same period (1575) to a man of the lower middle class, an average member of a Shakespearean audience, has been preserved for us. It is to be found in a very quaint account of the Kenilworth festivities, sent by Robert Laneham, a London mercer, to a brother mercer of the same city. Laneham states how an acquaintance of his, Captain Cox, a mason by trade, had in his possession, not only " Kyng Arthurz book, Huon of Burdeaus, The foour suns of Aymon, Bevis of Hampton," and many of those popular romances, illustrated with woodcuts of which a few specimens are to be seen above, but also, mason as he was, the very same Italian book, the " Lucres and Eurialus," of which we have just given an account.[1]

With the diffusion of these small handy volumes

[1] "Captain Cox, his ballads and books, or Robert Laneham's Letter . . . 1575," ed. F. J. Furnivall, London, Ballad Society, 1871, 8vo. p. 29.

of tales of all kinds, from all countries, a quite modern sort of literature, a literature for travellers, was being set on foot. Manuscript books did not easily lend themselves to be carried about; but it was otherwise with the printed pamphlets. Authors began to recommend their productions as convenient travelling companions, very much in the same manner as the publishers recommend them now as suitable to be taken to the Alps or to the seaside. Paynter, for example, who circulated in England from the year 1566 his collection of tales translated or imitated from Boccaccio and Bandello, Apuleius and Xenophon, the Queen of Navarre, and Bonaventure Desperriers, Belleforest and Froissart, Guevara and many others, assures his reader that: "Pleasaunt they be for that they recreate, and refreshe weried mindes defatigated either with painefull travaile or with continuall care, occasioning them to shunne and to avoid heavinesse of minde, vaine fantasies and idle cogitations. Pleasaunt so well abroad as at home, to avoide the griefe of winters night and length of sommers day, which the travailers on foote may use for a staye to ease their weried bodye, and the journeours on horsback, for a chariot or lesse painful meane of travaile in steade of a merie companion to shorten the tedious toyle of wearie wayes." [1]

It is pleasant to think of Shakespeare in some journey from Stratford to London, sitting under a tree, and in order to forget "the tedious toyle of wearie wayes," taking out of his pocket Paynter's book to dream of future Romeos and possible Helenas.

[1] Epistle to the reader, prefacing the "Palace of Pleasure."

III.

The Italian and French languages were held in great honour; both were taught at Oxford and Cambridge; the latter especially was of common use in England, and this peculiarity attracted the notice of foreigners. "As regards their manners and mode of living, ornaments, garments and vestments," writes the Greek Nicander Nucius, in 1545, "they resemble the French more than others, and, for the most part, they use their language."[1] But besides these elegant languages, Greek and Latin were becoming courtly. They were taught in the schools and out of the schools; the nobles, following the example of King Henry VIII. and his children, made a parade of their knowledge. Ignorance was no longer the fashion, no more than the old towers without windows. The grave Erasmus went to hear Colet, the Dean of St. Paul's, and "he thought he was hearing Plato"; Sir T. More, according to Erasmus, is the "sweetest, softest, happiest genius nature has ever shaped." In a word, "literature is triumphant among the English. The king himself, the two cardinals, almost all the bishops, favour with all their soul and adorn Letters."[2] To learn Greek and Latin was to move with the times and to follow the fashion. "All men," says Ascham, less displeased with this novelty than with the travelling propensities

[1] That there was also in London a public for Italian books is shown, among many other proofs, by the early publication there of an edition of the "Pastor Fido" of Guarini in the original, London, 1591, 12mo.

[2] "Epistolarum . . . libri xxxi.," London, 1642, fol., col. 308, 533, 364, &c. A.D. 1497 and 1519.

of his compatriots, "covet to have their children speake latin"; and "Sophocles and Euripides are more familiar now here than Plautus was formerly."[1] Dazzled by what he saw and heard, Erasmus was announcing to the world in enthusiastic letters that "the golden age" was to be born again in this fortunate island.[2] His only regret was that he would perhaps not live long enough to see it. Well might he regret it, even though it were not to follow exactly as he had foreseen; for the golden apple of the golden age was not to be plucked in the Greek Hesperides' garden, but in a plain Warwickshire orchard: nor was it the less golden.

This fermentation of mind lasted for more than a century; lives were often shortened by it, but they had been doubly well filled. From this restless curiosity, bent towards past ages and foreign countries, towards everything that was remote, unknown and different, came that striking appearance of omniscience and universality, and that prodigious wealth of imagery, allusions and ideas of every kind that are to be found in all the authors of that time, small as well as great, and which unites in one common bond Rabelais and Shakespeare, Cervantes and Sidney and the "master of the enchanters of the ear," Ronsard.

When the armour, worn less often, began to grow rusty in the great halls, and the nobles, coming forth

---

[1] "The Scholemaster," p. 2, and Letter to Brandesby (in Latin), 1542-3; "Works," ed. Giles, tom. i. p. 25.
[2] "Equidem aureum quoddam seculum exoriri video, quo mihi fortassis non continget frui, quippe qui jam ad fabulæ meæ catastrophem accedam" (Letter to Henry of Guildford, May, 1519, "Epistolarum . . . libri xxxi.," London, 1642, fol., col. 368)

from their coats-of-mail like the butterfly from the
chrysalis, showed themselves all glistening in silk, pearls
in their ears, their heads full of Italian madrigals and
mythological similes, a new society was formed, salons
of a kind were organized, and the rôle of the women
was enlarged. English mediæval times had been by no
means sparing of compliments to them. But there is a
great difference between celebrating in verse fair, slim-
necked ladies, and writing books expressly for them:
and it is one of the points in which, during the Middle
Ages and even until the middle of the sixteenth century,
England differed from the nations of the south. In
England no Lady Oisille had gathered round her in the
depth of green valleys tellers of amorous stories; no
thickly-shaded parks had seen Fiammettas or Philomenas
listening to all kinds of narratives, forgetful of the
actual world and its sorrows. The only group of
story-tellers, bound together by a true artist's fancy,
Chaucer's pilgrims, had ridden in broad daylight on
the high road to Canterbury, led by Harry Bailly, the
jovial innkeeper of Southwark, a blustering, red-faced
dictator, who had regulated the pace of the nags, and
silenced the tedious babblers: very different in all
things from Fiammetta and the Lady Oisille.

Under the influence of Italy, France and mythology,
the England of the Tudors, changed all that. Women
appeared in the foreground: a movement of general
curiosity animated the age, and they participated in it
quite naturally. They will become learned, if necessary, rather than remain in the shade; they will no
longer rest contented with permission to read books
written for their fathers, brothers, lovers, or husbands;

some must be written especially on their account, consulting their preferences and personal caprices; and they had good reason to command: one of them sat on the throne.

They, too, began to read Greek. Latin, Italian and French; knowledge was so much the fashion that it extended to women. Here Ascham bears testimony in their favour; the Queen herself gives the example: "She readeth now at Windsore more Greeke every day than some prebendarie of this chirch doth read Latin in a wole weeke."[1] In this she has innumerable imitators, so much so that Harrison sums up as follows his judgment concerning English ladies: "To saie how many gentlewomen and ladies there are, that beside sound knowledge of the Greeke and Latin toongs are thereto no lesse skilfull in the Spanish, Italian and French or in some one of them, it resteth not in me."[2]

It must not be believed, however, that so much Greek and Latin in any way imperilled the grace and ease of their manners, or that when you met them you would be welcomed with a quotation from Plato and dismissed with a verse from Virgil. Far from it. It was the custom at that time with English ladies to greet their friends and relations, and even strangers, with kisses, and strange as it may appear to our modern ideas, accustomed as we are to stare in amazement at such practices when by any chance we observe them in southern countries, the custom was so strikingly

---

[1] "The Scholemaster," p. 21.
[2] "Description of Britaine," 1577, ed Furnivall, New Shakspere Society, part i. p. 271.

prevalent in England that travellers noticed it as one of the strange sights of the land ; grave Erasmus cynically calls it one of its attractions. "This custom," says he, " will never be praised enough." [1] The above-named Nicander Nucius, of Corcyra, who came to England some fifty years later, notices the same habit as a great local curiosity. According to him, the English "display great simplicity and absence of jealousy in their usages towards females. For not only do those who are of the same family and household kiss them . . . with salutations and embraces, but even those, too, who have never seen them. And to themselves this appears by no means indecent." [2] The very Queen herself, even in the middle of the most imposing ceremonies, could not help indulging in familiarities contrary to our ideas of decorum, but quite in accordance with the freedom of manners then prevalent. Sir James Melville relates in his memoirs how he was present when Robert Dudley was made " Earl of Leicester and baron of Denbigh ; which was done at Westminster with great solemnity, the Queen herself helping to put on his ceremonial, he sitting upon his knees before her with a great gravity. But she could not refrain from putting her hand in his neck, smilingly tickling him,

---

[1] "Est præterea mos nunquam satis laudatus. Sive quo venias omnium osculis exciperis; sive discedas aliquo, osculis dimitteris; redis, redduntur suavia . . . denique quocumque te moveas, suaviorum plena sunt omnia" ("Epistolarum . . . libri.," London, 1642, col. 315, A.D. 1499).

[2] "The second book of the travels of Nicander Nucius," ed. Cramer, London, Camden Society, 1841, 4to, p. 10. Nucius resided in England in 1545-6.

the French Ambassadour and I standing by. Then she turned, asking at me, 'how I liked him?'"[1]

The earliest attempts at the novel in the modern style bore a resemblance to these social and intellectual manners. Let us not be surprised if these works are too heavily bedizened for our liking : the toilettes and fashions of that time were less sober than those of to-day; it was the same with literature. Queen Elizabeth, who was wholly representative of her age, and shared even its follies, liked and encouraged finery in everything. All that was ornament and pageantry held her favour ; in spite of public affairs, she remained all her life the most feminine of women ; on her gowns, in her palaces, with her poets, she liked to find ornaments and embellishments in profusion. The learned queen who read Plutarch in Greek, a thing Shakespeare could never do, and translated Boetius into English,[2] found, in spite of her philosophy, an immense delight in having herself painted in fantastic costumes, her thin person hidden in a silken sheath, covered by a light gauze, over which birds ran. Around her was a perpetual field of cloth of gold, and the nobles sold their lands in order to appear at Court sufficiently embroidered. She liked nothing better than to hear and take part in conversations on dresses and fashions. This was so well known, that when Mary, Queen of Scots, sent the same Sir James Melville on his mission to the

[1] "The Memoires of Sir James Melvil, of Hal-hill," ed. G. Scott. London, 1683, fol. p. 47.

[2] The autograph manuscript of her translations, which comprise a part of the works of Plutarch, Horace and Boetius, was found in 1883, at the Record Office.

English Court, in 1564, she was careful to advise him not to forget such means to propitiate her " dear sister." The account left by Melville of the way in which he carried into effect this part of his instructions is highly characteristic of the times, and gives an idea of the way in which a courtly conversation was then conducted :

"The Queen my mistress," says Melville, in his "Memoires," "had instructed me to leave matters of gravity sometimes, and cast in merry purposes, lest otherwise I should be wearied [wearying], she being well informed of that queens natural temper. Therefore in declaring my observations of the customs of Dutchland, Poland and Italy, the buskins of the women was not forgot, and what countrey weed I thought best becoming gentlewomen. The Queen said she had cloths of every sort, which every day thereafter, so long as I was there, she changed. One day she had the English weed, another the French, and another the Italian and so forth.

"She asked me which of them became her best?

"I answered, in my judgment the Italian dress, which answer I found pleased her well, for she delighted to shew her golden coloured hair, wearing a caul and bonnet as they do in Italy. Her hair was more reddish than yellow, curled in appearance naturally.

"She desired to know of me what colour of hair was reputed best, and which of them two was fairest.

"I answered the fairness of them both was not their worst faults.

"But she was earnest with me to declare which of them I judged fairest?

"I said she was the fairest Queen of England, and mine the fairest Queen of Scotland.

"Yet she appeared earnest.

"I answered they were both the fairest Ladies in their countries; that Her Majesty was whiter, but my Queen was very lovely.

"She inquired which of them was of highest stature?

"I said my Queen.

"Then saith she, she is too high, for I, my self, am neither too high nor too low. Then she asked what kind of exercise she used?

"I answered that when I received my dispatch, the Queen was lately come from the High-land hunting. That when her more serious affairs permitted, she was taken up with reading of histories; that sometimes she recreated her self in playing upon the lute and virginals.

"She asked if she played well? I said reasonably, for a Queen.

"That same day after dinner my Lord of Hunsdean drew me up to a quiet gallery, that I might hear some musick, but he said that he durst not avow it, where I might hear the Queen play upon the virginals. After I had hearkned a while, I took up the tapistry that hung before the door of the chamber, and seeing her back was toward the door, I entered within the chamber, and stood a pretty space hearing her play excellently well, but she left off immediately, so soon as she turned her about and saw me. She appeared to be surprized to see me, and came forward, seeming to strike me with her hand, alledging she used not to play before men, but when she was solitary to shun melancholly."

Fortunately she does not strike the ambassador, and is easily pacified. She wants to dazzle him also with her knowledge of languages:

"She said my French was good, and asked if I could speak Italian which she spoke reasonably well. . . . Then she spake to me in Dutch [*i.e.*, German], which was not good; and would know what kind of books I most delighted in, whether theology, history, or love matters." She manages to keep Melville two days longer than he had intended to stay "till I might see her dance, as I was afterward informed. Which being over, she inquired of me whether she or my Queen danced best? I answered the Queen danced not so high and disposedly as she did."

This woman, nevertheless, with so many frailties and ultra-feminine vanities, was a sovereign with a will and a purpose. Even in the midst of this talk about buskins, love-books and virginals, it shone out. So much so, that hearing she is resolved not to marry, the Scottish ambassador immediately retorts in somewhat blunt fashion: "I know the truth of that, madam, said I, and you need not tell it me. Your Majesty thinks if you were married, you would be but Queen of England, and now you are both King and Queen. I know your spirit cannot endure a commander."[1]

The same singular combination may be observed in the literary works of her time: flowers of speech and vanities abound, but they are not without an aim. Rarely was any sovereign so completely emblematic of his or her period. She may almost be said to be the key to it; and it may be very well asserted that whatever the branch of art or literature of this epoch you wish to understand, you must first study Elizabeth.

[1] "Memoires," London, 1683, pp. 49 *et seq.*

Her taste for finery and jewels remained to the last. Hentzner, a German, who saw her many years after Melville, describes her coming out of her chapel at Greenwich Palace, in 1598. She has greatly altered; she is no longer the young princess that would publicly forget etiquette at Westminster for the sake of Robert Dudley; but she still glitters with jewels and ornaments. "Next came the Queen, in the sixty-fifth year of her age, as we were told, very majestic; her face oblong, fair, but wrinkled, her eyes small, yet black and pleasant; her nose a little hooked, her lips narrow, and her teeth black. . . . She had in her ears two pearls, with very rich drops; she wore false hair and that red; upon her head she had a small crown. . . . Her bosom was uncovered as all the English ladies have till they marry, and she had on a necklace of exceeding fine jewels; her hands were small, her fingers long, and her stature neither tall nor low; her air was stately, her manner of speaking kind and obliging. That day she was dressed in white silk, bordered with pearls of the size of beans, and over it a mantle of black silk, shot with silver threads . . . Instead of a chain, she had an oblong collar of gold and jewels."[1]

These descriptions of her by Melville and Hentzner are supplemented, in highly characteristic fashion, not only by such fancy portraits as the one alluded to before, where she is represented as a shepherdess, a nymph, an imaginary being from Arcady, from mythology, or from nowhere, but by such grave, dignified, official portraitures as the very fine engraving left by Rogers. Round the sharp-featured face, with

[1] "Travels in England," ed. H. Morley, London, 1889, p. 47.

QUEEN CLEOPATRA, AS REPRESENTED ON THE ENGLISH STAGE IN THE EIGHTEENTH CENTURY.

closed, wilful lips, weary eyes, open, intelligent forehead, lace ruffs of various shapes, some very bushy, some quite flat and round-shaped like butterfly wings, are displayed in most imposing array. No imaginable kind of gum or starch could keep them straight; they were spread on iron wires. The gown itself, of cylindric shape, expanded by means of a farthingale, is covered with knobs, knots, pearls, ribbons, fringes, and ornaments of all sorts. Well does this figure deserve the attention of the student of Shakespeare, for in this and no other fashion was Cleopatra, the Egyptian queen, dressed, when she appeared on the boards of the Globe Theatre. Never did the author of "Antony" dream of Denderah's temple, and of the soft, voluptuous face, peacock-covered, representing there Isis-Cleopatra; but he dressed his Egyptian queen as the queen he had known had been dressed, and it was in the costumes of Rogers' engraving, and most appropriately too, that the Cleopatra of the Globe was heard to make the remarkable proposal, "Let's to billiards."[1]

Does this seem very strange or in any way incredible? But we must remember that many years, nay, several centuries, were to elapse before anything like historical accuracy was to affect dresses on the stage. Another Cleopatra trod the boards of the English theatre in the eighteenth century; she was very different from her Elizabethan elder sister; she wore *paniers* and a Louis XV. wig, and, as may be seen in our engraving, came in no way nearer the model at Denderah.

The architecture of this period corresponded with

[1] "Antony and Cleopatra," act ii. sc. 5. As for a reproduction of Rogers' engraving, see Frontispiece of this volume.

the richness and pomp of the costumes. A new style, partly from Italy, partly from dreamland, was introduced into England during the Tudor and early Jacobean times. There was lace, and knots and knobs and curious holes, pillars, and pilasters. The sincerest admirers of antiquity, such as Inigo Jones, who went to Italy with such good purpose, and there filled his albums with many exquisite sketches of antique and Renaissance masterpieces,[1] could not refrain from sometimes introducing Arcady and dreamland into their architecture. Inigo Jones died before finishing his Whitehall palace, and we know from his drawings that he intended to embellish the central circular court with a row of gigantic caryatides representing Persians, six or seven yards high.[2] A contriver of masks for the Court, Inigo Jones, was in this way tempted to build palaces, if one may say so, in *mask-style*. Such houses as

SKETCHES MADE BY INIGO JONES IN ITALY.

[1] An album of sketches of this sort, made by Inigo Jones while in Italy, 1614, was reproduced in fac-simile by the care of the Duke of Devonshire, London, 1832. See also drawings, by the same, for scenery and costumes in masks in the "Portfolio," May, June, and July, 1889, three articles by Mr. R. T. Blomfield. Isaac Oliver the famous Elizabethan miniature painter, has left also drawings, one of which is reproduced at the head of this chapter, testifying to his careful study of Italian models.

[2] A view of this court, with the caryatides, is to be seen in W. Kent, "The Designs of Inigo Jones," London, 1835, two vol. fol. We give a reproduction of the caryatides.

Audley End, Hatfield, and especially Burghley, this last being mostly Elizabethan,[1] are excellent representations of the architectural tastes of the time; the thick windowless towers of a former age are replaced by palatial façades, where countless enormous windows occupy more space in the wall than the bricks and stones themselves. Not a few people of a conservative turn of mind were heard to grumble at these novelties: " And albeit," said Harrison, in 1577, at the very time when Lord Burghley was busy building his house in Northamptonshire, " that in these daies there be manie

INIGO JONES'S PERSIANS STANDING AS CARYATIDES.

goodlie houses erected in the sundrie quarters of this Iland ; yet they are rather curious to the eie, *like paper worke* than substantiall for continuance ; whereas such as he [Henry VIII.] did set up, excel in both and therefore may justlie be preferred farre above all the

[1] It was built on the plans, as is supposed, of J. Thorpe, possibly with the help of the Italian John of Padua. Above one of the doors of the inner court is the date 1577 ; the clock tower is dated 1585 ; see the engraving p. 69. Hatfield bears on its façade the date 1611. Audley End was built 1603–1616.

rest." But notwithstanding such a threatening prophecy neither at Burghley nor at Hatfield has the "paper worke" put there been yet blown away by storm or time, and these houses continue to afford a safe residence to the descendants of the Cecils. According to Harrison's judgment the interior of the new houses, no less than the exterior, testified to a decadence: "Now have we manie chimnies; and yet our tenderlings complaine of rheumes, catarhs and poses. Then had we none but reredosses; and our heads did never ake. For as the smoke in those daies was supposed to be a sufficient hardening of the timber of the house, so it was reputed a far better medicine to keepe the goodman and his familie from the quacke or pose, wherewith, as then verie few were acquainted." [1]

But Harrison's blame does not seem to have greatly affected the taste for chimneys, any more than his sinister prophecies concerning Elizabethan houses have been fulfilled; chimneys have continued, and paper-work houses remain still to help us if need be to understand the poetry, the drama, and the novel of the period.

[1] "Description of Britaine," ed. Furnivall, New Shakspere Society, part i. pp. 268 and 338.

VIRGO.

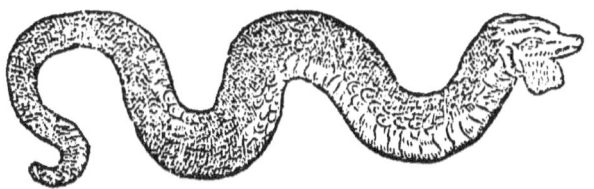

A DRAGON, ACCORDING TO TOPSELL, 1608.

CHAPTER III.

LYLY AND HIS "EUPHUES."

I.

THE romance which, at this period, received a new life, and was to come nearer to our novels than anything that had gone before, has many traits in common with the fanciful style of the architecture, costume, and conversation described above. What have we to do, thought men, with things practical, convenient, or of ordinary use? We wish for nothing but what is brilliant, unexpected, extraordinary. What is the good of setting down in writing the incidents of commonplace lives? Are they not sufficiently known to us? does not their triviality sadden us enough every day? If we are told stories of imaginary lives, let them at least be dissimilar from our own; let them offer unforeseen incidents; let the author be free to turn aside from reality provided that he leaves the trivial and the ordinary. Let him lead us to Verona, Athens, into Arcadia, where he will, but as far as possible from Fleet Street! And if by ill-luck he sets foot in Fleet Street, let him at least speak the language of Arcadia!

Authors found this advice excellent, and took good care to relieve themselves of difficult search after the mere truth. The public who imposed these laws, this exacting public of women who read Plutarch and Plato, who judged the merits of great men as learnedly as the cut of a ruff, found at the very moment they most wanted him the author who could please them in the person of a novel writer, the famous Lyly. At twenty-five years of age, John Lyly, a *protégé* of Lord Burghley, who was at this same time busy with his own architectural poem, if one may say so, of Burghley House, wrote "Euphues,"[1] a new kind too of "paperwork" with which people were enraptured.

It was written expressly for women, and not only did the author not conceal the circumstance, but he proclaimed it aloud. Their opinion alone interested him, to that of the critics he was indifferent. "It resteth Ladies," he said, "that you take the paines to read it, but at such times, as you spend in playing with your little dogges, and yet will I not pinch you of that pastime, for I am content that your dogges lie in your laps: so 'Euphues' may be in your hands, that when you shall be wearie in reading of the one, you may be ready to sport with the other. . . . 'Euphues' had

---

[1] "'Euphues' the anatomy of wyt . . . wherin are contained the delights that wyt followeth in his youth by the pleasauntnesse of Love, and the happynesse he reapeth in age by the perfectnesse of wisedome"; London [1579], 4to; reprinted by Arber, London, 1869. Lyly was born in 1553 or 1554; he died in 1606.

rather lye shut in a Ladyes casket, then open in a Schollers studie." Yet after dinner, "Euphues" will still be agreeable to the ladies, adds Lyly, always smiling; if they desire to slumber, it will bring them to sleep which will be far better than beginning to sew and pricking their fingers when they begin to nod.[1]

There is no possibility of error; with Lyly commences in England the literature of the drawing-room, that of which we speak at morning calls, productions which, in spite of vast and many changes, still occupy a favourite place on the little boudoir tables. We must also notice what pains Lyly gives himself to make his innovation a success, and so please his patronesses, and how he ornaments his thoughts and engarlands his speeches, how cunningly he imbues himself with the knowledge of the ancients and of foreigners, and what trouble he gives himself to improve upon the most learned and the most florid of them. His care was not thrown away. He was spoiled, petted, and caressed by the ladies; with an impartial heart they extended to the author the same favour they granted to the book, and to their little dogs. He was proclaimed king of letters by his admirers, and became, in fact, king of the *précieux*. He created a school, and the name of his hero served to baptize a whole literature. This particular form of bad style was called *euphuism*.

---

[1] Dedication of the second part: "To the Ladies and Gentlewoemen of England." There is afterwards a sort of second preface addressed to the "Gentlemen readers," but Lyly puts into it much less animation, and appears to have written it only for conscience' sake in order not to forget any one.

II.

Euphuism owes to him its name and its diffusion in England; but not, although it is usually so stated, its birth. This strange language, as Dr. Landmann[1] has well demonstrated, was imported from Spain into England, and Lyly was not the first to use it in this country. The works of Guevara, turned into English by five or six different translators, had a considerable vogue and acclimatized this extraordinary style in Great Britain. One of his writings especially, "The golden boke of Marcus Aurelius, emperour," enjoyed a very great popularity; it was translated by Lord Berners in 1532, and by Sir Thomas North in 1557,[2] and went through

---

[1] In his excellent work, "Shakspere and Euphuism," *Transactions of the New Shakspere Society*, 1884, Dr. Landmann was the first to break up Lyly's style into its different parts, and point out the true sources where he found not only the elements of his language, but even many of his ideas. The same essay contains very useful information on Gongorism and other kinds of affected styles of the sixteenth century. See also Dr. Landmann's "Der Euphuismus," Giessen, 1881; his edition of part of "Euphues," Heilbronn, 1887; and an article by Mr. S. L. Lee, *Athenæum*, July 14, 1883.

[2] The "Libro aureo" appeared in 1529; it was translated into French in 1531, and went through a great many editions, entitled sometimes "Le Livre doré de Marc-Aurèle"; sometimes "L'Horloge des princes." North's translation, which followed the French editions, is entitled, "The Diall of Princes, by Guevara, englyshed out of the Frenche," London, 1557, fol.; it had several editions. It is to the Marcus Aurelius of Guevara that La Fontaine alludes in his "Paysan du Danube"; the story of the peasant was one of the most popular of the "Golden Boke." Guevara's style, with all the supplementary embellishments that Lyly has added, was already to be seen in the

many editions. The moral dissertations of which it is full enchanted serious minds ; the unusual language of Spain delighted frivolous souls. Before Lyly, English authors had already imitated it ; but when Lyly appeared and embellished it even more, enthusiasm ran so high that its foreign progenitor was forgotten, and this exotic style was rebaptized as proof of adoption and naturalization in England.

Since it is not a natural product, but the mere result of ingenious artifices, nothing is easier than to reduce it to its component parts, to take it to pieces so to speak. It consists in an immoderate, prodigious, monstrous use of similes, so arranged as to set up antitheses in every limb of the sentence. What is peculiar to the English imitators, is the employment of alliteration, in order to better mark the balance of the sentences written for effect. Finally, the kind of similes even has something peculiar : they are for the most part borrowed from an imaginary ancient history and a fantastical natural history, a sort of mythology of plants and stones to which the most extraordinary virtues are attributed.

In the important parts, when he means to use a noble style, Lyly cannot relate the most trivial incident without setting up parallels between the sentiments of his characters and the virtues of toads, serpents, unicorns, scorpions, and all the fantastical animals mentioned in Pliny or described in the bestiaries of the Middle Ages. His knowledge of zoology resembles that of Richard

collection of short stories by Pettie, 1576 (*supra*, p. 81) of which one of the early editions begins like " Euphues," with an epistle to the " gentlewomen readers."

de Fournival, who, in the thirteenth century, lamented in his "Bestiaire d'Amour," [1] that he was like the wolf, who, when instead of first noticing the man, allowed the man to see him first, lost all his courage ; or like the cricket who loves chirping so much that he forgets to eat and allows himself to be caught. Richard was overcome in like manner by the glances of his mistress, and all his songs only served to accomplish his ruin. The woman he loves resembles the bird called "Kalander," or again, the animal called "cockatrice" or "cocodrille," which is often mentioned by Lyly. "Its nature is such that when it finds a man, then it devours him, and when it has devoured him, then it laments him all the days of its life." [2] Such is the conduct, says Richard, of women too beautiful and too much beloved.

Bestiaries had enjoyed an immense popularity from the earliest times. They were not all, far from it, like Richard de Fournival's, love-bestiaries ; most of them had a religious tendency. Such were, for example, in England, the well-known Anglo-Saxon bestiary,[3] or the English bestiary of the thirteenth century, in which we read of the world-famous wickedness of the whale who allows sailors to rest on her back, and even to light a fire thereon, in order to

[1] "Le Bestiaire d'Amour," ed. Hippeau, Paris, 1840, 8vo. Richard de Fournival died about 1260. The MS. followed in this edition is dated 1285.

[2] "Sa nature si est que quand il trouve un homme, si le dévore, et quand il l'a dévoré, si le pleure tous les jours de sa vie."

[3] Fragments of which remain in the "Codex Exoniensis," ed. Thorpe, London, 1842, 8vo. The Panther, p. 355 ; the Whale, p. 360, &c.

THE "EGYPTIAN OR LAND CROCODILE," 1608.

[*p.* 109.

warm themselves; but as soon as she feels the heat she dives and drowns them all: an example of what may be expected from the devil. There is, too, the elephant that leans against a tree to take his rest. People cunningly cut the tree, and replace it; when the elephant comes the tree falls and so does he, and is caught, an emblem of our father Adam, who also owed his fall to a tree.[1] Again the "Contes Moralisés" of Nicole Bozon, written in French by a friar who lived in England in the first half of the fourteenth century, are also full of the most curious comparisons between the properties of animals, plants, and minerals, and the sinful tendencies and frailties of mankind.[2]

These are old, far-off examples, and it might be supposed that people of education in Elizabethan England would have possessed a sounder knowledge of natural history. This was, however, not the case. And if we wish to know what were the current beliefs among well-informed men of the time about animals, we have only to open the two folio volumes penned with greatest care by painstaking Topsell, concerning "Foure-footed beastes" and "Serpents."[3] We shall then willingly set Lyly and his followers free from all blame of exaggeration and improbable inventions. Most often indeed

---

[1] "An old English Miscellany, containing a bestiary," ed. R. Morris, London, Early English Text Society, 1872.

[2] Recently published by Miss Lucy Toulmin Smith and M. Paul Meyer, Paris, Société des anciens textes Français, 1889, 8vo.

[3] "The historic of Foure-footed beastes, describing the true and lively figure of every beast," London, 1607, fol. "The historic of Serpents or the second book of living creatures," London, 1608, fol.

they did not invent; they knew. Topsell's books are nothing but a careful summary of the then generally accepted reports concerning animated creation.

His histories are the more curious as his scruples and earnestness are obvious. His purpose is high, and he means to write only for the Creator's glory, considering his subject to be a "part of Divinity that was never known in English. I take my owne conscience to witness, which is manifest to my Judge and Saviour, I have intended nothing but his glory, that is the creator of all." Secondly, his serious attention to his subject is shown by what he says of accessible animals; the engravings he gives of them, of dogs, for instance, of bulls, asses, and many others being really excellent. Even rare animals, when by any chance he had secured a glimpse of them, are represented with the utmost care; such, for instance, is his chameleon, of which he gives a very good engraving, not long after careless Robert Greene had been writing of "this byrd, a camelion."[1]

But, then, nature is full of surprises, and so is Topsell's book. His antelopes are very dangerous things: "They have hornes . . . which are very long and sharpe; so that Alexander affirmed they pierced through the sheeldes of his souldiers, and fought with them very irefully: at which time his companions slew as he travelled to India, 8,550; which great slaughter may be the occasion why they are so rare and sildome seene to this day." Undoubtedly.

The blood of the elephant has a very strange pro-

[1] "Alcida, Greenes metamorphosis," licensed 1588; earliest known edition, 1617.

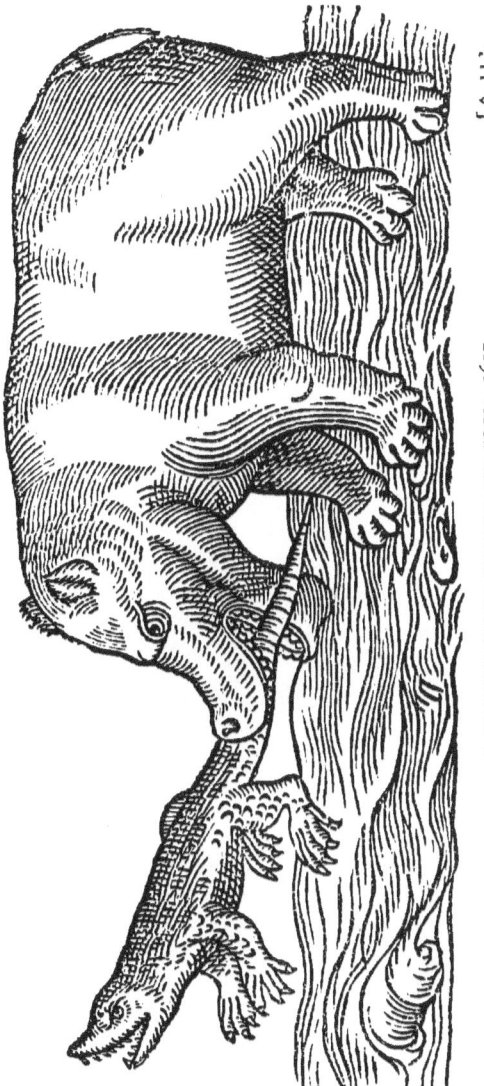

A HIPPOPOTAMUS TAKING ITS FOOD, 1607.

perty: "Also it is reported that the blood of an elephant is the coldest blood in the world and that Dragons in the scorching heate of summer cannot get anything to coole them except this blood." The seahorse, or hippopotamus, "is a most ugly and filthy beast, so called because in his voice and mane he resembleth a horsse, but in his head an oxe or a calfe; in the residue of his body a swine. . . . It liveth for the most part in rivers; yet it is of a doubtful life, for it brings forth and breedeth on the land." According to the accompanying engraving he apparently feeds on crocodiles. The rhinoceros is remarkable for his breathing: he "hath a necke like unto a horsse and also the other parts of his body, but it is said to breath out aire which killeth men."

But in this world of animals, which includes the Mantichora, the Sphinga, the Papio, and a monster alive "in the territory of the bishop of Salceburgh," the most interesting is the Lamia. It is of such great interest because its very existence has been disputed, but quite wrongly. Some untrue reports were circulated concerning this animal, and as these accounts were fabulous, people have been found who disbelieved, not only the stories, but even the possibility that Lamiæ existed. Topsell wisely takes a middle course: "These and such like stories and opinions there are of Phairies, which in my judgment arise from the præstigious apparitions of Devils, whose delight is to deceive and beguile the minds of men with errour, contrary to the truths of holye scripture which doeth no where make mention of such inchaunting creatures; and therefore if any such be, we will holde them the workes of the

Devill and not of God." But, then, there are true Lamiæ, and "we shall take for granted by the testimony of holy scripture that there is such a beast as this." The particulars Topsell was able to gather about them are to the following effect : "The hinde parts of this beast are like unto a goate, his fore legs like a beares, his upper parts to a woman, the body scaled all over like a Dragon, as some have observed, by the observation of their bodies." Their wickedness is so great that it scarcely bears description : "They are the swiftest of foot of all earthly beasts, so as none can escape them by running, for by their celerity, they compasse their prey of beastes, and by their fraud, they overthrow men. For when as they see a man, they lay open their breastes, and by the beauty thereof entice them to come neare to conference, and so having them within their compasse, they devoure and kill them." So much for four-footed beasts.[1]

The "Historie of serpents" is not less instructive, for it contains, "with their lively figures : names, conditions, kindes and natures of all venomous beasts : with their severall poisons and antidotes ; their deepe hatred to mankind and the wonderfull worke of God in their creation and destruction." Among serpents are included : bees, drones, wasps, hornets, frogs, toads, tortoises, spiders, earthworms, and many other unexpected "venomous beasts." There is in this book information concerning the boas : "The Latines call it *Boa* and *Bossa* of *Bos* because by sucking cowes milke it so encreaseth that in the end it destroyeth all manner of herdes and cattels." The cockatrice, above named, "seemeth to be

[1] "Foure-footed beastes," *ut supra*, pp. 1, 199, 328, 453.

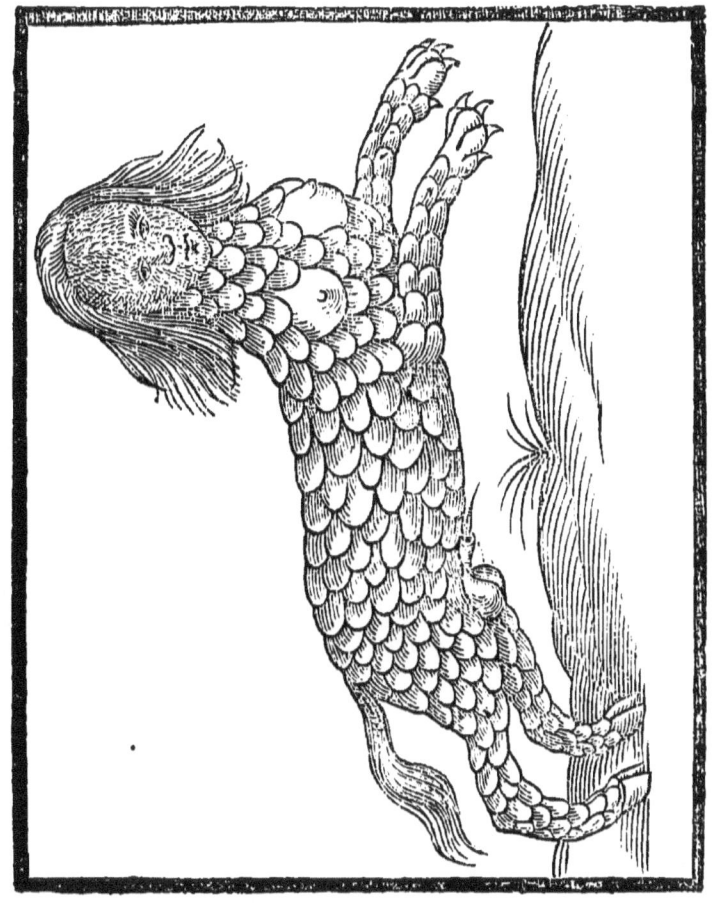

THE LAMIA, ACCORDING TO TOPSELL, 1607.

the king of serpents . . . because of his stately face and magnanimous mind." The crocodile is to be carefully avoided, "even the Egyptians themselves account a crocodile a savage and cruell murthering beast, as may appear by their Hieroglyphicks, for when they will decypher a mad man, they picture a crocodile." And Topsell goes on to relate the particular hatred which existed between crocodiles and the inhabitants of Tentyris, that exquisitely charming Denderah which overlooks the valley of the Nile, and still deserves its old fame as the chief temple of the Goddess Athor, the Egyptian Aphrodite.

The dipsas, the hydra, the dragon, are also endowed with the most remarkable qualities; but they seem to have disappeared since Topsell's day. Not so another very wonderful animal of whom we continue to hear from time to time, I mean the great sea-serpent; this marvellous beast is not only described, but depicted in our naturalist's book. Topsell gives a faithful portrait of it, and we do the same. These animals are so big that "many a time, they overthrow in the waters a laden vessell of great quantitie, with all the wares therein contained." The engraving shows one of them upsetting a three-masted Jacobean ship and swallowing sailors, apparently with great relish and voracity.[1]

Such being the current belief among students of the natural sciences, we may be the better prepared to excuse some eccentricities in a novelist. Lyly, who was well versed in the legendary lore of plants and animals, is never tired of making a display of his knowledge, but the wonder is that his readers had never too much of that.

[1] "Historie of serpents," *ut supra*, pp. 111, 140, 236, &c.

A single erudite or scientific simile never satisfies Lyly ; he has always in his hands a long bead-roll of them, which he complacently pays out : "The foul toade hath a faire stone in his head, the fine golde is found in the filthy earth : the sweet kernell lyeth in the hard shell : vertue is harboured in the heart of him that most men esteeme mishapen . . . Doe we not commonly see that in painted pottes is hidden the deadlyest poyson? that in the greenest grasse is ye greatest serpent? in the cleerest water the uglyest toade?" and four or five similes still follow. Tormented by examples, overwhelmed with similitudes, the adventurous reader, who to-day risks a reading of "Euphues," feels it impossible to keep his composure. He would like to protest, to defend himself, to say that he has lied, this imperturbable naturalist, that bitter kernels are found indeed in the hardest shells, that painted pots often contain something other than poison, and that if toads appear less ugly in foul water, it is perhaps because they are the less seen. But what does it matter to Lyly? He writes for a select coterie, and when a man writes for a coterie, the protestations of the discontented, of the envious, alas! of those of good sense, too, are scarcely of any consequence. Let the common herd then shriek themselves hoarse at Lyly's door : it is shut fast, he will hear nothing, and is indifferent even if among this common herd Shakespeare figures. He is happy ; "Euphues," in company with the little dogs, rumples the silken laps of ladies with the lace-plaited ruffs.

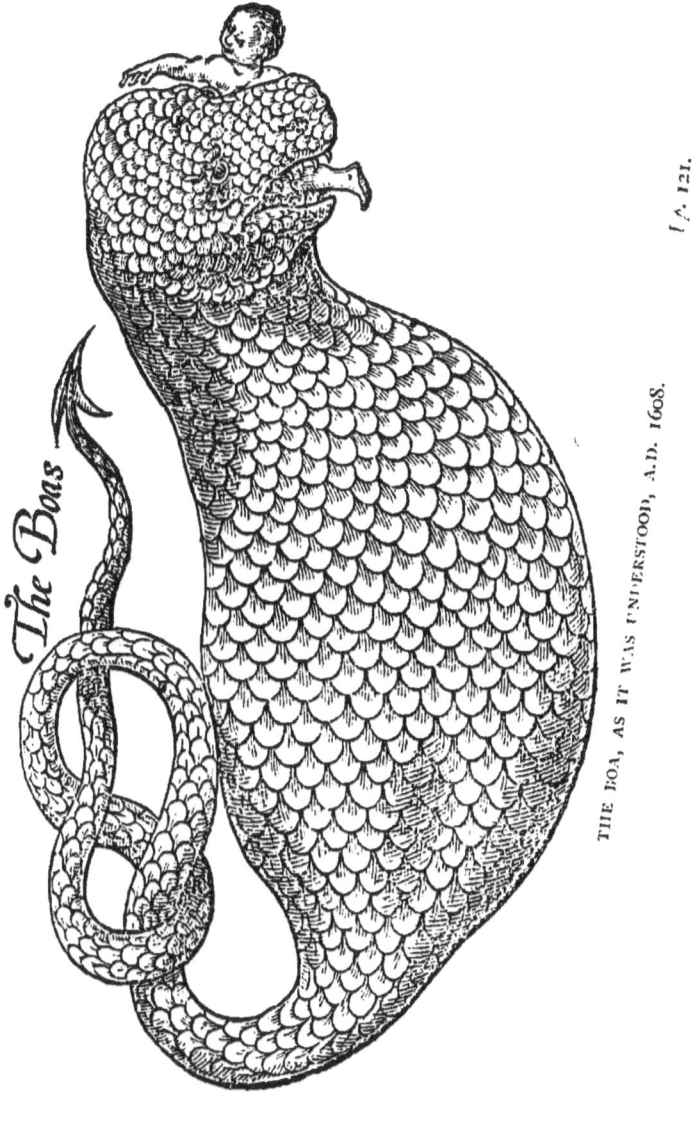

THE BOA, AS IT WAS UNDERSTOOD, A.D. 1608.

III.

But however important style may be, it is not everything in a literary work. It must be acknowledged that Lyly's success, if it is no commendation of the taste of his contemporaries, is greatly to the credit of their morality and earnestness. By the form of his sentences Lyly is a Spaniard; he surpasses the most bombastic, and could give points to that author mentioned by Louis Racine, who, discovering his mistress lying under a tree, cried: "Come and see the sun reclining in the shade!" But the basis of his character is purely English; he is truly of the same country as Richardson, and belongs at heart to that race which Tacitus said did not know how "to laugh at vices," a very high praise that Rousseau rendered later almost in the same terms.[1] From the time of Lyly until our own day, the English novel, generally speaking, has remained not only moral, but a moralizing agent; the author has recourse to a thousand skilful and fascinating devices, and leads us by the hand through all sorts of flowery paths; but whatever the manner may be, he almost invariably, without saying so, leads us to the sermon. There are sermons in Defoe, who strongly protested against some abbreviations of his "Robinson Crusoe": "They strip

[1] It should not, however, be thence concluded that Lyly is original in all his moral dissertations; as Dr. Landmann has pointed out (see *supra*, p. 106) he often borrows large passages from Plutarch and Guevara; but what is remarkable is the intense and persistent conviction, and also the success, at least success in so far that it was read, with which this young man of twenty-five, who was of the world and not of the church, preaches good morals to all classes of society.

it of all those reflections as well religious as moral, which are not only the greatest beauties of the work, but are calculated for the infinite advantage of the reader."[1] There are sermons in Richardson, so much so that it might rather be said that novels are to be noticed in Richardson's magnificent series of sermons. This is the way he himself would have spoken. Did he not write to Lady Bradsaigh, while forwarding her the last volumes of " Clarissa " : " Be pleased ... to honour these volumes with a place with your Taylor's Holy Living and Dying, with your Practice of piety, and Nelson's Fasts and Festivals, not as being worthy of such company, but that they may have a chance of being dipt into thirty years hence. For I persuade myself, they will not be found utterly unworthy of such a chance, since they appear in the humble guise of novel, only by the way of accommodation to the manners and taste of an age overwhelmed with luxury, and abandoned to sound and senselessness."[2] There are some sermons in Fielding, many in Dickens, not a few in George Eliot, and even in Thackeray. Splendid they are, most eloquent, most admirable in their kind, most beneficial in their way ; but there is no denying that sermons they are. Unfortunately for Lyly, what formerly constituted the attraction of " Euphues," and hid the sermon's bitterness, makes it to-day ridiculous and even odious : it is the style. Let us forget for a moment his unicorns and his scorpions ; taken in himself, his hero deserves attention, because he

[1] Preface to Part II.
[2] "Correspondence of Samuel Richardson," ed. Barbauld, London, 1804, 6 vols. 12mo.

THE GREAT SEA SERPENT, ACCORDING TO TOPSELL. 1608.

is the ancestor in direct line of Grandison, of Lord Orville, of Lord Colambre, and of all the sermonizing lords, and lords of good example, that England owed to the success of Richardson.

Euphues is a young Athenian, a contemporary not of Pericles, but of Lyly, who goes to Naples, thence to England, to study men and governments. Grave with that gravity peculiar to lay preachers, well-informed on every subject, even on his own merits, assured by his conscience that in making mankind sharer in his illumination, he will assure their salvation, he addresses moral epistles to his fellow men to guide them through life. Omniscient like the inheritors of his vein whom we have heard since, he instructs the world in the truth about marriage, travel, religion. He anticipates, in his discourses concerning aristocracy, the philosophical ideas of " Milord Edouard," of " Nouvelle Héloïse " fame ; he treats of love with the wisdom of Grandison, and of the bringing up of children with the experience of Pamela.[1]

When women are his subject he is especially earnest and eloquent, and having, as it seems, suffered much at their hands he concludes: " Come to me al ye lovers that have bene deceived by fancy, the glasse of pestilence, or deluded by woemen, the gate to perdition ; be as earnest to seeke a medicine, as you were eager

---

[1] The meaning of his name is thus given by Ascham in his " Scholemaster " (1570) : " Εὐφυής is he that is apte by goodnes of witte and appliable by readines of will, to learning, having all other qualities of the minde and partes of the bodie that must an other day serve learning, not troubled, mangled or halfed, but sounde, whole, full, and hable to do their office." So was Grandison.

to runne into a mischiefe." Having thus secured, as it seems, a fairly large audience, he begins his sermon, which he is pleased to call, " a cooling carde for Philautus, and all fond lovers." [1] His intention is to give men remedies, which shall cure them of loving. Some of his precepts resemble the wise advice of Rondibilis to Panurge; some do not. Philautus is to avoid solitude, and idleness; he must study. In the same way Panurge is recommended *labeur assidu* and *fervente estude*.[2] Philautus is advised to try law, " whereby thou mayest have understanding of olde and auntient customes;" if law proves of no avail, there is " Physicke," and if this again fails, then there is " the atteining of ye sacred and sincere knowledge of divinitie." Study then may be supplemented by contemptuous meditations about women;[3] a remedy which Rabelais, who probably knew more of life than twenty-five-years-old Lyly, refrains from recommending.

This part of the anathema, including as it does a description of the superfluities of Elizabethan dress, is especially worth noticing : " Take from them," cries Euphues, in a burst of eloquence, " their perywigges, their paintings, their jewells, their rowles, their boulstrings, and thou shalt soone perceive that a woman is the least part of hir selfe. When they be once robbed of their robes, then wil they appear so odious, so ugly, so monstrous, that thou wilt rather think them serpents then saints, and so like hags, that thou wilt

---

[1] Arber's reprint, pp. 106 *et seq*.
[2] " Pantagruel," bk. iii. ch. xxxi.
[3] Compare the meditations of the same sort of the Pedant in the " Pédant joué," of Cyrano de Bergerac.

feare rather to be enchaunted than enamoured. Looke in their closettes, and there shalt thou finde an appoticaryes shop of sweete confections, a surgions boxe of sundry salves, a pedlers packe of newe fangles Besides all this their shadows, their spots, their lawnes, their leefekyes, their ruffes, their rings, shew them rather cardinalls curtisans then modest matrons. . . . If every one of these things severally be not of force to move thee, yet all of them joyntly should mortifie thee." This was, however, by no means the case, and Philautus not so much "cooled" by this "carde" as his friend expected, behaved himself in such a way as to demonstrate that, according to his experience, here was gross exaggeration indeed.

Euphues shows better knowledge of the heart of woman when, continuing his analysis of women's foibles, he comes to give his friend information that teaches him in fact rather how to be loved than how to cease loving : "Yet if thou be so weake being bewitched with their wiles that thou hast neither will to eschue nor wit to avoyd their company . . . yet at the hearte dissemble thy griefe . . . cary two faces in one hood, cover thy flaming fancie with fained ashes . . . let thy hewe be merry when thy heart is melancholy, beare a pleasaunt countenaunce with a pined conscience. . . . Love creepeth in by stealth, and by stealth slideth away. If she breake promise with thee in the night, or absent hir selfe in the day, seeme thou carelesse, and and then will she be carefull ; if thou languish [*i.e.*, becomest slack in thy suit], then wil she be lavish of hir honour, yea and of the other strange beast her honestie."

He continues in this bitter vein, avenging, as it seems, his private wrongs, and vowing never, as far as he is himself concerned to have anything more to do with women. From them, he is naturally led to think of children who form an equally good theme on which to moralise. He does not fail in this duty, and writes for the good of his friend, and of the public at large, a little treatise very much in the style of some of Pamela's letters,[1] where we are taught how "Ephœbus," the child that is to be, should be brought up. Ephœbus is the Emile of this sixteenth-century Rousseau. Always thorough and exact, Lyly is careful to begin at the beginning, informing us at first " that the childe shoulde be true borne and no bastarde." [2]

Then he comes to the bringing up of the boy, and with as much earnestness as Jean-Jacques, and with true and moving eloquence, he beseeches the mother to be the nurse of her own progeny. "It is most necessary and most naturall in mine opinion, that the mother of the childe be also the nurse, both for the entire love she beareth to the babe, and the great desire she hath to have it well nourished : for is there any one more meete to bring up the infant than she that bore it? or will any be carefull for it, as she that bredde it? . . . Is the earth called the mother of all things onely bicause it bringeth forth? No, but

[1] For instance, the letter on the nursing of children by their mothers (vol. iii. of the original edition, letter 56), and the long letter where Pamela takes to pieces Locke's "Treatise on Education," and remodels it according to her own ideas (vol. iv. letters 48 *et seq.*).

[2] Arber's reprint, *ut supra*, "Euphues and his Ephœbus," pp. 123 *et seq.*

bicause it nourisheth those things that springe out of it. Whatsoever is bred in ye sea is fed in the sea; no plant, no tree, no hearbe commeth out of the ground that is not moystened, and as it were noursed of the moysture and mylke of the earth; the lyonesse nurseth hir whelps, the raven cherisheth hir byrdes, the viper her broode, and shal a woman cast away her babe?

"I accompt it cast away which in the swath clouts is cast aside, and lyttle care can the mother have which can suffer such crueltie: and can it be tearmed with any other title then cruelty, the infant yet looking redde of the mother, the mother yet breathing through the torments of hir travaile, the child crying for helpe which is said to move wilde beastes, even in the selfe said moment it is borne, or the nexte minute, to deliver to a straunge nurse, which perhappes is neither wholesome in body, neither honest in manners, whiche esteemeth more thy argent though a trifle, then thy tender infant, thy greatest treasure?" Here Lyly is at his best, and neither Richardson nor Rousseau spoke better on this point, which is one of their favourite subjects.

He goes on to show how his child should be brought up, with what principles he should be imbued; many of these principles again very much resembling those Rousseau was to accept and propagate two hundred years later: "It is good nurture that leadeth to virtue, and discreete demeanour that playneth the path to felicitie.... To be a noble man it is most excellent, but that is our ancestors ... as for our nobilytie, our stocke, our kindred, and whatsoever we ourselves have not done I scarcely accompt ours.... It is vertue, yea vertue, gentlemen, that maketh gentlemen....

These things [*i.e.*, knowledge, reason, good sense], neither the whirling wheele of Fortune can chaunge neither the deceitful cavilling of worldlings separate, neither sickenesse abate, neither age abolish." Then follows a dialogue between Euphues and an atheist,[1] in which I need not say the latter is utterly routed; and the book ends with a collection of letters[2] between Euphues and various people who ask and get his advice on their difficulties, oracle-wise, Pamela-wise too.

In the second part of his romance, which appeared in 1580,[3] Lyly gives a kind of *Lettres persanes*, but *Lettres persanes* reversed, Montesquieu making use of his foreigner to satirize France, and Lyly of his to eulogize his native land. Euphues comes to England with his friend Philautus, and, since he knows everything, instructs the latter as they go along. He warns him against wine, gambling, and debauchery, teaches him geography, and points out to him what is worth seeing. Philautus does not retort that Euphues is a pedant, which proves him to be very good tempered and a perfect travelling companion. The two friends are enchanted with the country: its natural products, its commerce, its agriculture, its inhabitants and their manners, its bishops and their flocks, the civil government, the religious government, everything is perfect.

---

[1] "Euphues and Atheos," Arber's reprint, *ut supra*, pp. 160, *et seq.*
[2] "Certeine Letters writ by Euphues to his friends," *ibid*, pp. 178 *et seq.*
[3] "Euphues and his England. Containing his voyage and adventures, myxed with sundry pretie discourses of honest love, the description of the countrey, the court and the manner of that Isle. . . . by John Lyly, Maister of Arte, London 1580," reprinted by Arber, *ut supra.*

English gentlewomen are prodigies of wisdom and beauty; and indeed that is the least Lyly can say of them, since it is for them that he is writing. When he spoke, as we have seen, disparagingly of women, he meant Italian women (none of whom, as a matter of fact, he had ever known or even seen), not Englishwomen. These spend their mornings "in devout prayer," and not in bed like the ladies of Italy; they read the Scriptures instead of Ariosto and Petrarch; they are so beautiful that the traveller is enraptured and cannot help crying out: "There is no beauty but in England." To sum up, "they are in prayer devoute, in bravery humble, in beautie chast, in feasting temperate, in affection wise, in mirth modest, in all their actions though courtlye, bicause woemen, yet Aungels, bicause virtuous." As for the women of other countries, they all have lovers and spend their time in painting their faces.[1]

Having verified such important differences, Philautus cannot do less than find a wife in England, and Euphues, whose unsociable humour prevents his doing likewise, carries away with him into his native land the remembrance of "a place, in my opinion (if any such may be on the earth) not inferiour to a paradise," and of a Queen "of singuler beautie and chastitie, excelling in the one Venus, in the other Vesta."

It is, however, appropriate to recollect that at the time of the Renaissance, before the blossoming in England of this literature for ladies, Caxton too had enumerated the chief qualities of the women of his country. They are the same as in Lyly, only, as we shall see, the honest

[1] "Euphues and his England," *ut supra*, p. 442.

printer closes his remarks with a slight reservation. In the preface placed at the beginning of a work translated from the French by Lord Rivers, he states that in the translation, several passages reflecting on the female sex were suppressed; that is easily understood; they would have no application in England; "for I wote wel," says he, "of whatsomever condicion women ben in Grece, the women of this contre ben right good, wyse, playsant, humble, discrete, sobre, chast, obedient to their husbandis, trewe, secrete, stedfast, ever besy and never ydle, attemperat in speking and vertuous in all their werkis"— "or," he is fain to add, "atte leste sholde be soo."[1] And thereupon, Caxton, on his own authority, restores the suppressed passages.

From the particular point of view of the historian of the English novel, Lyly with all his absurdities had yet one merit which must be taken into account. With him we leave epic and chivalrous stories and approach the novel of manners. There is no longer question of Arthur and his marvellous knights, but rather of contemporary men, who, in spite of excessive oratorical gew-gaws, possess some resemblance to reality. Conversations are reported in which we find the tone of well-born persons of the period. Lyly takes care also to be very exact in his dates. Having announced at the end of his first volume that Euphues was about to set out for England, he informs us in the beginning of the second, which appeared in 1580, that the embarkation took place on December 1, 1579. He would, for anything, have gone so far as to give an engraved portrait of his hero, just as we were to

[1] Preface to the "Dictes and Sayinges of the Philosophres," 1477.

see later, at the beginning of a book destined to make some noise in the world, the portrait of "Captain Lemuel Gulliver of Redriff." Undoubtedly his opinions on men and life, his analysis of sentiment, are rather clumsily blended with the story and savour of the awkwardness of a first attempt; but there was however merit in making the attempt, and it is not impossible at distant intervals to discover under the crust of pedantry some well-turned passage, possessing eloquence, as we have seen, or, more rarely, a sort of humour. It is thus that a tolerably good lesson may be drawn from the adventures of Philautus in London, who, deeply smitten with the charms of a young English lady, consults a sorcerer in order to obtain a philtre that will inspire love. Here was an excellent opportunity, which the magician does not fail to seize, of talking about serpents and toads. But, after a long enumeration of the bones, stones, and livers of animals that cause love, the alchemist, urged by Philautus, ends by confessing that the best sorcery of all to gain the loving regard of a woman, is to be handsome, witty, and charming.

IV.

By his defects and his merits, his wisdom, his gracefulness and also his bad style, Lyly could not fail to please. His public was ready when he began writing, a public with many frivolous tastes and many serious instincts. The lightness of tone and of behaviour which struck a foreigner coming for the first time to the English court or a professional censor who by trade is meant to see nothing else, was misleading as showing only the surface of the sort of mankind that was flourishing there at that time. This lightness of tone, however, did exist nevertheless, and those who assumed it were not slow to embellish their speeches with flowers from Lyly's paper garden. The austere French Huguenot, Hubert Languet, the friend and adviser of Sir Philip Sidney, who visited England in the very year "Euphues" was published, was very much astonished to see how English courtiers behaved themselves; accustomed as he was to the grave talk he enjoyed with his young friend, he had imagined, it seems, that no other was relished by him or by anybody in Queen Elizabeth's palaces. When he left the country he wrote to Sidney his opinion of the manners he had observed. It is simply a confirmation of what Ascham had stated sometime before, when he wrote of his travelled compatriots : neither of them did justice to the more serious qualities hidden under all this courtly trifling : "It was a delight to me last winter," says Languet, "to see you high in favour and enjoying the esteem of all your countrymen; but to speak plainly, the habits of your court seemed to me somewhat less manly than I could have wished, and most of your noblemen appeared to me to seek for a reputation more by a kind of affected courtesy than by those virtues which are wholesome to the State, and which are most becoming to generous spirits and to men of high birth. I was sorry therefore, and so were other friends of yours, to see you wasting the flower of your life on such things, and I feared lest that noble nature of yours should be brought to take pleasure in pursuits which only enervate the mind."[1]

Lyly's book proved well suited to this public; it went through numerous editions; it was printed five times during the first six years of its publication, and new editions were issued from time to time till 1636. It gave birth, as we shall see, to many imitations; the name of Euphues on the title-page of a novel was for years considered a safe conduct to the public, if not to posterity; books purporting to be Euphues' legacies or copies of Euphues' papers, or bearing in some way or other the stamp of his supposed approbation, multiplied accordingly. The movement increased rapidly, but it was not to last long; in fact, it did not continue beyond ten or twelve years; after this time the monuments of the euphuistic literature were still reprinted, but no addition was made to their number.

This period, however, was filled in a measure with the product of Lyly's brains or that of his imitators. All who prided themselves on elegance spoke his affected language, and studied in his book the mythology of plants. Edward Blount, a bookseller who reprinted Lyly's comedies in the following century, at a time when these courtly dramas were beginning to be forgotten, has well expressed the kindly and sympathetic favour accorded to Lyly by the ladies of Elizabethan days: "These papers of his," says he, "lay like dead lawrels in a churchyard; but I have gathered the scattered branches up, and by a charme, gotten from Apollo, made them greene againe and set them up as

[1] Antwerp, Nov. 14, 1579, "Correspondence of Sir Ph. Sidney and Hubert Languet," ed. Pears, London, 1845, 8vo, p. 167.

epitaphes to his memory. A sinne it were to suffer these rare monuments of wit to lye covered in dust and a shame such conceipted comedies should be acted by none but wormes. Oblivion shall not so trample on a sonne of the Muses; and such a sonne as they called their darling. Our nation are in his debt for a new English which he taught them. 'Euphues and his England' began first that language; all our ladyes were then his schollers; and that beautie in court, which could not parley eupheueisme was as little regarded, as shee which now there speakes not French."[1] It may be appropriately recalled here that this same Blount who thus eulogizes Lyly had published already another set of Elizabethan dramas, and a much more important one, viz., the first folio of Shakespeare in 1623.

Those comedies which Blount thought fit to reprint, considering that in so doing he was presenting to his readers "a Lilly growing in a grove of lawrels," are another proof of the success Lyly had, through his novel, secured for himself at court. His plays are mythological or pseudo-historical dramas, interspersed with some pretty songs and dialogues, and were performed by children before the Queen on holy-days. Among others were his "Campaspe," "played before the Queenes Majestie, on new yeares day at night, by Her Majesties children and the children of Paules," 1584; his "Sapho and Phao," performed also before the Queen by the same children, on Shrove Tuesday, 1584; his "Endimion, the man in the moone," played before

[1] Preface "to the Reader" in "Six Court Comedies . . . by the onely rare poet of that time, the wittie, comicall, facetiously-quicke and unparalelld John Lilly," London, 1632, 12mo.

the Queen "at Greenwich on Candlemass day at night, by the chyldren of Paules"; "Gallathea," played on New Year's Day; "Midas," performed on Twelfth Night, also before the Queen, &c.[1]

On love matters and women's affairs, he was considered an authority; the analysis of the passions and the knowledge of the deeper moods of the soul, which many consider to be, among novelists, a new-born science, were regarded by his contemporaries as a thing wholly his, a discovery made by himself; not foreseeing his successors, they proclaimed him a master of his newly invented art. Beginners would come to him for advice or for a preface, as they go now to the heirs of his art, especially when love is their theme. In this way Thomas Watson published in 1582 his " Passionate Centurie of Love," and prefaced it, as with a certificate of its worth, by a letter from Lyly : " My good friend, I have read your new passions, and they have renewed mine old pleasures, the which brought to me no lesse delight, then they have done to yourself commendations. . . . Such is the nature of persuading pleasure, that it melteth the marrow before it scorch the skin . . . not unlike unto the oyle of jeat which rotteth the bone and never rankleth the flesh." [2]

It was useless for wise minds to grumble; Lyly always found women to applaud him. In vain did Nash, twelve years after the appearance of "Euphues," scoff at the enthusiasm with which he had read the book

---

[1] "Dramatic Works," ed. Fairholt, London, 1858, two vols. 8vo.
[2] Watson was then about twenty-five years old. "Poems," reprinted by Arber, London, 1870, 4to.

when he was "a little ape in Cambridge";[1] vainly was Euphuism derided on the stage before a Cambridge audience: "There is a beaste in India call'd a polecatt ... and the further she is from you the less you smell her," a piece of information that contains more probability than perhaps any given by Lyly.[2] Vainly, too, Shakespeare showed his opinion of the style in lending it to Falstaff when the worthy knight wishes to admonish Prince Henry in the manner of courts. Grown old in his tavern, Falstaff has no idea that these refinements, fashionable at the time when he was as slender as his page, may be now the jest of the young generation: "There is a thing, Harry, which thou hast often heard of, and it is known to many in our land by the name of pitch: this pitch, as ancient writers do report, doth defile; so doth the company thou keepest: for, Harry, now I do not speak to thee in drink, but in tears; not in pleasure, but in passion; not in words only, but in woes also."[3]

Many persons to whom the book doubtless recalled the memory of their spring-time, shared Falstaff's ingenuousness, and remained faithful to Lyly; if men of letters, after some years of enthusiasm, ceased to imitate him, his book was for a long time continuously read, and it was reprinted again and again even in the

[1] "'Euphues' I read when I was a little ape in Cambridge, and I then thought it was *ipse ille;* it may be excellent still for ought I know, but I lookt not on it this ten yeare" ("Strange Newes," 1592).

[2] "The Pilgrimage to Parnassus," ed. Macray, Oxford, 1886, 8vo. "The Returne," part i. act v. sc. 2. This part was performed in 1600.

[3] "1 Henry IV.," act ii. sc. 4 (A.D. 1597-8, Furnivall).

reign of Charles I. It was translated into Dutch in the same century,[1] and was modernized in the following, under the title: "The false friend and the inconstant mistress: an instructive novel ... displaying the artifices of the female sex in their amours."[2] High praise is rendered by the editor to Lyly, who "was a great refiner of the English tongue in those days." The book appeared not very long before Richardson's "Pamela," a fact worthy of notice, the more so as in this abbreviation of Euphues, the letters contained in the original have been reproduced and look the more conspicuous in the little pamphlet. Quite Richardsonian, too, is the table of contents which is rather a table of good precepts and useful information, a very different table from the one appended by Harington to his "Ariosto." Here we find enumerated the many wise recommendations by which Lyly so long anticipated Richardson and Rousseau:

"The mother ought to be her own nurse p. 83.
"The wild beasts more tender of their young than those who nurse not their own children p. 83.
"Children not to be frightened with stories of spirits and bugbears (&c.) ... ... p. 86."

So much for the continuation of Lyly's fame. As for the period of imitation proper, the era of euphuism's

---

[1] "De vermakelijke historie Zee-een Landreize van Euphues," Rotterdam, 1671, 12mo. Another edition of the same, 1682.
[2] London, 1718, 16mo. "Price 2s." (on title-page). Defoe's "Robinson Crusoe" appeared the next year; Richardson's "Pamela" was published in 1740.

full glory, it lasted, as we have said, hardly more than twelve or at most fifteen years. But it saw the birth of works that are not without importance in the history of the origin of the novel in this country.

LIBRA.

10

KNIGHTLY PASTIMES. HAWKING, 1575.
Illustrative of Gerismond's life in Lodge's "Rosalynd."

[*p.* 144.

ANOTHER DRAGON, 1608.

CHAPTER IV.

LYLY'S LEGATEES.

I.

ALL Lyly's imitators, Greene, Lodge, Melbancke, Riche, Munday, Warner, Dickenson, and others, did not faithfully copy his style in all its peculiarities, at any rate in all their works; some of them borrowed only his ideas, others his plot; others his similes; most of them, however, when they first began to write, went the fullest length in imitation, and tricked themselves out in euphuistic tinsel. They were careful by choosing appropriate titles for their novels to publicly connect themselves with the euphuistic cycle. "Euphues" was a magic pass-word, and they well knew that the name once pronounced, the doors of the "boudoirs," or closets as they were then called, and the hands of the fair ladies, were sure to open; the book was certain to be welcome.

Hence the number of writers who declared themselves Euphues' legatees and executors. Year after year, for a while, readers saw issuing from the press such books as "Zelauto, the fountaine of Fame... containing a delicate disputation... given for a friendly entertainment to Euphues at his late arrival into England," by Munday, 1580; or as "Euphues his censure to Philautus, wherein is presented a philosophicall combat betweene Hector and Achylles," by Robert Greene, 1587: "Gentlemen," says the author to the readers, "by chance, some of Euphues loose papers came to my hand, wherein hee writ to his friend Philautus from Silexedra, certaine principles necessary to bee observed by every souldier." Or there was "Menaphon, Camillas alarum to slumbering Euphues," by the same, 1589; "Rosalynde, Euphues golden legacie, found after his death in his cell at Silexedra," by Thomas Lodge, 1590; "Arisbas, Euphues amidst his slumbers," by John Dickenson, 1594, &c.[1] All these authors continued their model's work in contributing to the development of literature written chiefly for ladies; in that way especially was Lyly's initiative fruitful.

Barnabe Riche, for example, publishes "Don Simo-

---

[1] "Prose and Verse" by John Dickenson, ed. Grosart, Manchester, 1878, 4to. At a later date Dickenson took Greene for his model when he wrote his "Greene in conceipt new raised from his grave, to write the tragique history of the faire Valeria of London," 1598. In this Dickenson imitates Greene's descriptions of the life of the courtezans of London (Troy-novant). See *infra*, pp. 187 *et seq.*

nides,"[1] a story of a foreigner who travels in Italy and then comes to London, like Euphues, mixes in good society, and makes the acquaintance of Philautus; he writes this romance "for the amusement of our noble gentilmen as well as of our honourable ladies." He wrote also a series of short stories,[2] this time "for the onely delight of the courteous gentlewoemen bothe of England and Irelande;" and, for fear they should forget his design of solely pleasing them, he addresses them directly in the course of his narrative: "Now, gentilwomen, doe you thinke there could have been a greater torment devised, wherewith to afflicte the harte of Silla?" Shakespeare, an assiduous reader of collections of this kind, and who, unfortunately for their authors, has not transmitted his taste to posterity, was acquainted with Riche's tales, and drew from this same story of Silla the principal incidents of his "Twelfth Night." Riche himself had taken it from the "Histoires tragiques" of Belleforest, and Belleforest had translated it from Bandello.

Munday's Zelauto[3] is also a traveller. A son of

[1] "The straunge and wonderfull Adventures of Don Simonides," London, 1581, 4to; in 1584 appeared "The second tome of the travailes ... of Don Simonides."

[2] "Riche his Farewell to Militarie profession: Conteining verie pleasaunt discourses fit for a peaceable tyme. Gathered together for the onely delight of the Courteous Gentlewoemen bothe of England and Irelande, for whose onely pleasure thei were collected together, and unto whom thei are directed and dedicated," London, 1581, 4to. By the same: "The Adventures of Brusanus, Prince of Hungaria," 1592; "Greenes newes both from heaven and hell," 1593, &c.

[3] London, 1580, 4to. One copy in the Bodleian Library.

the Duke of Venice, he goes on his travels, after the example of Euphues, visiting Naples and Spain, where he falls " in the company of certain English merchants," very learned merchants, " who, in the Latin tongue, told him the happy estate of England and how a worthy princes governed their common wealth." He comes accordingly to this country, for which he feels an admiration equal to Euphues' own. From thence he "takes shipping into Persia," and visits Turkey, prepared upon any emergency to fight valiantly or to speak eloquently, his hand and tongue being equally ready with thrusts and parries, or comparisons and similes.

Again we find Lyly's manner in Melbancke's "Philotimus,"[1] 1583, a book full, as " Euphues," of letters, dialogues, and philosophical discussions, and in Warner's " Pan his Syrinx," 1584. Warner, whose fame mainly rests on his long poem, " Albion's England," published in 1586, began his literary career as a novelist of the euphuistic school. In common with many youths of all times, of whom Lyly was one, he was scarcely out of " non-age," to use his own word, than he wanted to impart to his fellow-men his experience of a life, for him just begun, and to teach them how to behave in a world of which he knew only the outside. He lands his hero, Sorares, " in a sterile and harborlesse island," not a rare occurrence even in novels anterior to Defoe ; Sorares' sons start to find him. Both they and their father meet with sundry adventures, in the course of which they tell or hear stories and take part in various " controversies and complayntes." Many topics

[1] " Philotimus, the warre betwixt nature and fortune," London, 1583, 4to. A copy in the Bodleian Library.

are philosophically discussed ; the chief being, as in Lyly, woman. One of the speakers puts forward the assertion that there may be, after all, some good in women ; but another demonstrates that there is none at all ; and that their name of "wo-man" contains their truest definition. Whereupon, we are treated once more to a description of dresses and fashions : "Her face painted, her beautie borrowed, her haire an others, and that frisled, her gestures enforced, her lookes premeditated, her backe bolstred, her breast bumbasted, her shoulders bared and her middle straite laced, and then is she in fashion !" Of course this does not apply to English, but to Scythian and Assyrian ladies. This description is followed, as in Lyly, by a proper antidote, and with a number of rules to be observed by all the honest people who desire to escape the wiles of the feminine sex.

Warner's book had some success ; it reached a second edition in 1597,[1] in which the author states that two writers, at least, copied him, sometimes "verbatim" without any acknowledgment ; one of them seems to have been no less a person than Robert Greene, "a scholler," says Warner, "better than my selfe on whose grave the grasse now groweth green, whom otherwise, though otherwise to me guiltie, I name not." Several incidents in Greene's works resemble Warner's stories, especially the one called "Opheltes," the plot of which forcibly reminds us of "Francesco's Fortunes," and at

---

[1] "Syrinx or a seavenfold historic . . . newly perused and amended by the original author," London, 1597, 4to. Warner died in 1609.

the same time of a different work of greater fame, the "Two Gentlemen of Verona."[1]

When Warner spoke, apparently, of Greene as a "scholler" better than himself he was quite right, and as a matter of fact, Lyly's two most famous disciples were Thomas Lodge, a friend of Riche, who helped him to revise his works and corrected his faulty verses, and Robert Greene, a novelist and dramatist like Lodge and Lyly, and a friend of the former. Endowed with a less calm and sociable temperament than their model, Greene and Lodge led a chequered existence very characteristic of their epoch.

II.

With Robert Greene we are in the midst of Bohemia, not exactly the Bohemia which Mürger described and which dies in the hospital: the hospital

---

[1] "Episode of Julia and Proteus." This episode has been traced to the story of the shepherdess Felismena, in Montemayor's "Diana." But Shakespeare may have taken some hints also from Warner. Opheltes (Proteus) married (not betrothed) to the virtuous Alcippe (Julia), goes to "Sardis," where he becomes acquainted (in the same manner as Greene's Francesco) with the courtesan Phœmonoe (Greene's Infida). Alcippe hears of it, and wants at least to be able to see her husband; she enters the service of the courtesan, and there suffers a moral martyrdom. Opheltes is ruined, and, in words which Greene nearly copied, "Phœmonoe not brooking the cumbersome haunt of so beggerly a guest, with outragious tearms flatly forbad him her house." Alcippe makes herself known, and all ends well for the couple.

corresponds in some manner to ideas of order and rule; under Elizabeth men remained irregular to the end; literary men who were not physicians like Lodge, or shareholders in a theatre like Shakespeare, or subsidized by the Court like Ben Jonson, died of hunger in the gutter, or of indigestion at a neighbour's house, or of a sword-thrust in the tavern. Therein is one of the peculiarities of the period. It distinguishes the Bohemia of Elizabeth from other famous Bohemias, that of Grub Street, known to Dr. Johnson, and that of the *quartier latin* described by Mürger.

Greene was one of the most original specimens of the unfortunate men who in the time of Elizabeth attempted to live by their pen. He was as remarkable for his extravagances of conduct as for his talents, sometimes gaining money and fame by the success of his writings, sometimes sinking into abject poverty and consorting with the outcasts of society. Of all the writers of the Elizabethan period he is perhaps the one whose life and character we can best picture to ourselves; for in his last years, repentant and sorrow-stricken, he wrote with the utmost sincerity autobiographical tales and pamphlets, which are invaluable as a picture of the times; they are, in fact, nothing else than the "Scènes de la vie de Bohème" of Elizabethan England.

In these books Greene gives us the key to his own character, to his many adventures, and to his miserable end. There were two separate selves in him, and they proved incompatible. One was full of reasonable, sensible, and somewhat *bourgeois* tendencies, highly appreciating honour respectability, decorum, civic and patriotic virtues ; of women liking only those that were pure, of men those that were honest, religious and good citizens. Greene's other self was not, properly speaking, the counterpart of the first, and had no taste for vices as vices, nor for disorder as disorder, but was wholly and solely bent upon *enjoyment*, immediate enjoyment whatever be the sort, the cost, or the consequence. Hence the glaring discrepancies in Greene's life, his faults, not to say his crimes, his sudden short-lived repentances, his supplications to his friends not to imitate his example, his incapacity to follow steadily one course or the other. His better self kept his writings free from vice, but was powerless to control his conduct. This struggle between the forces of good and evil is exceedingly well depicted in Greene's Repentances, under his own or fictitious names ; of all the heroes of his tales he is himself the most interesting and the most deeply studied. As a novel writer and an observer of human nature, his own portrait is perhaps his masterpiece.

Greene was born at Norwich about 1560, and belonged to a family in easy circumstances. He was sent to Cambridge, where he was admitted to St. John's College on November, 1575. There, according to a propensity that was inborn, he at once associated with noisy, unprincipled young fellows. This propensity accompanied him through life, and led him to constantly surround himself with a rabble of merry companions, to be greatly liked by them, but to make few sincere friends, and to quarrel with these very often, to drop their acquaintance, to befriend them again, and so on to the last.

The universities at that time were not places of edification; and Lyly, who during the same period had a personal experience of them, was careful when, shortly afterwards, he wrote his advice for the education of "Ephœbus" to warn fathers of the dangers of university life : " To speak plainly of the disorder of Athens [that is, Oxford] who does not se it and sorrow at it? Such playing at dice, such quaffing of drink, such daliaunce with women, such dauncing, that in my opinion there is no quaffer in Flaunders so given to tipplyng, no courtier in Italy so given to ryot, no creature in the world so misled as a student in Athens." Many return from the universities "little better learned, but a great deal worse lived, then when they went, and not only unthrifts of their money, but also banckerouts of good manners." [1]

Greene did not fail to choose his associates among people of this sort, and with some of them he crossed over to the continent in his turn to visit "Circe." "Being at the University of Cambridge, I light amongst wags as lewd as my selfe, with whome I consumed the flower of my youth, who drew me to travell into Italy and Spaine, in which places I saw and practizde such villainie as is abhominable to declare. . . ." He comes back, and after the pleasures and excitement of travel, ordinary every-day life seems to him tasteless ; the mere idea of a regular career of any sort is abhorrent to him. "At my return into England, I ruffeled out in my silks, in the habit of *Malcontent*, and seemed so discontent that no place would please me to

[1] Arber's reprint, pp. 139 and 141.

abide in, nor no vocation cause mee to stay myselfe in." [1]

In this uncertainty, and with his head full of Italian remembrances and romantic adventures, he thought, being not yet twenty, to try his hand at writing. His first attempt was a novel, a love story in the Italian fashion, in which very much loving was to do for very little probability and less observation of character and nature. It was called "Mamillia"; it was finished in 1580, and published three years later.

Greene at that time was again in Cambridge, and strange to say, among the many whims that crossed his mind, a fancy took him to apply himself to study. Gifted as he was, this caused him no trouble; he acquired much varied knowledge, of which his writings show sufficient proof, and was received M.A. in 1583.[2] He then left the university and went to London, where the most curious part of his life, that was to last only nine years longer, began.

---

[1] "The Repentance of Robert Greene," 1592. "Works," ed. Grosart, vol. xii. p. 172.

[2] He belonged then to Clare Hall; the preface to the second part of "Mamillia" (entered 1583) is dated "from my studie in Clarehall." Later in life he seems to have again felt the want of increasing his knowledge, and he was, for a while, incorporated at Oxford, July, 1588; he, therefore, describes himself on the title-page of some of his works, not without touch of pride, as belonging to both universities. In common with his friend Lodge he had a taste for medical studies, and he appears to have attempted to open to himself a career of this kind; he styles himself on the title-page of "Planetomachia," 1585, as "Student in Phisicke," but as he never gave himself any higher appellation we may take it for granted that he never went beyond the preliminaries.

The reception awarded to "Mamillia" seems to have encouraged him to continue writing. It had, in fact, crude as it seems to us now, many qualities that would ensure it a welcome : its style was euphuistic ; its tone was Italian ; its plot was intricate, and, lastly, there was very much love in it. He continued therefore in this vein, writing with extreme facility and rapidity improbable love stories, with wars, kings, and princesses, with euphuism and mythology, with Danish, Greek, Egyptian and Bohemian adventures. There was a "Myrrour of Modesty" which has for its heroine the chaste Susannah, a "Gwydonius, the card of fancie," again a tale in the Italian style, an "Arbasto" which tells of the wars and loves of a Danish king, a "Morando," containing a series of discussions and speeches on love, all of them entered or published in 1584–6. Then came his "Planetomachia," 1585, where the several planets describe and exemplify their influence on human fate ; "Penelopes web," 1587, containing a succession of short stories ; "Perimedes," 1588, imitated from Boccaccio ; "Pandosto," a tale of Bohemian and Sicilian kings and shepherds, which had an immense success, much greater according to appearances than the exquisite drama of a "Winter's Tale," that Shakespeare drew from it. "Alcida," a story of the metamorphosis of three young love-stricken princesses of an island "under the pole antartike," was apparently published in the same year ; "Menaphon," a charming pastoral tale, appeared in 1589, and several others followed. His popularity was soon considerable ; his books were in all the shops ; several went through an extraordinary number of editions ; his name was better known than any : " I became," says he, "an author of playes, and a penner of love pamphlets, so that I soone grew famous in that qualitie," and who then "for that trade" was there "so ordinarie about London as *Robin Greene*?"[1]

As for his beginning to write plays, he has left a lively account of the casual meeting which led to his becoming attached to a company of players and to be for a time their playwright in ordinary. It was at a moment when his purse was empty; for as he quaintly puts it in one of his stories: "so long went the pot to the water, that at last it came broken home; and so long put he his hand into his purse that at last the emptie bottome returned him a writt of *non est inventus;* for well might the divell dance there for ever a crosse to keepe him backe."[2] In this difficulty he met by chance a brilliantly dressed fellow who seemed to be a cavalier, and happened to be a player. It is a well-known fact that if scenery was scanty in Elizabethan play-houses, the players' dresses were very costly, and if need there was, this would be an additional proof that no monetary consideration would have induced the young man who played, for example, the part of Shakespeare's Cleopatra, to appear in less than queenly ruffs and farthingales, such as Rogers has represented in his portrait of Elizabeth.

"What is your profession? said Roberto [that is, Robert Greene].[3]

[1] "The Repentance of Robert Greene," 1592, "Works" vol. xii. p. 173.
[2] "Greene's never too late," 1590, "Works," vol. viii. p. 101.
[3] "Greene's Groats-worth of wit," 1592, "Works," vol. xii. pp. 131 *et seq.* "Roberto ... whose life in most parts agreeing with mine, found one selfe punishment as I have done" (*Ibid.* p. 137).

"Truely, sir, said he, I am a player.

"A player, quoth Roberto; I tooke you rather for a gentleman of great living, for if by outward habit men should be censured, I tell you, you woud be taken for a substantiall man.

"So am I, where I dwell, quoth the player, reputed able at my proper cost, to build a windmill. What, though the worlde once went hard with me, when I was faine to carrie my playing fardle a footebacke; *tempora mutantur* . . . it is otherwise now; for my share in playing apparell will not be solde for two hundred pounds."

The player goes on relating his own successes, the parts he performs, and how he had been himself for a while the playwright of his troop, but that had been some time ago; tastes are changing and his wit is now out of fashion: "Nay, more, I can serve to make a prettie speech, for I was a countrie author, passing at a morall, for it was I that pende the moral of mans wit, the Dialogue of Dives, and for seaven yeeres space was absolute interpreter of the puppets. But now my Almanacke is out of date:

>   The people make no estimation
>   Of morals teaching education.

"Was not this prettie for a plaine rime extempore? If ye will, ye shall have more.

"Nay, it is enough, said Roberto, but how meane you to use mee?

"Why, sir, in making playes, said the other, for which you shall be well paid, if you will take the paines."

Greene did so, and with no mean success. He grew more and more famous, and, without becoming more wealthy, had the pleasure of being able to squander at one time much larger sums of money than before: "Roberto was now famozed for an arch-playmaking-poet; his purse, like the sea, somtime sweld, anon like the same sea fell to a low ebb; yet seldom he wanted, his labors were so well esteemed."

He had not yet broken all connection with his birth-place and his family, and some of his visits were for him memorable ones. During one of them he was seized with a sudden fit of repentance for the loose life he had been leading in London; the better man in him made himself heard, and he fell into such an abyss of misery and despair as to remind us of the great conversions of the Puritan epoch. In fact, his companions, when he again saw them, wondering at his altered countenance, called him a Puritan. "Once I felt a feare and horrour in my conscience, and then the terrour of Gods judgementes did manifestly teach me that my life was bad, that by sinne I deserved damnation, and that such was the greatnes of my sinne that I deserved no redemption. And this inward motion I received in St. Andrews church in the cittie of Norwich, at a lecture or sermon then preached by a godly learned man. . . . At this sermon the terrour of Gods judgementes did manifestly teach me, that my exercises were damnable, and that I should bee wipte out of the booke of life, if I did not speedily repent my loosenes of life, and reforme my misdemeanors."

In the same way, in the next century, George Fox the

Quaker, John Bunyan, and many others, were to find themselves awe-stricken at the thought of God's judgment ; in the same way also, and in almost the same words, the hero of a novel that was to be world-famous in the following age was to express the sudden horror he felt when remorse began to prey upon him. " No one," wrote Robinson Crusoe, in his journal, " that shall ever read this account will expect that I shall be able to describe the horrors of my soul at this terrible vision." But Greene differed from them all by the short duration of his anxieties : " This good notion lasted not long in mee, for no sooner had I met with my copesmates, but seeing me in such a solemn humour, they demaunded the cause of my sadnes . . . they fell upon me in a jeasting manner, calling me Puritane and Presizian, and wished I might have a pulpit." And soon the good effect of the godly vision in St. Andrew's church wore away.

He allowed another chance of escaping his final doom to pass in the same manner. Famous as he was all over the country, witty and brilliant, with such patrons as Leicester, Essex and Arundel, to whom several of his works are dedicated, he became acquainted with " a gentlemans daughter of good account." He loved her ; his suit was favoured, and he married her, about 1586. He lived with her for a year and they had a boy ; but she objected to his disorderly ways of life, and he, unable to alter them, " cast her off, having spent the marriage money." She returned to Lincolnshire, he to London, and they never met again. That Greene, however, had felt within himself what it is to be a father is shown by the exquisite " lullaby " he

composed shortly after for Sephestia in his "Menaphon."
It is the well-known song :

> "Weepe not my wanton ! smile upon my knee !
> When thou art olde, ther's griefe inough for thee !
>   Mothers wagge, pretie boy,
>   Fathers sorrow, fathers joy.
>   When thy father first did see
>   Such a boy by him and mee,
>   He was glad, I was woe.
>   Fortune changde made him so,
>   When he left his pretie boy,
>   Last his sorowe, first his joy.
>
> .   .   .   .   .
>
> Weepe not my wanton ! smile upon my knee !
> When thou art olde, ther's griefe inough for thee !
>   The wanton smilde, father wept;
>   Mother cride, babie lept :
>   More he crowde, more we cride ;
>   Nature could not sorowe hide.
>   He must goe, he must kisse
>   Childe and mother, babie blisse :
>   For he left his pretie boy,
>   Fathers sorowe, fathers joy."

In London he continued a favourite : "For these my vaine discourses [that is, his love novels] I was beloved of the more vainer sort of people, who being my continuall companions came still to my lodging, and there would continue quaffing, corowsing, and surfeting with me all the day long." One of his best friends has corroborated his statement, giving at the same time a graphic description of his physical appearance : " Hee inherited more vertues than vices," wrote Nash, " a jolly long red peake [beard] like the spire of a steeple he cherisht continually, without

ROBERT GREENE IN HIS SHROUD.
(*From Dickenson's "Greene in conceipt,"* 1598.)

cutting, whereat a man might hang a jewell, it was so sharp and pendant. . . He had his faultes. . . Debt and deadly sinne, who is not subject to? . . A good fellow he was. . . In a night and a day would he have yarkt up a pamphlet as well as in seaven yeare, and glad was that printer that might bee so blest to pay him deare for the very dregs of his wit. He made no account of winning credite by his workes. . . His only care was to have a spel in his purse to conjure up a good cuppe of wine with at all times." [1]

The few samples that have come to us of the talk in these meetings of Elizabethan literary men show, as might well have been supposed, that it was not lacking in freedom. Greene himself has left an account of one of these conversations, when he expressed, Bohemia-wise, his opinions of a future life and, without Aucassin's extenuating plea that he was love-mad, he exclaimed: "Hell, quoth I, what talke you of hell to me? I know if I once come there, I shall have the company of better men than my selfe; I shall also meete with some madde knaves in that place, and so long as I shall not sit there alone, my care is the lesse. But you are mad folks, quoth I, for if I feared the judges of the Bench no more than I dread the judgments of God, I would before I slept dive into one carles bagges or other, make merrie with the shelles I found in them so long as they would last." [2]

[1] "Strange Newes," 1592. A rough engraving, showing Greene at his writing table, is to be seen on the title-page of "Greene in conceipt," a novel by T. Dickenson, 1598; his "peake" exists, but is not quite so long as Nash's description would have led us to expect.
[2] "Repentance," "Works," vol. xii. p. 164.

His associations at that time were getting lower and lower. He was leaving Bohemia for the mysterious haunts of robbers, sharpers, loose women, and "conny-catchers." He had once for a mistress the sister of a famous thief nicknamed Cutting Ball that ended his days on the gallows, and he had a child by her, called Fortunatus, who died in 1593. He thought it a sort of atonement to communicate to the public the experience he derived from his life among these people, and accordingly printed a series of books on "conny-catching," in which he unveiled all their tricks and malpractices. The main result was that they wanted to kill him.[1]

It was, in fact, too late to reform; all that was left for him was to repent, an empty repentance that no deed could follow. Though scarcely thirty his constitution was worn out. The alternations of excessive cheer and of scanty food had ruined his health; it was soon obvious that he could not live much longer. One day a "surfet which hee had taken with drinking"[2] brought him home to his room, in a poor shoemaker's house, who allowed him to stay there by charity on credit. He was not to come out alive. His illness lasted some weeks, and as his brain power was unimpaired he employed his

---

[1] See especially vol. x. of the "Works." Greene's example gave a great impetus to these strange kinds of works, but he was not the first to compose such; several came before him, especially T. Audeley, with his "Fraternitye of vacabondes," 1560-1, and Thomas Harman, "A caveat or warening for common cursetors vulgarely called vagabones," 1566 or 1567; both reprinted by Viles and Furnivall, Early English Text Society, 1869.

[2] See the note added by the editor to his "Repentance," "Works," vol. xii. p. 184.

time in writing the last of his autobiographical pamphlets. Considering the extravagance of his life, in which he had known so many successes, and the sorrows of his protracted illness, they read very tragically indeed. He addressed himself to the public at large, to his more intimate friends, to his wife confessing his wrongs towards her, and asking pardon. Yet to the last, broken as he was in body, he remained a literary man, and while confessing all round and pardoning every one, he could not drop his literary animosities nor forget his life-long complaint against plagiarists.

His complaint was one of which the world of letters was to hear much more in after time, and which in fact is constantly renewed in our own day; it is the complaint of the novelist against the dramatist, claiming as his own incidents transferred by the playwright from readers to spectators. As novels proper were just beginning then in England, and as drama was also beginning to spread, Greene's protest is one of the first on record, and thousands were to follow it. Strange to say of all the men of whom he complains, the one he has picked out to hold up to disdain and to scorn, and towards whom in his dying days he seems to have entertained the strongest animosity, was a young man of twenty-eight, who was just then becoming known, and whose fame was to increase somewhat in after years, namely, William Shakespeare. Greene beseeches the three principal friends he still had, Marlowe, Nash, and Peele, to cease writing plays; what is the good of it? others come, turn to account what has been written before them, give never a thank-you for it, and get the praise. Let them stop publishing and these new-comers, among them this "upstart" Shakespeare, unable as they obviously are to invent anything, will have their careers cut short. Be warned by my fate, says Greene, and mind " those puppits . . . that speake from our mouths, those anticks garnisht in our colours. Is it not strange that I, to whom they al have beene beholding: is it not like that you to whome they all have been beholding, shall (were ye in that case that I am now) be both at once of them forsaken? Yes, trust them not, for there is an upstart crow, beautified with our feathers, that with his *Tigers heart wrapt in a players hide*, supposes he is as well able to bombast out a blanke verse as the best of you; and being an absolute *Joannes fac totum*, is in his owne conceit the onely shake-scene in a countrie. O that I might intreate your rare wits to be imployed in more profitable courses: and let those apes imitate your past excellence and never more acquaint them with your rare inventions." [1]

This savage abuse of young Shakespeare, who had probably mended at that time more plays than we know, and more, surely, than he had personally written, must not pass without the needful comment that his abuser was, according to his own testimony, as ready, for a trifle, to make an acquaintance and start a friendship as to turn a friend into a foe. "Though," says he, "I

---

[1] Epilogue to the " Groats-worth of wit," directed "to those gentlemen, his quondam acquaintance, that spend their wits in making plaies," " Works," vol. xii. p. 144. The verse quoted by Greene occurs in the third part of Henry VI., with the difference of " womans " for " players." About this, see Furnivall, Introduction to the " Leopold Shakspere," p. xvi. As to the identification of Greene's three friends, see Grosart's memorial introduction and Storojenko's " Life," in " Works," vol. i.

knew how to get a friend, yet I had not the gift or reason how to keepe a friend." He quarrelled, in fact, with most of them, not excepting Nash and Marlowe, to whom he is now appealing against Shakespeare ; and his prefaces contain numerous attacks on the writers of the time. It must be remembered, too, how bitter was the end of poor Greene, how keenly he felt, he the boon companion *par excellence*, finding himself " forsaken " in his need, and left alone in the shoemaker's desolate room. It is curious to think that among the men whose absence from his bedside he most resented was Shakespeare, and that this want of a visit whetted his already ill-disposed mind into expressing the only abuse known to have been directed by his contemporaries against the author of " Hamlet."

Shakespeare, of course, did not answer ; [1] his plea might have been that if he did not pay much attention to others' authorship, much less did he pay to his own ; for he never published his own dramas, nor did he protest when mangled versions of them were circulated by printers. He only showed that Greene's criticisms had not much affected him by turning later on another

[1] The exaggeration in the attack was so obvious that it raised some protest, and Henry Chettle, who had edited Greene's " Groats-worth " after his death, felt obliged to print a rectification in his next book, as was the custom then, when newspapers did not exist. This acknowledgment, that would to-day have been published in the *Athenæum* or the *Academy*, was inserted in his " Kind Heart's Dream," issued in the same year, 1592, and is to the effect that so far as Shakespeare (for Chettle can allude here to no other) is concerned : " divers of worship have reported his uprightnes of dealing, which argues his honesty, and his facetious grace in writing that approoves his art."

of the complainer's novels into a drama. Shakespeare's friend, Ben Jonson, who was not accustomed to so much reserve, speaks very disparagingly of Greene; he represents him as being a perfectly forgotten author in 1599, which was untrue, and as for the particular work in which Shakespeare was abused, he describes it as only fit for the reading of crazy persons.

"*Trusty*. . . Every night they read themselves asleep on those books [one of the two being the "Groats-worth"].

"*Epicoene*. Good faith it stands with good reason. I would I knew where to procure those books.

"*Morose*. Oh!

"*Sir Amorous La Foole*. I can help you with one of them, mistress Morose, the 'Groats-worth of wit.'

"*Epicoene*. But I shall disfurnish you, Sir Amorous, can you spare it?

"*La Foole*. O yes, for a week or so; I shall read it myself to him," &c.[1]

With the exception just mentioned, Greene's thoughts were all turned to repentance. He had the consolation of receiving from his wife a kindly message on the eve of his death, "whereat hee greatly rejoiced, confessed that he had mightily wronged her, and wished that hee might see her before he departed. Whereupon, feeling his time was but short, hee tooke pen and inke and wrote her a letter to this effect:

"Sweet wife, as ever there was any good will or friendship betweene thee and mee, see this bearer (my host) satisfied of his debt: I owe him tenne pound, and

[1] "The Silent Woman," act iv. sc. 2; and "Every man out of his humour," act ii. sc. 1.

but for him I had perished in the streetes. Forget and forgive my wronges done unto thee, and Almighty God have mercie on my soule. Farewell till we meet in heaven, for on earth thou shalt never see me more. This 2d of September, 1592. Written by thy dying husband."[1]

He died a day after.

III.

Greene's non-dramatic works are the largest contribution left by any Elizabethan writer to the novel literature of the day. They are of four sorts: his novels proper or romantic love stories, which he called his love pamphlets; his patriotic pamphlets; his conny-catching writings, in which he depicts actual fact, and tells tales of real life forshadowing in some degree Defoe's manner; lastly, his Repentances, of which some idea has already been given.[2]

[1] "Repentance," "Works," vol. xii. p. 185.

[2] The "Life and Complete Works" of Greene have been published by Dr. Grosart, London, 1881, 15 vols. 4to. His principal non-dramatic writings may be classified as follows:

1. *Romantic novels, or "love pamphlets":* "Mamillia," 1583; "The second part," 1583; "Myrrour of Modestie," 1584; "Card of fancie," 1584 (?); "Arbasto," 1584 (?); "Planetomachia," 1585; "Morando, the Tritameron of love," 1586 (?); "Second part," 1587; "Debate betweene follie and love," 1587; "Penelopes web," 1587; "Euphues his censure to Philautus," 1587; "Perimedes," 1588; "Pandosto" (*alias* "Dorastus and Fawnia"), 1588; "Alcida," 1588 (?); "Menaphon," 1589; "Ciceronis amor," 1589; "Orpharion," 1590 (?); "Philomela," 1592.

2. *Civic and patriotic pamphlets:* "Spanish Masquerado," 1589; "Royal Exchange," 1590; "Quip for an upstart courtier," 1592.

3. *Conny-catching pamphlets:* "A notable discovery of coosnage,"

His love pamphlets, which filled the greatest part of his literary career, connect him with the euphuistic cycle, and he is assuredly one of Lyly's legatees. Possessing a much greater fertility of invention than Lyly, he follows as closely as the original bent of his mind allows him, the manner of his master. He is euphuistic in his style, wise in his advice to his readers, and a great admirer of his own country.

His moral propensities do not lie concealed behind pretty descriptions or adventures; they are stamped on the very first page of each of his books and are expressly mentioned in their titles. In this too, like his master Lyly, he may be considered a precursor of Richardson. He writes his " Mamillia " to entreat gentlemen to beware how, " under the perfect substaunce of pure love, [they] are oft inveigled with the shadowe of lewde luste ; " his " Myrrour of Modestie " to show " howe the Lorde delivereth the innocent from all imminent perils and plagueth the bloudthirstie hypocrites with deserved punishments." " Euphues his censure to Philautus " teaches " the vertues necessary in every gentleman ; " " Pandosto " shows that " although by the meanes of

---

1591 ; " Second part of Conny-catching," 1591 ; " Third and last part," 1592 ; " Disputation betweene a Hee conny-catcher and a Shee conny-catcher," 1592 (attributed to Greene) ; " The Blacke bookes messenger " (*i.e.*, " Life of Ned Browne "), 1592.

4. *Repentances:* " Greenes mourning garment," 1590 (?); " Greenes never too late to mend," 1590 ; " Francescos fortune or the second part of Greenes never too late," 1590 (these two last belong also to Group 1) ; " Farewell to follie," 1591 (entered 1587) ; " Greenes Groats-worth of wit," 1592 ; " The Repentance of Robert Greene," 1592.

sinister fortune truth may be concealed, yet by Time
in spight of fortune, it is most manifestly revealed."[1]
Quiet, wealthy, comfortable Richardson had no better
aim, and had, in fact, a very similar one, when he wrote
his "Pamela," as he is careful to state on the title-page,
"in order to cultivate the principles of virtue and
religion in the minds of the youth of both sexes;" and
his "Clarissa," to show "the distresses that may attend
the misconduct both of parents and children in relation
to marriage." Be it said to the praise of both authors
and readers, this moral purpose so prominently stated
did not in the least frighten the public of ladies, whose
suffrage, the two men, different as they were in most
things, were especially courting. Richardson's popularity among them needs not to be recalled, and as for
Greene, he was stated at the time of his greater vogue
to be nothing less than "the Homer of women."[2]

Greene's praise of England is as constant as Lyly's;
he is careful to show that whatever appearances may
be, he is proud to be a citizen of London, not, after
all, of Bohemia; if he represents himself shipwrecked
near the coast of an island where, like Robinson Crusoe,
he is alone able to swim, finding the country pleasant,
he describes it as "much like that faire England the

---

[1] The same virtuous tone and purpose appear invariably in the
dedications of his books to his patrons or friends. To all of them
he wishes "increase of worship and vertue," and he commends
them all "to the tuition of the Almightie."

[2] Thomas Nash, "The Anatomie of Absurditie," London, 1590,
4to, written in 1588. There seems to be no doubt that Nash
refers to Greene in the passage: "I but here the Homer of
women hath forestalled an objection," &c., sig. A ii.

flower of Europe."[1] Euphues' praise of London is matched by Greene's description of its naval power in his " Royal Exchange " : " Our citizens of London (Her Majesties royal fleet excepted) have so many shyppes harboured within the Thames as wyll not onelie match with all the argosies, galleyes, galeons and patashes in Venice, but to encounter by sea with the strongest cittie in the whole world."[2] As for foreign women, Greene agrees with Lyly that they all paint their faces, and cannot live without a lover. French women, for example, are "beautifull," it is true, but "they have drugges of Alexandria, minerals of Egypt, waters from Tharsus, paintings from Spaine, and what to doe forsooth? To make them more beautifull then vertuous and more pleasing in the eyes of men then delightful in the sight of God. . . . Some take no pleasure but in amorous passions, no delight but in madrigals of love, wetting Cupid's wings with rose water, and tricking up his quiver with sweete perfumes."[3]

But Greene's style marked him most indelibly as a pupil of Lyly. He has taken Euphues' ways of speech with all their peculiarities, and has sometimes crowded his tales with such a quantity of similes, metaphors and antitheses as to beat his master himself on his own ground.[4] Here, again, we are in the middle of scor-

[1] "Alcida," "Works," vol. ix. p. 17.
[2] "The Royal Exchange, contayning sundry aphorismes of phylosophie . . . fyrst written in Italian," 1590, "Works," vol. vii. p. 224.
[3] "Greenes never too late," 1590, "Works," vol. viii. p. 25.
[4] Greene and Lyly are placed on a par by J. Eliote, a friend of

pions, crocodiles, dipsas, and what not. Take, for instance, "Philomela the lady Fitzwaters nightingale;"[1] as it is written expressly for ladies, and dedicated to one of them, and as, in addition, the characters are of high rank, the novel is nearly one unbroken series of similes: "The greener the alisander leaves be, the more bitter is the sappe," says Philip, the jealous husband, to himself; "the salamander is most warm when it lyeth furthest from the fire;" thus his wife may well be as heart-hollow as she seems lip-holy. He charges his friend Lutesio to tempt her, by way of trial. "Lutesio," the lady replies to the young man's declaration, "now I see, the strongest oake hath his sap and his worms [and] that ravens will breed

ANOTHER DRAGON. 1608.

the former; in the sonnet, in Stratford-at-Bow French, he wrote in commendation of Greene's "Perimedes":

"Greene et Lylli tous deux raffineurs de l'Anglois."

See also the commendatory verses by H. Upchear, prefacing "Menaphon":

"Of all the flowers a *Lillie* one I lov'd."

[1] 1592, "Works," vol. xi.

in the fayrest ash." These observations appear unanswerable to Lutesio, and the husband would share his conviction if he did not reflect that "the onix is inwardly most cold, when it is outwardly most hot." The experiment must be tried again, and the friend returns to the charge: "Madam, I have been stung with the scorpion and cannot be helpt or healed by none but by the scorpion."

"I see now," replies the lady to this compliment, "that hemlocke wheresoever it bee planted, will be pestilent [and] that the serpent with the brightest scales shroudeth the most fatall venome." Is there anything more certain? But that does not prevent the halcyon from hatching when the sea is calm, and the phœnix from spreading her wings when the sunbeams shine on her nest. This is what the husband remarks, and, guided by the onyx, the alexander, &c., after a mock trial, he divorces his wife.

What did the people think of it? They thought "all was not golde that glistered, . . . that the Agate, bee it never so white without, yet it is full of black strokes within."

During this time, Philomela, the wife who had been driven away, retires to Palermo, where her knowledge of natural history allows her to observe that the more the camomile is trodden on, the faster it grows. Scarcely separated from her, the husband loses his confidence in the onyx and alexander, and sets out in search of her. He does not know her place of retreat, but, happily, among all possible routes, he chooses precisely that leading to Palermo. He finds his wife again, and his joy is so great that he is choked by it, and dies; a just punishment for his confidence in Lyly's botany.[1]

In the same way as patient Grisell's story had been in the same period transferred to the stage, this new example of feminine virtue, from the pen of the "Homer of women," was, in later years, worked into a drama. At that time Greene had long been dead and could not complain of the new "shake-scene" tortures inflicted upon him by Davenport.[2]

This story, characteristic as it is of Greene's style when he means to be euphuistic, can scarcely be taken as a fair sample of the improbability he is able to crowd into a single novel. Most of his tales (and in this he greatly differs from Lyly) take place we do not know when, we do not know where, among men we have never anywhere come across. Learned as he was, versed in the Greek, Latin, French and Italian tongues, able to translate passages from the Italian of Ariosto, to dress in English language the charming "Débat de Folie et d'Amour"[3] of Louise Labé, to imitate (as he thought) Cicero's style, while describing (as he thought) the great orator's loves,[4] his turn of mind was as little critical as can be

---

[1] Some faint resemblance has been pointed out by Dunlop between this story and the tale of Tito and Gisippo in the "Decameron," giornata x. novella 8.

[2] "The City Nightcap, or crede quod habes et habes, a tragicomedy," London, 1661, 4to, licensed 1624, reprinted in Dodsley's "Old plays."

[3] "The debate betweene Follie and Love, translated out of French," 1587, "Works," vol. iv.

[4] "Ciceronis amor Tulies love . . . a work full of pleasure, as following Ciceroes vaine," 1589, "Works," vol. vii. This work

imagined, and his wide popularity served to spread geographical and historical absurdities, some of which were preserved by Shakespeare himself, for the amusement of a learned posterity. Greene's picture of Ulysses' Penelope is not more Greek than the exquisite painting by Pinturicchio at the National Gallery, where the wise king of Ithaca appears under the guise of a red-hosed Italian youth with flowing hair; while his wife sits at her "web" in a Florentine blue dress. In Greene, Penelope is represented telling stories to while away the time, which, unless we endow her with a prophetical gift, are impossibilities. Her first story begins thus: "Saladyne the Souldan of Ægipt, who by his prowesse had made a generall conquest of the south-east part of ye world tooke to wife Barmenissa, the onely daughter and heire of the great chan." No wonder that such tales could chain the attention and awaken the curiosity of her maids, and keep them quiet till the time when "a messenger came hastily rushing in, who tolde Penelope that Ulisses was arryved that night within the port of Ithaca. . . . Penelope called for her sonne and that night sent him post to the sea." [1]

is noteworthy as being an almost if not quite unique example of an attempt in Elizabethan times to write a pseudo-historical novel in the style of the period referred to. Greene set to work expressly with such a purpose, and he states it in the title of the book and in its preface: "Gentlemen, I have written of Tullies love, a worke attempted to win your favours, but to discover mine owne ignorance in that coveting to counterfeit Tullies phrase, I have lost myself in unproper words." In this tale Cicero is represented standing at the tribune and haranguing the senate: "Conscript fathers and grave senators of Rome," &c.

[1] "Penelopes web," 1587, "Works," vol. iv. p. 233.

Not less wonderful are the stories of "Arbasto," King of Denmark, or of "Pandosto," King of Bohemia. They may be taken as typical specimens of the sort of romantic novel the Elizabethan public enjoyed, and which was sure to make an author popular. We must remember when reading these tales that they were the fashion, the craze, at a time when "Midsummer Night's Dream" and "Romeo and Juliet" were being played. Chaotic, improbable, and in some parts ridiculous as they appear to us, they would have made their author wealthy if anything could, so much so that, as we have seen, the publishers, according to Nash, considered themselves "blest to pay Greene deare for the very dregs of his wit." He was, if anything, an author that sold. What were his wares?

In "Arbasto" Greene represents himself reaching in his travels the island of Candia. He meets in a cell a solitary old man, and without any ceremony makes bold to ask him for his story. The old man is at first somewhat shocked at this inquisitiveness, and gets very angry; but he grows calmer and complies. He is Arbasto, late King of Denmark, and was once very happy: "I feared not the force of forraigne foes, for I knewe none but were my faithfull friends," says he, in a style that reminds one of the King Herod of miracle-plays. Living in such content, he thought it advisable to invade France, where at that time a king was reigning, named Pelorus, about whom chroniclers are silent. Arbasto came straight to Orleans, and after some siege operations, "had so shaken the walles with cannon shot, that they were forced to strengthen them with counter mures."

A three months' truce is agreed to on both sides, and the two sovereigns entertain each other. At the French court, Arbasto meets the two daughters of the king, Myrania and Doralicia, two wonderful creatures, especially the latter, who was "so adorned with more then earthlie perfection as she seemed to be framed by nature to blemishe nature, and that beautie had skipt beyond her skil in framing a peece of such curious workemanship." Arbasto cannot cease gazing at her; he addresses to himself euphuistic speeches several pages long, but they do him no good. It so happens that while his love is set on Doralicia, the other princess falls in love with him. But this again does him no good. He ceases to find anything worth living for; even the possible destruction of France seems to him tasteless. His nobles observe his changed mood, and wonder, and his confidant, Duke Egerio, vainly tries on him the effect of a new series of euphuistic examples and similes. Arbasto continues loving, and Doralicia perseveres in her coldness; they meet once, and argue one against the other with the help of salamanders and scorpions, and empty their whole herbaria over each other's head; but things remain *in statu*.

King Pelorus, who, for all that, does not lose his head, offers Arbasto an interview in Orleans to sign the peace. Arbasto comes, the gates are shut, he is thrown into prison; his army is cut to pieces, and a great scaffold is erected in a conspicuous place, on which the prisoner is to be publicly executed in ten days' time.

The royal Dane tries to console himself in his prison with what remains of his herbarium and zoology. But better help comes in the shape of the loving princess, Myrania, who is resolved to save him. By her command her maid entices the gaoler to her room, and causes him to tread "upon a false bord" that had apparently been there in all times, ready for this very emergency. The gaoler falls "up to the shoulders;" then he disappears into a hole, where he dies, and his keys are taken from him.

Arbasto is very happy, and promises Myrania to love and marry her; they go "covertly out of the citie, passing through France with many fearefull perils" and reach Denmark. Pelorus and Doralicia are extremely angry; she even takes to "blaspheming . . . but as words breake no bones, so we cared the lesse for her scolding."

But Arbasto learns to his cost that no man when truly in love can cease to love as he pleases. Before keeping his word to Myrania he wants once more to appeal to her fair sister. But the fair sister continues in her blaspheming mood, and sends a very sharp and contemptuous answer.

Both letters fall into the hands of Myrania, who is so struck by this piece of treachery that she dies of her sorrow; hearing which Pelorus rather unexpectedly dies of his sorrow for her death. Doralicia then is queen, and at last discovers that in the innermost part of her heart there is love for Arbasto. She writes accordingly, but the Dane this time returns a contemptuous answer. Receiving which, the poor French queen dies of her sorrow. And thereupon, for no apparent reason, except to add yet more sorrow to the conclusion of this tragical tale, the confidant of the

Danish king turns traitor, usurps his crown, and Arbasto goes to Candia, where Greene had the good fortune to hear from his own lips this wondrous and authentic tale. " Merry and tragical ! tedious and brief ! " as Duke Theseus would think.

However complete the success awarded to Arbasto's adventures, it was nothing compared with the popularity of " Pandosto." If this was not the best it was the most famous of Greene's tales. The plot is well known, for Shakespeare, unmoved by the dying maledictions of his late companion, drew from it the materials of his " Winter's Tale " (1611 ?). He kept many of the improbabilities of Greene, rejected a few, and added some of his own. But the great change he made was to give life to the heroes, and as they had been shaped by Greene they sorely needed it. Rarely did a more unlikely and a cruder tale come from the pen of our novelist.

The events of the story take place among kings and shepherds : " In the countrey of Bohemia there raygned a king called Pandosto." This is the usual beginning of novels of the time ; hundreds of them commence in this manner ; [1] the very first lines transport the reader to an unknown country, and place him before an unknown king, and if, after reading only those few words, he is surprised to find himself entangled in extraordinary, inexplicable adventures, he must be of

---

[1] " There dwelled in Bononia a certaine Knight called Signior Bonfadio " (" Morando "). " There dwelled in the citie of Metelyne a certain Duke called Clerophantes " (" Greenes carde of fancie "). " There dwelled . . . in the citie of Memphis a poore man called Perymedes " (" Perimedes "), &c.

a very naïve disposition. But in Elizabethan times adventures were liked for their own sake; probability was only a very secondary motive of enjoyment. "Pandosto," in any case, deserves our attention, for, if it commenced like many other novels of the time, it led, as we have said, to "Winter's Tale," to which it is worth while to go. When the two are read together and compared, it seems as if Shakespeare had chosen on purpose one of the worst of Greene's tales, to show by way of an answer to the accusations of the dead writer, that he was able to form something out of nothing. Greene had, in truth, only modelled the clay; Shakespeare used it, adding the soul.

Greene simply states his facts and takes little trouble about explaining them; the reader must rest satisfied with the author's bare word. There is no attempt at the study of passions; his heroes change their minds all of a sudden, with the stiff, sharp, improbable action of puppets in a show. Pandosto (Leontes) loves and hates, and becomes jealous, and repents always in the same brusque wire-and-wood manner; the warmth of his passions, so great and terrible in Shakespeare, is here simply absent; when he begins to suspect his friend Egistus (Polixenes) of feeling an unlawful love for Bellaria (Hermione), we are barely informed that the Bohemian king "concluded at last to poyson him." When Dorastus and Fawnia (Florizel and Perdita) seek refuge in Pandosto's kingdom, Pandosto at once falls in love with his own daughter, Fawnia, whom he does not know; then on the receipt of a letter from Egistus, "having his former love turned to a disdainful hate," he wishes to have her killed. Very differently is the couple received by Shakespeare's Leontes:

> "Were I but twenty-one,
> Your father's image is so hit in you,
> His very air, that I should call you brother,
> As I did him; and speak of something wildly
> By us performed before. Most dearly welcome!
> And you, fair princess, goddess!—O, alas,
> I lost a couple, that 'twixt heaven and earth
> Might thus have stood, begetting wonder as
> You gracious couple do."

In Greene the exquisite figure of Perdita appears as a very rough sketch under the name of Fawnia. She loves her Dorastus not merely because he is lovable, but because "hoping in time to be advaunced from the daughter of a poore farmer to be the wife of a riche king." Dorastus comes to her disguised as a shepherd, and as she does not recognize him "she began halfe to forget Dorastus and to favor this prety shepheard whom she thought shee might both love and obtaine." It would be cruel to make further comparisons, but it is necessary to say thus much in order to show what a hold adventures, however crude, surprises, unexpected meetings and recognitions, had upon Elizabethan minds. They were quite sufficient to insure success; to add life and poetry was very well, but by no means necessary. Shakespeare did so because he could not do otherwise; and he did it thoroughly, as was his wont, endowing with his life-giving faculty the most insignificant personage he found embryo-like in Greene. The least of them has, in Shakespeare, his own moods, his sensitiveness, a mind and a heart that is his and his alone; even young Mamillius, the child who lives only the length of one scene, is not any child, but tells his tale, his sad tale, with a grace that is all his own.

> "A sad tale's best for winter.
> . . . I will tell it softly;
> Yond crickets shall not hear it."

Living people, too, are his Paulina, his Antigonus, his Camillo, his Autolycus, all of them additions of his own creation. Living also, his shepherds, for whom he received only insignificant hints from Greene. In "Pandosto" we hear of "a meeting of all the farmers daughters in Sycilia," without anything more, and from this Shakespeare drew the idea of his sheep-shearing feast, where he delights in contrasting with the rough ways of his peasants the inborn elegance of Perdita: "O Proserpina," says she, in her delicious mythological prattle:

> "For the flowers now, that, frighted, thou lett'st fall
> From Dis's wagon! daffodils,
> That come before the swallow dares . . ."

And Florizel, wondering at her with his young admiring eyes, answers in the same strain:

> "When you speak, sweet,
> I'd have you do it ever; when you sing,
> I'd have you buy and sell so; so give alms;
> Pray so; and, for the ordering your affairs,
> To sing them too: when you do dance, I wish you
> A wave o' the sea, that you might ever do
> Nothing but that."

Very different is the old shepherd's tone; though kindly, it is quite conformable to his estate and situation:

> " Fie, daughter ! when my old wife lived, upon
> This day she was both pantler, butler, cook,
> Both dame and servant; welcomed all, served all,
> Would sing her song, and dance her turn ; now here,
> At upper end o' the table, now i' the middle ;
> On his shoulder and his ; her face o' fire
> With labour, and the thing she took to quench it,
> She would to each one sip. You are retired,
> As if you were a feasted one, and not
> The hostess of the meeting."

Never has the language of country people been better transferred to literature ; their manners, tone, and language in Shakespeare have remained true to nature even to the present day, so much so that it is difficult, while writing, not to think of harvest and vintage scenes, which every year brings round again in our French valleys, and the sort of kindly talk very similar to the old shepherd's that many of us remember, as well as I do, to have heard in the country, from peasant associates in early days. This unsurpassed fidelity to nature is the more remarkable as it dates from the Arcadian times of English literature, days that were to last long, even down to the time of Pope and of Thomson himself, to stop at Burns, when at last a deeper, if not truer, note was to be struck.

But with regard to mere facts, Shakespeare was in no way more careful than Greene, and he seems to have known, and it was in fact visible enough, the greediness of his public to be such that, ostrich like, they would swallow anything. He, therefore, changed very little. In Greene, ships "sail into Bohemia," a feat that cannot be repeated to-day; the Queen is tried by a jury "panelled" for that purpose; the nobles go "to the isle of Delphos, there to enquire of the oracle of Apollo whether she had committed adultery." Very much the same things happen in Shakespeare. The survival of Hermione is his own invention; in Greene she dies for good at the beginning of the novel, when she hears of the death of her son. With the same aptitude to die for no other cause than to improve a story, Pandosto dies also in Greene's tale: he remembered his faults and "fell in a melancholie fit, and to close up the comedie with a tragicall stratageme he slewe himselfe." Merry and tragical! But otherwise Dorastus and Fawnia would have had to wait before becoming king and queen, and such a waiting was against the taste of the time and the rules of novel writing.

Such as it is, Greene's tale had an extraordinary success. While Shakespeare's drama was not printed, either in authentic or pirated shape, before the appearance of the 1623 folio, the prose story had a number of editions throughout the seventeenth century and even, under one shape or another, throughout the eighteenth. It was printed as a chap-book during this last period, and in this costume began a new life. It was turned into verse in 1672, under the title, "Fortune's tennis ball: or the most excellent history of Dorastus and Fawnia, rendred into delightful english verse"; [1] it begins with this "delightful" invocation:

> "Inspire me gentle love and jealousie,
> Give me thy passion and thy extasie,
> While to a pleasant ayr I strik the strings
> Singing the fates of lovers and of kings."

But the highest and most extraordinary compliment to Greene's performance was its translation into French, not only once, as has been said, but twice. The first time was at a moment when the English language and literature were practically unknown and as good as nonextant to French readers. It appeared in 1615, and was dedicated to "très haute and très illustre princesse, Madame Christine Sœur du Roy." [2] The second translation, that has never yet been noticed, was made at a time when France had a novel literature of its own well worth reading, and when Boileau had utterly routed and discomfited the writers of romantic and improbable tales. Nevertheless, it was thought that a public would be found in Paris for Greene's novel, and it was printed accordingly in French in 1722, this time adorned with engravings.[3] They show "Doraste" dressed as a mar-

[1] London, 1672.
[2] "Histoire tragique de Pandosto roy de Bohème et de Bellaria sa femme. Ensemble les amours de Dorastus et de Faunia ; où sont comprises les adventures de Pandosto roy de Bohème, enrichies de feintes moralités, allégories, et telles autres diversités convenables au sujet. Le tout traduit premièrement en Anglois de la langue Bohème et de nouveau mis en françois par L. Regnault," Paris, 1615, 12mo. A copy in the Bodleian Library.
[3] "Histoire tragique de Pandolphe roy de Bohème et de Cellaria sa femme, ensemble les amours de Doraste et de Faunia ; enrichie de figures en taille douce," Paris, 1722, 12mo.

quis of Louis XV.'s time; while "Pandolphe" wears a flowing wig under his cocked hat, and sits on a throne in rococo style. A copy of the book was purchased for the royal library, and is still to be seen at the Bibliothèque Nationale in Paris, with the crown and cipher of his Most Christian Majesty on the cover.

Greene's story of "Menaphon"[1] is hardly more probable, but it takes place in the country of Arcadia, a fact that predisposes us to treat with indulgence any lack of reality; moreover, it contains touches of true poetry, and is perhaps, all considered, the best of Greene's romantic novels. In common with most of this author's tales it abounds in monologues and dialogues; heroes think aloud and let us into their secret thoughts, a device adapted from the classic drama and very common in all the English novels of the period. There is also, according to Greene's custom, a great abundance of songs and verses, the best piece being the lullaby quoted above. Propriety and the truth of characters are not much better observed here than in Greene's other stories. Everybody in this romance speaks with infinite grace and politeness. The shepherd Menaphon, introducing himself to the Princess Sephestia and her child, who have been cast ashore through a shipwreck, says to them: "Strangers, your degree I know not, therefore pardon if I give lesse title than your estates merit." And, falling desperately in love with the beautiful young woman, who gives as her name Samela of the island of Cyprus, he describes to her with ardour and not without grace the pastoral life that he would like to lead

[1] "Menaphon. Camillas alarum to slumbering Euphues, in his melancholie cell at Silexedra," 1589. "Works," vol. vi.

with her : "I tell thee, faire nymph, these plaines that thou seest stretching southward, are pastures belonging to Menaphon : ther growes the cintfoyle, and the hyacinth, the cowsloppe, the primrose and the violet, which my flockes shall spare for flowers to make thee garlands, the milke of my ewes shall be meate for thy pretie wanton, the wool of the fat weathers that seemes as fine as the fleece that Jason fet from Colchos, shall serve to make Samela webbes withall ; the mountaine tops shall be thy mornings walke, and the shadie valleies thy evenings arbour : as much as Menaphon owes shall be at Samelas command if she like to live with Menaphon."

The romance goes on its way, strewn with songs whose refrains of varied and tuneful metres afford charming melody. In the end two knights, Melicertus and Pleusidippus, both enamoured of Sephestia, fight a duel ; they are separated. The king of the country interferes, and comprehending nothing of these intricate love affairs, he is on the point of cutting off all their heads, when it is discovered that Melicertus is the long lost husband of Sephestia ; the other duellist is the child of the shipwrecked woman, who, in the course of the tale, has been stolen from her on the shore and has grown up in hiding. They embrace one another ; and, as for Menaphon, whose sweetheart finds herself thus provided with a sufficiently fond husband and son, he returns to his old love, Pesana, who had had patience to wait for him, doubtless without growing old : for, in these romances, people do not grow old. Pleusidippus has become a man, without the least change in his mother's face ; she has remained as beautiful as in the first page of the book, and is, according to appearances, still " sweet-and-twenty."

In his tales of this sort Greene was mostly describing delights with which he was not personally acquainted, lands of which he had no practical knowledge, princely adventures for which no historian could vouch. He was perfectly free and unimpeded. The taste of the public was similar to his ; no Boileau was there to stop him, and he wrote accordingly, following his fancy, not caring in the least for nature and possibility, letting his pen go as fast as it would, and turning out " in a night and a day " a tale like his " Menaphon." But if he did not choose to paint from life and to describe realities in his " love pamphlets," he did so on purpose, not because he was unable to do it. In several of his other writings his subject was such that the work would have been nothing if not true ; and there we find a clear view of human passions, foibles and peculiarities, which show that if the taste of the romance readers of the time had been such as to encourage him in this line, he would have proved no mean realistic novelist. His Repentances abound in portraits and scenes, showing the keen eye he had for realities. His conny-catching literature is full of exact descriptions of the sordid life of the sharpers and low courtesans of Elizabethan London. In more than one of these pamphlets he foreshadows, though I need not say with a much lesser genius, the " Moll Flanders " and the " Colonel Jack " of a later period. The resemblance is especially great in the " Life and death of Ned Browne,"[1] in which the hero, according to

[1] "The blacke bookes messenger, laying open the life and death

the custom in picaresque novels, of which more hereafter, himself tells his own story in the first person. Greene is particularly bitter in his denunciations of the professional courtesans of London, about whom he knew probably more than any of his contemporaries. But with all the hatred he felt towards them so long as he had pen in hand, he cannot help repeating that, however objectionable they are in many ways, they have for themselves this advantage, that they are extremely beautiful, so that if their morals are exactly the same as in other countries they excel at least in something which in itself is not contemptible. They are "a kinde of women bearing the faces of Angels, but the hearts of devils, able to intrap the elect if it were possible."[1] Greene had no pretension to be one of the elect, and was only too often "intraped"; but for all his miseries his words show a scarcely less intense admiration for his diabolical angels than Des Grieux's famous rapturous phrase when he meets Manon on her way to the ship that is to convey her to America: "Son linge était sale et dérangé; ses mains délicates exposées à l'injure de l'air; enfin tout ce composé charmant, *cette figure capable de ramener l'univers à l'idolatrie*, paraissait dans un désordre et un abattement inexprimables." "Again," writes Greene: "let me say this much, that our curtizans . . . are far superiour in artificiall allurement to them of all the world, for, although they have

---

of Ned Browne one of the most notable of cutpurses . . . in England. Heerein hee telleth verie pleasantly in his owne person such strange prancks . . . as the like was yet never heard of," 1592, "Works," vol. xi.

[1] "Groats-worth of wit," "Works," vol. xii. p. 140.

not the painting of Italie, nor the charms of France, nor the jewelles of Spaine, yet they have in their eyes adamants that wil drawe youth as the jet the strawe. ... Their lookes... containe modesty, mirth, chastity, wantonness and what not." [1]

Besides the personal reminiscences with which he made up his repentance tales and stories, Greene as an observer of human nature is seen at his best in his curious, and at the time famous, dialogue "between velvet breeches and cloth breeches." [2] It is in fact a disputation between old England and new England; the England that built the strong houses praised by Harrison, and the England that adorned itself with the Burghley House paper work; traditional England and italianate England. Velvet breeches is "richly daubde with gold, and poudred with pearle," and is "sprung from the auncient Romans, borne in Italy, the mistresse of the worlde for chivalry." Cloth breeches is of English manufacture and descent, and deplores the vices that have crept into "this glorious Iland" in the wake of Italian fashions. Both plead before Greene, each giving very graphic accounts of the

[1] "Greenes never too late," "Works," vol. viii. p. 67.

[2] "A quip for an upstart courtier, or a quaint dispute between velvet breeches and cloth breeches," London, 1592; "Works," vol. xi. In the year of its publication it went through three editions and had several afterwards. It was translated into Dutch: "Een seer vermakelick Proces tusschen Fluweele-Broeck ende Laken-Broek," Leyden, 1601, 4to. Greene had as his model in writing this book F. T.'s "Debate between pride and lowliness," and he drew much from it, though not so much by far as he has been accused of by Mr. Collier. "The Debate," &c., Shakespeare Society, 1841, preface. (F. T. is not Francis Thynne.)

behaviour of the other. Here, for example, is a scene, assuredly from the life, at a barber's shop:

"Velvet breeches he sittes downe in the chaire wrapt in fine cloathes . . . then comes [the barber] out with his fustian eloquence, and making a low conge, saith:

"Sir, will you have your wor[ship's] haire cut

VELVET BREECHES AND CLOTH BREECHES, 1592.

after the Italian maner, shorte and round, and then frounst with the curling yrons, to make it looke like a halfe moone in a miste? or like a Spanyard, long at the eares and curled like the two endes of an old cast periwig? or will you be Frenchified, with a love locke downe to your shoulders, wherein you may weare your mistresse favour? The English cut is base and gentlemen scorne it, novelty is daintye; speake the woord sir, and my sissars are ready to execute your worships wil.

"His head being once drest, which requires in combing and rubbing some two howers, hee comes to the bason : then being curiously washt with no woorse then a camphire bal, he descends as low as his berd, and asketh whether he please to be shaven or no, whether he will have his peak cut short and sharpe, amiable like an *inamorato*, or broad pendant like a spade, to be terrible like a warrior and a Soldado . . . if it be his pleasure to have his appendices primed or his mustachios fostered to turn about his eares like ye branches of a vine. . . ."

The question pending between cloth and velvet is submitted to a jury ; men of the various professions are called and accepted, or rejected, according to their merit ; each is described, often in a very lively manner. Here is, for example, the portrait of a poet or rather of *the* poet of the Elizabethan period ; for the specimen here represented stands as a type for all his class ; and it is worth notice, for if Shakespeare himself was different, many of his associates at the " Mermaid," we may be sure, well answered the description. " I espied far off a certain kind of an overworne gentleman, attired in velvet and satin ; but it was somewhat dropped and greasie, and bootes on his legges, whose soles wexed thin and seemed to complaine of their maister, which treading thrift under his feet, had brought them unto that consumption. He walked not as other men in the common beaten way, but came compassing *circumcirca*, as if we had beene divells and he would draw a circle about us, and at every third step he looked back as if he were afraid of a baily or a sarjant." Cloth Breeches, who seems to be describing here Greene himself, is not too severe in his appreciation of the character of the poor troubled fellow: "If he have forty pound in his purse together, he puts it not to usury, neither buies land nor merchandise with it, but a moneths commodity of wenches and capons. Ten pound a supper, why tis nothing if his plough goes and his ink horne be cleere . . . But to speak plainely I think him an honest man if he would but live within his compasse, and generally no mans foe but his own. Therefore I hold him a man fit to be of my jury."

Judgment is passed in favour of cloth England against velvet England; and in this ultra-conservative sentence the views of the Bohemian novelist are summed up in this premature essay on the "philosophy of clothes."

IV.

The fame and success of Greene encouraged writers to follow his example. He had shown that there was a public for novels, and that it was a sort of literature that would pay, both in reputation and money. He had, therefore, many rivals and imitators who were thus only second-hand disciples of Lyly. Among these Nicholas Breton and Emmanuel Ford may be taken as examples. Both were his contemporaries, but survived him many years. In both traces of euphuism survive, but they are faint; at the time they wrote euphuism was on the wane, and it is only on rare occasions that Ford reminds us that "the most mightie monarch Alexander, aswel beheld the crooked counterfeit of Vulcan as the sweet picture of Venus. Philip of Macedon accepted...."[1]

What Ford especially imitated from Greene was the art of writing romantic tales with plenty of adventures, unexpected meetings and discoveries, much love, and improbabilities enough to enchant Elizabethan readers and sell the book up to any number of editions. In this he rivalled his model very successfully, and his romances were among the most popular of the time of Shakespeare. The number of their editions was extraordinary, and they were renewed at almost regular intervals up to the eighteenth century; there was a far greater demand for them than for any play of Shakespeare.[2] Besides imitating Greene, who obviously revealed to him the success to be won by writing romantic tales, he imitated at the same time the Italians and the Spaniards, introducing into his romances a licentiousness quite unknown to Greene, but well known to Boccaccio, and heroic adventures similar to those his friend Anthony Munday was just then putting into English. These last were to be the chief delight of novel-readers in the seventeenth century, and did more than anything for the great popularity of Ford's novels during that period.

Ford's earliest and most characteristic work was

---

[1] Dedication of "Parismus," 1598.
[2] The thirteenth edition of "Parismus" appeared in 1649; there were others in 1657, 1663, 1664, 1665, 1658, 1671, 1677, 1684, 1690, 1696, 1704, &c. (Sidney L. Lee.)

called "Parismus, the renowned prince of Bohemia
... conteining his noble battailes fought against
the Persians... his love to Laurana... and his
straunge adventures in the desolate Iland," &c., &c.[1]
As the title informs us there are loves and wars in this
romance, deeds of valour and of sorcery, there are
pageants and enchanters. The adventures take place
in purely imaginary lands, which the author is pleased
to call Bohemia, Persia, &c., but which might have
been as well baptized Tartary or Mongolia. The
manners and costumes, however, when there is an
attempt at describing them, are purely Elizabethan.
There are masques such as were shown at court in
Shakespeare's time, and during one such fête, as in
"Romeo and Juliet," Parismus for the first time
declares his love to Laurana: "The maskers entred
in this sort: first entred two torch bearers, apparelled
in white satten, beset with spangles of gold, after
whom followed two Eunuches, apparelled all in greene,
playing on two instruments, then came Parismus attired
all in carnation satten ... next followed ... when came
two knights ... next followed ... "[2] and so on; in
the same style as in Shakespeare's play, "enter Romeo,
Mercutio, Benvolio, with five or six maskers, torch-
bearers and others."[3] But, alas, this is the only
place where there is any resemblance between the two

---

[1] London, 1598, 4to. [2] Sig. C iii. *et seq.*
[3] Act i. sc. 4. "Romeo" was first printed in 1597. A contemporary representation of such an *entrée* of maskers is to be
seen in the curious painting representing Sir H. Unton and the
principal events in his life; now kept in the National Portrait
Gallery (painted about 1596).

styles ; though the situation developes under Ford's pen in a manner to suggest that he must have read "Romeo" not without a purpose. Had his purpose been to show his contemporaries the height of Shakespeare's genius by giving, side by side with it, the measure of an ordinary mind, he could not have tried better nor succeeded less. For contemporaries and successors consumed innumerable editions of "Parismus," and only too easily numbered editions of "Romeo."

Parismus and Laurana talk, in the midst of the ball, of their new-born love, and after an exchange of highly polite phrases she thus confesses her feelings : " My noble lord . . . I heartily thanke you for taking so much paines for my sake, being unwoorthie thereof, and also unable to bee sufficiently thankfull unto you for the same, and for that you say your happinesse resteth in my power, if I can any way work your content to the uttermost of my endeavour I will do it." Parismus, of course, has nothing to answer except that no one could require more.

It had been, however, with her also, love at first sight ; but Laurana does not say :

> "Go, ask his name : if he be married,
> My grave is like to be my wedding bed."

She is far too well bred and courtly, and she explains as follows what she has felt : " My Lord, I assure you, that at such time as I sawe you comming first into this court, my heart was then surprised, procured, as I think by the destinies, that ever since I have vowed to rest yours." This speech is made at a nightly garden meeting, similar to the one where Romeo went " with love's light wings," and where was heard the sweetest and gravest lovers' music that ever enchanted human ears:

> "At lovers' perjuries,
> They say Jove laughs. O gentle Romeo,
> If thou dost love, pronounce it faithfully:
> Or if thou think'st I am too quickly won,
> I will frown and be perverse. . . .
> Well, do not swear: although I joy in thee,
> I have no joy of this contract to-night.
> It is too rash, too unadvised, too sudden;
> Too like the lightning, which doth cease to be
> Ere one can say, It lightens." . . .

He of Bohemia had not come with "love's light wings," but "somewhat before the hour, was gone forth in his night gowne, with his sworde under his arme, and comming to the gate he was wont to goe in at into the gardeine, found it shut, and having no other meanes, he gott over the wall." We picture him clambering over the wall, his night-gown flowing about him to do duty for love's wings. The lovers meet, and "thus they spent the night in kinde salutations and curteous imbracings to the unspeakable joy and comfort of them both."

To complete the external resemblance of the two situations, there is in Ford's novel a young lord to play the part of "County Paris." He is called Sicanus, and Laurana's family greatly favours his suit: "Laurana, my cheefest care is to see thee married, according to thy state, which hath made me send for thee, to know whether thou hast alreadie placed thy affection or no : otherwise there is come into this country, a knight of great estate," &c., &c. "Laurana departed with a heavie heart."

Then again, as in "Romeo," there is another meeting of the lovers, this time in Laurana's chamber ; and they spend the hours " in sweete greetings, but farre from anie thought of unchastnesse, their imbracings being grounded upon the most vertuous conditions that might bee : and sitting together upon the beds side, Laurana told him. . . ." As in Romeo, they are parted by morn :

> "Wilt thou be gone ? it is not yet near day :
> It was the nightingale, and not the lark. . . .
> —It was the lark, the herald of the morn,
> No nightingale : look, love, what envious streaks
> Do lace the severing clouds in yonder east. . . .
> —Yond light is not daylight. . . ."

A very different morn shines in at Laurana's windows : " Nowe the dismall houre of their parting being approached, by reason of the light that the sunne began to give into the chamber, Parismus taking Laurana in his armes, drawing sweete breath from her lippes, told her that now, to his greefe, he must leave her to be courted by his enemie."

Without any very great grief on our side we shall leave them to follow from this point a series of adventures very different from Romeo's. Parismus becomes a chief of outlaws, and acquires great fame under the name of the Black Knight; he wages war against Sicanus, he encounters young Violetta, and their meetings read like a tale from Boccaccio rather than like a play of Shakespeare ; at last he marries Laurana " with admirable pompe " in the " temple of Diana." We shall leave them in this holy place, though many more adventures are in store for them. We shall only state that Ford, encouraged by the great success of this first attempt, wrote several other novels exactly in the same style, containing the same improbable monsters and wonders, and the same licentious adventures. In spite, however, of the condemnation he suffered at the hands of wise people on account of the undeniable immorality of several of his episodes, his reputation went on increasing for years and long survived him.[1]

Another follower of Greene was Nicholas Breton,[2] eighteen years his senior ; but he did not begin novel-writing until after the death of his model, when this kind of literature had taken a firm hold of the public. Very little euphuism remains in Breton ; we do not find in him those clusters of similes with which Lyly and Greene were fond of adorning their novels, and alliteration is there only to remind us that through Greene, Breton may be considered a secondary legatee

---

[1] " Parismenos, the second part of . . . Parismus," 1599 ; " Ornatus and Artesia," of uncertain date, but surely anterior to 1598 ; " Montelion, Knight of the Oracle," of uncertain date ; the earliest known copy bears date, 1633. Francis Meres, in his celebrated " Palladis Tamia," gives a list of books " hurtful to youth," and which are to be " censured " ; among them, besides " Gargantua," " Owlglass," &c., he names " Ornatus and Artesia " and the " Black Knight," which might perhaps be " Parismus," for such was our hero's nickname.

[2] "Works in verse and prose," ed. Grosart, London, 1879, 2 vols., 4to. Breton was born in 1542-3 ; he studied at Oxford, and travelled on the continent ; he died in 1626.

of Lyly. The subjects and the form of his writings, much better than his style, prove him a pupil of Greene. He imitated his dialogues, publishing in succession his conference " betwixt a scholler and an angler," his discussion between " wit and will"; his disputation of a scholar and a soldier, " the one defending learning, the other martiall discipline," and several others on travels, on court and country, &c. He imitated Greene's tales of low life, anticipating in his turn Defoe's novels, with his " Miseries of Mavillia ; " he remained, however, far below the level not only of Defoe, but of Greene, whose personal knowledge of the misfortunes he was describing enabled him to give in his writings of this kind pictures of reality that contrasted strangely with the fanciful incidents of his romantic novels. The only things worth remembering in these " miseries," besides their subject, are a few thoughtful observations such as the one (in alliterative style) which opens the story : " Sorrow sokes long ere it slayes ; care consumes before it killes ; and destinie drives the body into much miserie, before the heart be strooken dead ; " a far juster observation than Greene's fancies, according to which heroes of novels may be got rid of as quickly by sorrow as by poison or apoplexy.

There are also in Breton imitations of the romantic novel of Italian origin such as Greene understood it and such as the Elizabethan public loved it. Breton published in 1600 his " Strange fortunes of two excellent princes," which his modern editor does not hesitate to declare " a bright and characteristic little book." This little masterpiece begins thus, in very characteristic fashion indeed : " In the Ilandes of Balino, neere unto the

city of Dulno, there lived a great duke named Firente.
. . . This lord had to wife a sweete ladie called Merilla,
a creature of much worth. . . . This blessed lord and
ladie had issue male, onlie one sonne named Penillo
and female one onlie daughter named Merilla." These
two children were famous for their wit and beauty.
"But I will . . . entreat of another Duke, who dwelt
in the Ilands of Cotasie. . . . This duke had to name
Ordillo, a man famous for much worth as well in wit
as valour. . . . This duke had to wife a gratious ladie.
. . . She had by her lord the duke two blessed children,
a sonne and a daughter; her sonne named Fantiro and
her daughter Sinilla." These two children begat wonder
for their wit and their beauty.

Such is the introduction. What do you think will
follow? That the two perfect young men will marry
the two unique young women? This is exactly what
happens; and the only perceptible interest in the tale
is to see from what improbable incidents such likely
consequences are derived. We can safely, it seems,
class this novel in the same category as "Arbasto,"
"Mamillia," and other products of Greene's pen; not,
however, without remarking that Breton's stories, as well
as those of his model, were not meant to delight nurseries,
but were destined to give pleasure to grown-up people,
to people in society; they were offered them as
jucunda oblivia vitæ, exactly in the same fashion as
the three-volume novels of to-day. Breton himself is
positive on this point, and he has been careful to inform
us that his intention was to write things " which being
read or heard in a winters evening by a good fire, or a
summers morning in the greene fields may serve both

to purge melancholy from the minde and grosse humours from the body."[1]

Again, he was connected with the Greene and Lyly group by the pleasure he felt in composing imaginary letters. A number of such letters had been inserted by Lyly in his "Euphues," and had proved one of the attractions of the book; Greene and the other novelists of the period never missed an opportunity of making their heroes write to each other, and they always transcribed their letters in full, a process inherited from the romance writers of the Middle Ages. Breton, following the example already given by some of his contemporaries, went beyond that, and published a volume of imaginary letters from everybody to anybody on any subject, many of them rather coarse, some good, some rather slow in their gait and heavy in their wit.[2] The public taste

[1] This forms part of the title of his "Wonders worth the hearing," 1602 (a dialogue with anecdotes).

[2] "A poste with a packet of mad Letters." The earliest dated edition is of the year 1603. Breton published, besides the writings above mentioned, some religious, pastoral, and other poetry. Part of it is dedicated to Mary Sidney, Countess of Pembroke, the famous sister of Sir Philip: "The Countesse of Pembrookes love," 1592; "The Countesse of Pembroke's passion" (no date). His pastoral poetry is among the best of his time. He left also moral essays and characters or typical portraits: "Characters upon essaies morall and divine, 1615," dedicated to Bacon, and concerning wisdom, learning, knowledge, patience, love, peace, war and other, even then, rather trite subjects. "The good and badde," 1616, contains characters of a knave, an usurer, a virgin, a parasite, a goodman, an "atheist or most badde man: hee makes robberie his purchase, lecherie his solace, mirth his exercise, and drunkennesse his glory," &c. These books of "Characters" were extremely popular. *Cf.* "Characters of virtues and vices," by Hall, 1608; Sir Thomas Overbury's "Characters," 1614; John Earle's

was so decidedly in favour of these compositions that this was the most successful of Breton's enterprises. It was often reprinted; a number of similar collections were circulated in the seventeenth century, and their popularity had not abated when Richardson was asked, by the publishers Osborne and Rivington, to compose one for country people. He did so, and the only difference, and a sufficiently important one, was that in his series the letters were connected by the thread of a story.

Greene had a rival of much higher stature in his friend Thomas Lodge. Lodge was a little older than Greene, and survived him long, so that he happened to be a contemporary both of Greene and of his imitators. He rivalled Greene, but did not imitate him, being himself a direct legatee of Lyly. The sort of life he led differed greatly from that of his friend, but it was scarcely less characteristic of the period. Lodge was the son of a rich London grocer who had been Lord Mayor. Born in 1557, he had known Lyly at Oxford; had studied law; then, yielding to those desires of seeing the dangers and beauties of the world which drove the English youths of the period to seek preferment abroad, he closed his books for a while, and became a corsair, visiting the Canary Isles, Brazil, and Patagonia. He brought back, as booty from his expeditions, romances written at sea to beguile the tedium of the passage and the anxieties of the tempest. One was called " The Margarite of America"; another " Rosa-

" Microcosmographie," 1628, and a great many others. The last-named was translated into French by J. Dymocke, " Le vice ridicule," Louvain, 1671, 12mo. One of his most curious works is his " Fantasticks," 1626.

lynde. The latter fell into Shakespeare's hands and pleased him; he drew from it the plot of "As you like it."[1] Coming before the literary public, Lodge does not altogether forget his profession of corsair, and in order to deprive the critics of the temptation to sneer, he is careful to brandish his rapier from time to time, and to write prefaces that make one's hair stand on end. " Roome for a souldier and a sailer, that gives you the fruits of his labors that he wrote in the Ocean !" he cries to the reader at the beginning of his " Rosalynde," and let fault-finders keep silence; otherwise he will throw them overboard " to feed cods."

After such a warning there would be nothing it seems but to hold our tongue; but perhaps, taking the practical side of the question, we may consider that by this time Lodge's rapier must have grown very rusty, and would not offer more danger than any critic is

---

[1] The principal novels or short stories of Lodge are: "Forbonius and Prisceria," 1584, reprinted by the Shakespeare Society, 1853; "Rosalynde, Euphues golden legacie found after his death in his cell at Silexedra . . . fetcht from the Canaries," 1590, reprinted by Hazlitt, 1875, and again in a popular form by Prof. H. Morley, 1887; " The famous, true, and historicall life of . . . Robin the divell," 1591; "Euphues shadow the battaile of the sences wherein youthful folly is set downe," 1592; it was edited by Greene in the absence of his friend, who was at sea "upon a long voyage." The story takes place in Italy at the time when "Octavius possessed the monarchy of the whole world." "The Margarite of America," 1596, reprinted by Halliwell, 1859. In this romance (p. 116), Lodge incidentally eulogizes his contemporary the French poet Philippe Desportes, and he mentions the popularity of his works in England. The "Complete Works" of Lodge have been published by the Hunterian Club, ed. Gosse, Glasgow, 1875, *et seq.*

bound to incur in the performance of his duty. Besides that admiration may in all sincerity be blended with criticism when it is a question of Lodge's masterpiece, " Rosalynde."

The tale itself bears a somewhat curious history. Twice at two hundred years' distance it took the fancy of the greatest genius of the period. In the Middle Ages it was called the " Tale of Gamelyn," [1] and Chaucer apparently intended to work it into his " Canterbury Tales," but he died before he had completed his wish, and some copy of the rough old poem having, as it seems, been found among his papers, it was in after time inserted in the manuscripts of his works as the " Cooke's Tale." As it stood in the fourteenth century this story recited mere deeds of valour, of strong, sinewy fighters ; love and women played no part in it ; and it is a great loss for us not to know whether old Chaucer would have made this very necessary addition, and what sort of mediæval Rosalind he would have depicted.

As things went, we are indebted to our gentleman adventurer for the invention of Rosalind. Lodge took up the tale and remodelled it entirely ; he gave place in it to the fair she-page and to her friend Alinda and to Phœbe, the hard-hearted shepherdess, in such a way that when Shakespeare in his turn bethought himself of this story, he had nothing to add to fit it for his own stage, nothing except genius.

But if Lodge cannot be considered a man of genius, he is certainly a writer of very remarkable gifts. His

[1] "The tale of Gamelyn, from Harleian MS., 7334," ed. Skeat, Oxford, 1884, 16mo.

novel is a pastoral tale that takes place somewhere in France, near Bordeaux, and reads as pleasantly as any story in " Astrée," no mean compliment. Probability, geography and chronology, are not Lodge's strong points; we are in fact again in the country of nowhere, in an imaginary kingdom of France over which the usurper Torismond reigns. The true king has been deposed and leads a forester's life, untroubled, unknown, in the thick woods of Arden. Rosalind, a daughter of the deposed king, has been kept as a sort of hostage at the court of the tyrant in Bordeaux, presumably his capital. All of a sudden she is exiled in her turn, without more explanation than " I have heard of thy aspiring speaches and intended treasons."[1] Alinda, her friend, the daughter of the tyrant, refuses to leave her, and both fly the court, Rosalind being dressed as a page, a rapier at her side, her wit full of repartees, her mind full of shifts, and equal, in fact, as in Shakespeare, to any emergency. " Tush, quoth Rosalynd, art thou a woman and hast not a sodaine shift to prevent a misfortune? I, thou seest, am of a tall stature, and would very well become the person and apparell of a page ; thou shalt bee my mistris, and I will play the man so properly, that, trust me, in what company so ever I come, I will not bee discovered. I will buy mee

PREPARING FOR THE HUNT, 1575.

[1] "Works," vol. ii. p. 12 (each work has a separate pagination)

a suite, and have my rapier very handsomely at my side, and if any knave offer wrong, your page will shew him the point of his weapon. At this Alinda smiled, and upon this they agreed, and presentlie gathered up all their jewels which they trussed up in a casket. . . . They travailed along the vineyards, and by many by-waies, at last got to the forrest side," the forest of Arden, which at that time happened to be near the vineyards of Gascony.

But this geographical situation is the least of the wonders offered by the forest. In it live not only Gerismond, the lawful king, very happy and contented, free and without care, wanting nothing; but, in the valleys, the most lovable shepherdesses and the most loving shepherds; they feed their flocks while piping their ditties; they inscribe their sonnets on the bark of trees; they are very learned, though mere shepherds; they quote Latin and write French; they know how to ask the god of love that the heart of their mistress may not be " de glace."

"Bien qu'elle ait de neige le sein."

They live in the shade of the most unaccountable woods, woods composed of pine-trees, fig-trees, and lemon-trees. " Then, comming into a faire valley, compassed with mountaines whereon grewe many pleasant shrubbs, they might descrie where two flocks of sheepe did feede. Then looking about they might perceive where an old shepheard sat, and with him a yong swaine, under a covert most pleasantlie scituated. The ground where they sat was diapred with Floras riches, as if she ment to wrap Tellus in the glorie of her vestments:

round about, in the forme of an amphitheater were most curiouslie planted pine-trees, interseamed with limons and citrons, which with the thicknesse of their boughes so shadowed the place, that Phœbus could not prie into the secret of that arbour. . . . Fast by . . was there a fount so christalline and cleere that it seemed Diana and her Driades and Hemadriades had that spring as the secret of all their bathings. In this glorious arbour sat these two shepheards seeing their sheepe feede, playing on their pipes. . . ." It is like a landscape by Poussin. Alinda and her page find the place very pleasant, and decide to settle there, especially when they have heard what a shepherd's life is like. "For a shepheards life, oh! mistresse, did you but live a while in their content, you would saye the court were rather a place of sorrowe than of solace . . . Envie stirres not us, wee covet not to climbe, our desires mount not above our degrees, nor our thoughts above our fortunes. Care cannot harbour in our cottages, nor doo our homely couches know broken slumbers." Fine assertions, to which some hundred and fifty years later Prince Rasselas was most solemnly to give the lie. But his time had not yet come, and both princesses resolve to settle there, to purchase flocks, and " live quiet, unknowen, and contented." [1]

Many other pleasant things are to be found in the forest; in fact, the two ladies meet their lovers there; brave Rosader, the Gamelyn of Chaucerian times, the Orlando of Shakespeare, and wicked but repentant and reformed Saladin, who loves Alinda as Rosader loves Rosalind. They meet, too, the shepherdess Phœbe, " as

[1] "Works," vol. ii. pp. 14, 16, 19, 20.

faire as the wanton that brought Troy to ruine," but in a different dress; "she in a peticoate of scarlet, covered with a greene mantle, and to shrowde her from the sunne, a chaplet of roses;" in a different mood, too, towards shepherds, thinking nothing of her Paris, poor Montanus whom she disdains while he is dying for her.

Yet there were even more wonders in this forest of Arcadian shepherds, exiled princesses, and lemon-trees. There were "certaine rascalls that lived by prowling in the forrest, who for feare of the provost marshall had caves in the groves and thickets";[1] there were lions, too, very dangerous, hungry, man-eating lions. Such animals appear in Shakespeare also, as well as "palm trees," and Shakespeare moreover takes the liberty of doubling his lion with a serpent.

> "A wretched ragged man o'ergrown with hair
> Lay sleeping on his back: about his neck
> A green and gilded snake had wreath'd itself
> Who with her head, nimble in threats, approach'd
> The opening of his mouth; but suddenly,
> Seeing Orlando, it unlink'd itself,
> And with indented glides did slip away
> Into a bush: under which bush s shade
> A lioness, with udders all drawn dry,
> Lay couching."[2]

Let us not be too much troubled; here will be good opportunities for lovers to show the sort of men they are, to be wounded, but not disfigured, and finally to be loved.

[1] "Works," vol. ii. pp. 63, 46, 42.
[2] "As you like it," act iv. sc. 3.

So many rare encounters of men and animals, and shepherds and lovers, give excellent occasions for Rosalind to display the special turn of her mind, and if, in Lodge, she has not all the ready wit that Shakespeare has given her, she is by no means slow of speech; she possesses besides much more of that human kindness in which we sometimes find the brilliant page of the play a little deficient. The conversations between her and Alinda are very pleasant to read, and show how at last, not only on the stage, but even in novels, the tongues of the speakers had been loosened.

"No doubt, quoth Aliena,[1] this poesie is the passion of some perplexed shepheard, that being enamoured of some fair and beautifull shepheardesse suffered some sharpe repulse, and therefore complained of the cruelty of his mistris.

"You may see, quoth Ganimede [Rosalind's page-name], what mad cattell you women be, whose hearts sometimes are made of adamant that will touch with no impression, and sometimes of waxe that is fit for everie forme; they delight to be courted and then they glorie to seeme coy, and when they are most desired, then they freeze with disdaine. . . .

"And I pray you, quoth Aliena, if your roabes were off, what mettall are you made of that you are so satyricall against women? . . . Beware, Ganimede, that Rosader heare you not. . . .

"Thus, quoth Ganimede, I keepe decorum, I speake now as I am Alienas page, not as I am Gerismonds daughter; for put me but into a peticoate, and I will stand in defiance to the uttermost, that

[1] Her forest name for Alinda.

women are courteous, constant, virtuous, and what not."

Thus there is much merry prattle between these two, especially when the presence of the lover of the one sharpens the teasing disposition of the other; when, for example, Rosader finding, not without good cause, some resemblance between the page and his Rosalind, pities the former, for not equalling the perfection of his mistress.

"He hath answered you, Ganimede, quoth Aliena, it is inough for pages to waite on beautifull ladies and not to be beautifull themselves.

"Oh! mistres," answers the she-page, who cannot help feeling some spite, "holde your peace, for you are partiall; who knowes not, but that all women have desire to tie sovereigntie to their peticoats, and ascribe beautie to themselves, where if boyes might put on their garments, perhaps they would proove as comely; if not as comely, it may be more curteous."

There are also some morning scenes full of pleasant mirth and cheerful light, in which perhaps there is more of Phœbus than of the sun, and more of Aurora than of the dawn; but this light, such as it is, is worth the looking at, so merrily it shines; and the talk of these early risers well suits the half-classic landscape.

"The sunne was no sooner stept from the bed of Aurora, but Aliena was wakened by Ganimede, who restlesse all night, had tossed in her passions; saying it was then time to goe to the field to unfold their sheepe.

"Aliena . . . replied thus : What? wanton, the sun

is but new up, and as yet Iris riches lies folded in the bosom of Flora; Phœbus hath not dried the pearled deaw, and so long Coridon hath taught me it is not fit to lead the sheepe abroad lest the deaw being unwholesome they get the rot. But now see I the old proverbe true . . ." (and here comes some euphuism).

"Come on," answers Ganimede, who does not seem in a mood to appreciate euphuism just then, "this sermon of yours is but a subtiltie to lie still a bed, because either you think the morning colde, or els I being gone, you would steale a nappe; this shifte carries no palme, and therefore up and away. And for Love, let me alone; Ile whip him away with nettles and set Disdaine as a charme to withstand his forces; and therefore, looke you to your selfe; be not too bolde, for Venus can make you bend; nor too coy, for Cupid hath a piercing dart that will make you cry *Peccavi*.

"And that is it, quoth Aliena, that hath raysed you so early this morning?

"And with that she slipt on her peticoate, and start up; and assoone as she had made her readie and taken her breakfast, away goe these two with their bagge and bottles to the field, in more pleasant content of mind than ever they were in the court of Torismond."

In the same way as in Shakespeare, fair Phœbe, deceived by Rosalind's dress, Phœbe, who thought herself beyond the reach of love, becomes enamoured of the page and feels at last all the pangs of an unrequited passion. Lodge's Rosalind, more human we think than her great Shakespearean sister, uses, to persuade Phœbe into loving Montanus, a kindly, tender language, meant to heal rather than irritate the poor shepherdess's wounds. "What!" will exclaim the great sister, . . .

> ". . . What though you have no beauty . . .
> Must you be therefore proud and pitiless?
> Why, what means this? Why do you look on me?
> I see no more in you than in the ordinary
> Of nature's sale-work : Od's my little life!
> I think she means to tangle my eyes too :—
> No, 'faith, proud mistress, hope not after it ;
> 'Tis not your inky brows, your black silk-hair,
> Your bugle eyeballs, nor your cheek of cream
> That can entame my spirits to your worship." [1]

Very spiritless, and tame, and old fashioned, will the other Rosalind appear by the side of this impetuous, relentless deity. A few perhaps will consider that her tame, kindly, old-fashioned, mythological piece of advice to the shepherdess, makes her the more lovable : " What, shepheardesse, so fayre and so cruell? . . . Because thou art beautifull, be not so coye : as there is nothing more faire, so there is nothing more fading, as momentary as the shadowes which growes from a cloudie sunne. Such, my faire shepheardesse, as disdaine in youth, desire in age, and then are they hated in the winter, that might have been loved in the prime. A wrinkled maid is like a parched rose, that is cast up in coffers to please the smell, not worn in the hand to content the eye. There is no folly in love to had-I-wist, and therefore,

[1] "As you like it," act iii. sc. 5.

be rulde by me. Love while thou art young, least thou be disdained when thou art olde. Beautie nor time cannot bee recalde, and if thou love, like of Montanus; for if his desires are manie, so his deserts are great." [1] And it is indeed quite touching to see poor Montanus in the simplest lover fashion verify by his acts this description of himself; for while reduced to the last degree of despair, seeing the unconquerable love Phœbe entertains for the page, he beseeches Rosalind to save her by returning her love; sorrow will kill him any way, but he will die contented if he thinks that even through another's love Phœbe will live happy in her Arcadian vale.

I need not add that all these troubles end as happily as possible; the storms pass away and a many-coloured rainbow encompasses Arden, Arcady, and the kingdom of France; every lover becomes loved, the three couples get married, and while the music of the bridal fête is still in our ears, news is brought that "hard by, at the edge of this forest, the twelve peers of France are up in arms" to recover Gerismond's rights. They accomplish this feat in a twinkling, as French peers should; why they did not do it before does not appear: probably because the treble marriage would not have looked so pretty in Notre Dame as under the lemon trees. There is much bloodshed of course, but it is blood we do not care for, and we are allowed to part from our shepherd friends with the pleasing thought that they will see no end to their loves and happiness.

Such is "Euphues golden legacy," one of the best

[1] "Works," vol. ii. pp. 29, 30, 31, 49.

examples of the sort of novel that was being written at this period. It has all the characteristics of this kind of writing such as it had come to be understood at that date; prose is mixed with verse, and several of Lodge's best songs are included in " Rosalynde "; it is full of meditations and monologues like those with which the neo-classic drama of the French school has made us familiar.[1] In the more important places, in monologues, speeches and letters euphuistic style usually prevails;[2] the chronology and geography of the tale, its logic and probability, the grouping of events are of the loosest description; but it has moreover a freshness and sometimes a pathos which is more easily felt than expressed and of which the above quotations may have given some idea.

In " Rosalynde" we see Lodge at his best. Perhaps,

---

[1] "Saladin's meditation with himself: 'Saladin, art thou disquieted in thy thoughts?'" &c. " Rosalind's passion : ' Unfortunate Rosalind, whose misfortunes are more than thy years,'" &c. " Aliena's meditation : ' Ah ! me ; now I see, and sorrowing sigh to see that Diana's laurels are harbours for Venus doves,' " &c.

[2] For example, in "the schedule annexed to Euphues testament," by which the dying man leaves the book to Philautus for the benefit of his children. They will find in it what is fit for the God Love, "roses to whip him when he is wanton, reasons to whistant him when he is wilie." In the same manner Sir John of Bourdeaux informs his sons that "a woman's eye as it is precious to behold, so is it prejudicial to gaze upon "; Rosalind observes to herself that " the greatest seas have the sorest stormes, the highest birth is subject to the most bale and of all trees the cedars soonest shake with the wind," &c. The same style is used in " Euphues shadow " in " Robin the divell," &c. : " Thou art like the verven (Nature) poyson one wayes, and pleasure an other, feeding me with grapes in shewe lyke to Darius vine, but not in substance lyke those of Vermandois " (" Robin the divell ").

remembering his threats, it is better not to try to see him at his worst ; it will therefore be sufficient to add that, having published also satires and epistles imitated from Horace, eclogues, some other short stories or romances, a translation of the philosophical works of Seneca, two or three incoherent dramas (in one of which a whale comes on to the stage, and without any ceremony vomits forth the prophet Jonah),[1] Lodge changed his profession once again, abandoned the sword for the lancet, became a physician, gained a fortune, and died quietly a rich citizen in 1625.

He had thus lived beyond the period of Lyly's fame, of Greene's reputation, of Shakespeare's splendour, and saw, before he died, the beginnings of a new and very different era in which both the drama and the novel were to undergo, as we shall see, many and vast transformations.

[1] "A Looking glasse for London and England." This drama was written by Lodge and by his friend Greene. The following stage direction occurs in it : "Ionas the prophet cast out of the whales belly upon the stage."

SCORPIO.

PENSHURST, SIDNEY'S BIRTHPLACE.

CHAPTER V.

SIR PHILIP SIDNEY AND PASTORAL ROMANCE.

WHEN nowadays we see our shepherds, wrapped in their long brown cloaks, silently following the high roads in the midst of a suffocating dust which seems to come out of their sheep, it is difficult to explain the enthusiasm that has ascribed to this race of mutes such fine speeches and such pleasant adventures. Greeks, Romans, Italians, Spaniards, the French and the English, have differed in a multitude of points, but they have one and all delighted in pastorals. No class of heroes either in history or fiction has uttered so much verse and prose as the keepers of sheep. Neither Ajax son of Telamon, nor the wise king of Ithaca, nor Merlin, Lancelot, or Charlemagne, nor even the inexhaustible Grandison, can bear the least comparison with Tityrus. It is easy to give many reasons for this; but the phenomenon still remains somewhat strange. The best explanation is perhaps that the pastoral is one of the most convenient pretexts existing for saying what would otherwise be embarrassing. To many authors the eclogue is like a canvas for trying their colours and brushes. Many would not willingly confess it, and Pope would have vowed a mortal hatred to any one who explained his eclogues thus: but it is better for his reputation to believe that he had at least that reason for writing them. For some, the pastoral is an allegory, where, if one would, place can be given to Cynthia, Queen of the Sea, that is to say, to Elizabeth, and to a Shepherd of the Ocean who is Raleigh; it allows the poet to speak to kings, to ask alms discreetly of them, and to thank them.

In England in Shakespeare's time people were passionately fond of the country of Arcadia, not the Arcady "for better for worse" that can be seen anywhere outside London,[1] but the old poetical Arcadia, the Arcadia of nowhere, which was the more cherished on account of its non-existence. They could invent at their ease, imagine prodigious adventures and wonderful amours; since no one had ever been in Arcadia, it was hardly possible for any one to protest that events happened differently there. To-day we think in quite another way; we must be told of well-ascertained facts, of warranted catastrophes, at once certified and

[1] And which has been faithfully and touchingly described in Dr. Jessopp's book: "Arcady: For better, for worse," recently published in London.

provable. That is why the action of our novels, far from carrying us into Arcadia, often unfolds itself in our kitchens and on our back staircases. It is not at all as it was in the time of Robert Greene.

Very rarely now does any one ask if perchance some of these "Arcadias," so cherished by our fathers, contained their share of enduring beauty, or if their lasting success is to be explained otherwise than by their improbabilities and their artificial embellishments. Nevertheless the study might be profitable, for it must be borne in mind that the readers of these romances went in the afternoon to the "Globe" to see Shakespeare play his own pieces, and that, admitting their fondness for such dramas, in which, without speaking of other merits, the kitchen is sometimes the place represented, it would be surprising to find only mere nonsense in the whole collection of their favoured romances. Let these suggestions justify us at need in examining one more Arcadia: besides, it is not that of a penniless Bohemian; it is the Arcadia of Sir Philip Sidney, the pattern of chivalrous perfection under Elizabeth. His life is not, in its way, less characteristic of his time than that of starving Robert Greene, or of Thomas Lodge the corsair.

I.

Born in 1554, in the noble castle of Penshurst in Kent,[1] Sidney passed a part of his childhood in Ludlow

[1] Besides its fine collection of family portraits, one of which is reproduced in this volume, by the kind permission of Lord de

Castle, where in the next century Milton's "Comus" was to be represented. At college he was famous for his personal charm, his knowledge, and the thoughtful turn of his mind. "I knew him," wrote in later years his friend and companion Fulke Greville, "with such staiednesse of mind, lovely and familiar gravity, as carried grace and reverence above greater years."[1] During the year 1572 he was staying in France, where he had been appointed by King Charles IX. one of the gentlemen of his chamber. It was the time of the St. Bartholomew massacre, and Sidney, who belonged to the English mission, remained in the house of Sir Francis Walsingham, the Queen's ambassador, and escaped the perils of that terrible day.

He left France shortly after and travelled in several countries of Europe, studying men and nations, storing his mind with information; he was comparatively free from prejudice, and believed that useful examples and precepts might be obtained even from "the great Turk." "As surely," did he write some years later to his brother Robert, "in the great Turk, though we have nothing to do with him, yet his discipline in war matters is ... worthy to be known and learned. Nay even the kingdom of China which is almost as far as the Antipodes from us, their good laws and customs are to be learned."[2] In such a

---

l'Isle and Dudley, Penshurst is remarkable because it offers to this day a perfect example of a fourteenth-century hall with the fireplace in the middle.

[1] "Life of the renowned Sr Philip Sidney," London, 1652, 12mo.

[2] "The Correspondence of Sir Ph. Sidney and Hubert Languet," ed. Pears London, 1845, 8vo, Appendix; A.D. 1579 (?)

disposition of mind he visited successively Germany, Austria, Hungary, and Italy. The most interesting incident of his journey was the acquaintance he made with a Frenchman, the political thinker Hubert Languet, from whom Milton, a long time before Rousseau, probably derived his ideas of the social contract "fœdus," says Languet, "inter [principem] and populum," and his theories on the right of insurrection.[1] A most tender friendship was formed between the revolutionary writer and the aristocratic Sidney. They began a correspondence which did not cease till the former's death in 1581. Languet had great influence over his young friend, and was constantly giving him most manly advice and that best suited to strengthen his character, warning him especially in very wise fashion against a melancholy unsuitable to his age, which in the grave Huguenot's opinion was only a useless impedimentum in life. "I readily allow," wrote Sidney, in answer to his friend's remonstrances, "that I am often more serious than either my age or my pursuits demand."[2] That this tendency to pensiveness left its trace on his features may be seen in most of his portraits, among others in that by Isaac Oliver, of which we give a reproduction.

The most interesting of Sidney's portraits is unfortunately lost. He sat for it while in Italy, at the request of his friend, and chose no mean artist to paint it: "As soon as ever I return to Venice, I will have it done, either by Paul Veronese or by Tintoretto, who hold by far the highest place in the art." He decided

[1] "Vindictæ contra tyrannos," Edinburgh, 1579, part iii.
[2] Padua, February 4, 1574, "Correspondence," p. 29.

for Veronese, and sent the picture to Languet, who wrote shortly after: "As long as I enjoyed the sight of you, I made no great account of the portrait you gave me, and scarcely thanked you for so beautiful a present. I was led by regret for you on my return from Frankfort to place it in a frame and fix it in a conspicuous place. When I had done this, it appeared to me so beautiful and so strongly to resemble you that I possess nothing that I value more ... The painter has represented you sad and thoughtful. I should have been better pleased if your face had worn a more cheerful look when you sat for the painting."[1] When Languet died, Sidney described his sentiments for him in a touching poem, inserted in his "Arcadia"; it was sung by the shepherd Philisides, who represents the author himself and whose name is a contraction of the words Philip Sidney:

> "I sate me downe; for see to goe ne could,
> And sang unto my sheepe lest stray they should.
> The song I sang old Lan[g]uet had me taught,
> Lan[g]uet, the shepeard best swift Ister knew,
> For clearkly reed, and hating what is naught,
> For faithfull heart, cleane hands and mouth as true.
> With his sweet skill my skillesse youth he drew,
> To have a feeling taste of him that sits
> Beyond the heaven, farre more beyond our wits ...
> With old true tales he wont mine eares to fill,
> How shepeards did of yore, how now they thrive ...
> He liked me, but pitied lustfull youth:
> His good strong staffe my slipperie yeares upbore:
> He still hop'd well because I loved truth."[2]

---

[1] A.D. 1573, "Correspondence," p. 94. [2] "Arcadia," bk. iii.

In 1575, when twenty-one years old, Sidney returned to shine at court, where his uncle Leicester, the Queen's favourite was to make all things easy for him. He assisted that year at the fêtes given in Elizabeth's honour at Kenilworth, in those famous gardens "though not so goodly," writes a witness of the festivities, "as Paradis, for want of the fayr rivers, yet better a great deal by the lack of so unhappy a tree."[1] Then Sidney accompanied the Queen to Chartley, and these ceremonies mark a great epoch in his existence. While Elizabeth listened to the compliments of her entertainers, Sidney's eyes were fixed on a child. A sentiment, the full strength of which he was to feel only in after time, sprang up in his heart for Penelope Devereux, the twelve-year-old daughter of the Earl of Essex, who was as beautiful as Dante's Beatrice. He began to visit at her father's house frequently; it seemed as if a marriage would ensue; Essex himself was favourable to it, but for some cause or other Sidney did not press his suit; and while his friend Languet strongly advised him to marry, he was answering him in the leisurely style of one who believes himself heart-whole: " Respecting her of whom I readily acknowledge how unworthy I am, I have written you my reasons long since, briefly indeed, but yet as well as I was able."[2] He was soon to write in a very different manner. Penelope, the Stella of Sidney's verse, was, very much against her will, compelled at last by her family to marry the wealthy Lord Rich,

[1] "Captain Cox his ballads . . . or Robert Laneham's Letter, 1575," ed. Furnivall, London, Ballad Society, 1871, 8vo, p. 53.
[2] "Correspondence," *ut supra*, March 1, 1578.

and then Sidney awoke to his fate: what he had believed to be mere inclination, a light feeling of which he would always remain the master, had from the first been Love, irrepressible, unconquerable love:

> "I might;—unhappie word—O me, I might,
> And then would not, or could not see my blisse;
> Till now wrapt in a most infernall night,
> I find how heav'nly day, wretch! I did miss."[1]

He remained a lover of Stella, saw her, wrote to her, sang of her, and at length ascertained that she too, despite her marriage ties, loved him. He continued then, in altered tones, the magnificent series of sonnets dedicated to her and which read still like a love-drama of real life, a love-drama which is all summarized in the beautiful and well-known dirge:

> "Ring out your belles, let mourning shewes be spread;
> For Love is dead:
> All Love is dead, infected
> With plague of deep disdaine:
> Worth, as nought worth, rejected
> And Faith faire scorne doth gaine.
> From so ungratefull fancie,
> From such a femall franzie
> From them that use men thus,
> Good Lord, deliver us!
>
> Weepe, neighbours, weepe; do you not heare it said
> That Love is dead?
>   .   .   .   .   .   .

---

[1] "Sir Philip Sidney's Astrophel and Stella . . . edited from the folio of 1598," by Alfred Pollard, London, 1888, 8vo, sonnet 33. Penelope's marriage with Lord Rich seems to have taken place in April, 1581.

> Alas! I lie: rage hath this errour bred;
> Love is not dead;
> Love is not dead, but sleepeth
> In her unmatchèd mind,
> Where she his counsell keepeth,
> Till due desert she find.
> Therefore from so vile fancie
> To call such wit a franzie,
> Who Love can temper thus,
> Good Lord, deliver us!"

Love that was not dead but asleep awoke, and Sidney's raptures were again expressed in his verse:

> "O joy too high for my low stile to show! . . .
> For Stella hath, with words where faith doth shine,
> Of her high heart giv'n me the monarchie:
> I, I, O I, may say that she is mine.' [1]

This lasted some time and when love faded away, at least in Stella's fickle heart, "Astrophel" wrote the real dirge of his passion.

Sidney had nevertheless continued his active life all this while, sometimes at court and sometimes on the continent, recognized as a statesman by statesmen, as a poet by poets, as a perfect knight by all experts in knightly accomplishments. Spenser dedicated in 1579 his "Shepheardes Calender" to "the most noble and vertuous gentleman, most worthy of all titles, both of learning and chevalrie, M. Philip Sidney"[2]; and

---

[1] "Astrophel and Stella," *ut supra*, pp. 170 and 72 (sonnet 69).
[2] " Goe little booke! thy selfe present
    As childe whose father is unkent
    To him that is the President
    Of noblenesse and chevalree. . . ."
Dedication of the "Shepheardes Calender." Sidney seems to

William the Silent, Prince of Orange, once said to Fulke Greville that "Her Majesty had one of the ripest and greatest counsellors of estate in Sir Philip Sidney that at this day lived in Europe." The remaining years of his short life were well filled; he had been ambassador to the German Emperor in 1577; he had taken part at home, though unasked, in the negotiations concerning the Queen's marriage, and he lost favour for a while on account of the extraordinary freedom with which he had written to Elizabeth against the French match. He retired from court at that moment and went to live in the country; while staying with his sister at Wilton in the midst of congenial surroundings, he wrote most of his "Arcadia" (1580). He was a member of Parliament in 1581 and 1584, and married in 1583 the daughter of Sir Francis Walsingham. He all but accompanied Drake to America, where he had received from the Queen a large grant of lands; he became at last Governor of Flushing in the Netherlands. He died in that country at thirty-one years of age, in 1586, of a wound received at Zutphen; a premature death that gave the finishing touch to men's sympathy and love for him; all England wept for him.[1] Even now, it is difficult to

---

have had a right and not over-enthusiastic appreciation of Spenser's eclogues; in his "Apologie for Poetrie" he is content to say that "the Sheapheardes Kalender hath much poetrie in his eglogues: indeede worthy the reading if I be not deceived" (Arber's reprint, p. 62).

[1] The elegies written on this occasion are counted by the hundred. A splendid series of engravings were published by T. Laut to perpetuate the memory of Sidney's funeral, London, 1587

think unmoved of his well-filled career ending on the eve of the great triumphs of his country, to call to our memory this brave man who died with his face to the enemy without knowing that victory would be declared for his side, without having known Shakespeare, without having seen the defeat of the Armada.

As for his Stella she survived him only too long. A few years after Sidney's death she deserted her husband by whom she had had seven children, and became the mistress of Charles Blount, Lord Mountjoy, afterwards Earl of Devonshire, to whom she gave three sons and two daughters. Lord Rich, a man full of prudence it seems, waited for the death of the Earl of Essex, his wife's brother, to divorce her. She then married her lover in 1605. But till her death, which happened in 1608 she was mostly remembered as having been Sidney's friend, and books were dedicated to her because she had been Astrophel's " Stella." Thus Yong's translation of the " Diana " of Montemayor, a pastoral from which Sidney had taken many hints, is dedicated to her.[1] Thus again Florio asks her conjointly with Sidney's daughter[2] to patronize the second book of Montaigne's Essays, addressing Penelope, in the extraordinary style that belonged to him : " I meane you (truely richest Ladie Rich) in riches of fortune not deficient, but of body incomparably richer, of minde most rich : who yet, like Cornelia, were you out-vied, or by rich shewes envited to shew your richest jewelles,

---

[1] London, 1598, fol.
[2] Sidney left only one daughter who became Countess of Rutland. His wife remarried twice, first with the Earl of Essex, brother of Penelope, then with Lord Clanricarde.

would stay till your sweet images (your deere-sweete children) came from schoole." And then, addressing the ladies together, both the daughter and the mistress of the departed hero : " I know not this nor any I have seen, or can conceive, in this or other language, can in aught be compared to that perfect-imperfect Arcadia, which all our world yet weepes with you, that your all praise-exceeding father (his praise-succeeding countesse) your worthy friend (praise-worthiest lady) lived not to mend or end it."[1] Once Astrophel had sung of Stella, and now Lady Rich was praised by the pedant Rombus.

II.

Sidney's works well accord with his life ; in these few years he had time to take in with a clear and kindly glance all those beauties of ancient or modern times, of distant countries or of his own which set the hearts

---

[1] "Essayes," London, 1603, fol. Dedication of Book II. This "Epistle" is followed by two sonnets, one to each lady, again praising them for their connection with Sidney. The sonnet to Penelope begins thus :

" Madame, to write of you, and doe you right,
  What meane we, or what meanes to ayde meane might ?
  Since HE who admirably did endite,
  Entitleing you perfections heire, joies light,
  Loves life, lifes gemme, vertues court, Heav'ns delight,
  Natures chiefe worke, fair'st booke, his muses spright,
  Heav'n on earth, peerlesse Phœnix, Phœbe bright,
  Yet said he was to seeke, of you to write " (p. 191).

This last line alludes to Astrophel's first sonnet to Stella (quoted below, p. 233).

of his contemporaries beating, and he is therefore
perhaps, on account of his catholicity, the most worthy
of Shakespeare's immediate precursors. The brilliance
of the Spaniards enchants him, and he translates
fragments of Montemayor [1]; the Kenilworth fêtes
amuse him and he writes a masque, "The Lady of
May," [2] to be used at like festivities. A true Christian
he translates the Psalms of David; a tender and
passionate heart, he rhymes the sonnets of Astrophel to
Stella; enamoured of chivalry and great exploits, he
writes, with fluent pen, his "Arcadia," where he
imitates the style made fashionable in Europe by Montemayor in his "Diana"; a lover of *belles lettres*, he
defends the poet's art in an argument charming from
its youthfulness, vibrating with enthusiasm, which
holds in English literature the place filled in French by
Fenelon's "Lettre à l'Académie." [3] This work is very

---

[1] "What changes here," &c. "translated out of the 'Diana' of
Montemayor in Spanish. Where Sireno a shepheard pulling out a
little of his mistresse Diana's haire, wrapt about in greene silke,
who now had utterly forsaken him, to the haire hee thus bewayled
himselfe."—"The same Sireon . . . holding his mistresse glasse . . .
thus sung." "Certaine sonnets written by Sir Philip Sidney,
never before printed."

[2] This masque was written in 1578; and was performed before
the Queen when staying with the Earl of Leicester at Wanstead.
Sidney wrote also for festivities of the same kind a "Dialogue
betweene two shepheards, uttered in a pastorall shew at Wilton"
(the seat of his sister the Countess of Pembroke). Both works are
to be found in divers old editions of the "Arcadia" (*e.g.*, the
eighth, 1633, fol.), which in fact contain, very nearly, Sidney's
complete works.

[3] The "Apologie" written about 1581, which circulated in
MS. during Sidney's life-time, was published only after his death:

important with regard to the subject that now occupies us, not only because Sidney gives in it his opinion on works of fiction in general ; but because here we have at last a specimen of flexible, spirited, fluent prose, without excessive ornament of style, or learned *impedimenta*, a specimen of that prose which is exactly suited to novels and that no one—Roger Ascham perhaps excepted—had until then used in England.

Perhaps it will be found, he writes at the beginning of his work, with the elegant gracefulness of a man who knows how to do everything that he does well, that I carry my apology to excess ; but that is excusable : listen to what Pietro Pugliano, my master of horsemanship, at the Emperor's Court, said : ' Hee sayde souldiours were the noblest estate of mankinde, and horsemen, the noblest of souldiours. Hee sayde, they were the maisters of warre, and ornaments of peace : speedy goers and strong abiders, triumphers both in camp and courts." For a prince no accomplishment is comparable to that of being a good horseman ; " skill of government was but a Pedanteria in comparison : then would hee adde certaine prayses, by telling what a peerlesse beast a horse was. The onely serviceable courtier without flattery, the beast of most beutie, faithfulnes, courage, and such more, that if I had not beene a peece of a logician before I came to him, I think he would have perswaded mee to have wished my selfe a horse. But thus much at least with his no fewe words hee drave into me, that selfe-love is

---

" An Apologie for Poetrie, written by the right noble, vertuous and learned Sir Philip Sidney, Knight," London, 1595, reprinted by Arber, London, 1869.

better then any guilding to make that seeme gorgious, wherein our selves are parties. Wherein, if Pugliano his strong affection and weake arguments will not satisfie you, I wil give you a neerer example of my selfe, who (I knowe not by what mischance) in these my not old yeres and idelest times, having slipt into the title of a poet, am provoked to say somthing unto you in the defence of that my unelected vocation."

Set at ease by Pugliano's example, who seems to have had the same veneration for the horse as his countryman Vinci, Sidney enters on his defence and does not restrain himself from extolling poetry beyond any product of the human mind. Poetry is superior to history, to philosophy, to all forms of literature. Poets have, by the charm of their works, surpassed the beauties of nature and they have succeeded in making "the too much loved earth more lovely." He gives to poetry, in effect, an immense domain: everything that is poetic or even merely a work of the imagination is poetry for him : " there have beene many most excellent poets, that never versified, and now swarme many versifiers that neede never aunswere to the name of poets." For him, the romance of " Theagines and Cariclea" is a " poem " ; Xenophon's " Cyrus " is " an absolute heroicall poem." To the great joy of their author he would certainly have seen an epic in Chateaubriand's " Martyrs." "It is not riming and versing that maketh a poet, no more then a long gowne maketh an advocate : who though he pleaded in armor should be an advocate and no soldiour." Even historians have sometimes to do the work of poets, that is imagining, inventing, " although theyr lippes sounde of things doone and veritie be written in theyr foreheads."

In spite of his fondness for the ancients, whose unities and messenger he greatly approves, and of his contempt for the modern drama, such as it was understood in those pre-Shakespearean times, he remains, at bottom, entirely English; he adores the old memorials of his native land, and does not know his Virgil better than his Chaucer, or even the popular songs hummed by the wayfarer along the high roads. Irish ballads, English ballads of Robin Hood, Scottish ballads of Douglas, are familiar to him, and some of them make him start as at the sound of a trumpet: "Certainly, I must confesse my own barbarousnes, I never heard the olde song of Percy and Douglas, that I found not my heart mooved more then with a trumpet: and yet it is sung by some blind crouder, with no rougher voyce then rude stile; which being so evill apparelled in the dust and cobwebbes of that uncivill age, what would it worke, trymmed in the gorgeous eloquence of Pindar?" He would have loved, like Molière, the song of the "roi Henri," and like La Fontaine, the story of Peau d'Ane. But his closest sympathies were reserved for poetical tales, for the adventures of Roland and King Arthur, which are a soldier's reading, and even for the exploits of Amadis of Gaul. "I dare undertake 'Orlando furioso' or honest King Arthur will never displease a souldier. ... Truely, I have knowen men, that even with reading 'Amadis de Gaule,' which God knoweth wanteth much of a perfect poesie, have found their hearts mooved to the exercise of courtesie, liberalitie and especially courage." He imagines nothing more enchanting or more powerful than the charm of poetical prose stories, "any of which holdeth children from play, and old men from the chimney corner." Their attraction has something superior, divine ; for, he adds with a depth of emotion that appears quite modern, "so is it in men, most of which are childish in the best things, till they bee cradlid in their graves." [1]

He closes with a witty and delightful ending, a kindly wish for the hardened enemies of poetry: "Yet this much curse I must send you, in the behalfe of all Poets, that while you live, you live in love, and never get favour, for lacking skill of a sonnet : and when you die, your memory die from the earth, for want of an epitaph."

Neither did Sidney lack epitaphs ; all the poets wept for him ; nor was he wanting in those favours that a sonnet can win, for he wrote the most passionate that appeared in England before those of Shakespeare. Like the "Apologie" they move us by their youth and sincerity; they come from the heart :

"Loving in truth, and faine in verse my love to show,
  That She, dear She ! might take some pleasure of my paine :
    .   .   .   .
  I sought fit words to paint the blackest face of woe,
  Studying inventions fine, her wits to entertaine ;
  Oft turning others' leaves, to see if thence would flow
  Som fresh and fruitfull showers upon my sun-burn'd brain:
  But words came halting forth . . .

---

[1] Arber's reprint, pp. 46, 55, 41, and 40.

> Biting my trewand pen, beating myselfe for spite :
> 'Foole!' said my Muse to me, 'looke in thy heart, and
> write!'"[1]

Unfortunately, when Sidney took up his pen to write his "Arcadia,"[2] he no longer looked into his heart; he loosed the rein of his imagination, and, without concerning himself with a critical posterity for whom the book was not destined, he only wished, like Lyly, to write a romance for ladies, or rather for one lady, his sister, the Countess of Pembroke, famous as his sister, famous as a patron of letters,[3] famous also as the mother of William Herbert, the future friend of Shakespeare, the "W. H." for whom in all probability the sonnets of the great poet were written. Sidney sent the sheets to his sister as fast as he penned them, charging her to destroy them, a thing she did not do.

---

[1] "The Complete Poems of Sir Philip Sidney," ed. Grosart, London, 1877, 3 vol. 8vo; "Sir Philip Sidney's Astrophel and Stella . . . edited from the folio of 1598," by Alfred Pollard, London, 1888, 8vo.

[2] The "Arcadia" begun in 1580, appeared after Sidney's death : "The Countesse of Pembrokes Arcadia, written by Sir Philippe Sidnei," London, 1590, 4to. Several of the numerous poems inserted in the "Arcadia" are written in classical metres; for Sidney took part with several of his contemporaries in the futile effort made in England as in France to apply to modern languages the rules of ancient prosody. The pages referred to in the following notes are those of the edition of 1633, "now the eighth time published with some new additions."

[3] And compared as such to Octavia, sister of Augustus, by Meres in his "Paladis Tamia," 1598. She helped her brother in translating the Psalms of David and published various works, one of them being a translation of one of Garnier's neo-classical tragedies : "The tragedie of Antonie," written in 1590, printed in 1595,

The poet knight only saw in it an amusement for himself and for the Countess, and he gave free vent to his fondness for poetical prose : "For severer eyes it is not," says he to his sister, "being but a trifle and that triflingly handled. Your deare selfe can best witnesse the manner, being done in loose sheets of paper, most of it in your presence, the rest by sheetes, sent unto you as fast as they were done. In summe, a young head, not so well staied as I would it were (and shall bee when God will) having many fancies begotten in it, if it had not beene in some way delivered, would have growne a monster, and more sorry might I bee that they came in than that they gat out." His "Apologie" was perhaps from its style more useful to the development of the novel than the "Arcadia"; but the latter, in spite of its enormous defects of style and composition, was also of use, and it is not unimportant to note that its influence lasted until and even beyond the time of Richardson.

Sidney's romance is not, as might be believed, an enormous pseudo-Greek pastoral, with tunic-wearing shepherds in the foreground, piping their ditties to which contains, conformably to Sidney's taste, messengers, monologues and choruses. It begins thus in the regular classical style of that time :

"Since cruel Heav'ns against me obstinate,
Since all mishappes of the round engin doo
Conspire my harme : since men, since powers divine.
Aire, earth, and sea are all injurious :
And that my queene her selfe, in whom I liv'd
The idoll of my harte, doth me pursue,
It's meete I dye."

their flocks, to their nymphs, to Echo. Elizabethan Arcadias were knightly Arcadias. Sidney's heroes are all princes or the daughters of kings. Their adventures take place in Greece, undoubtedly, and among learned shepherds, but the great parts are left to the noblemen, and the distance between the two classes is well marked. However intelligent and well bred the shepherds may be, they are only there for decoration and ornament, to amuse the princes with their songs, and to pull them out of the water when they are drowning. There are Amadises and Palmerins in Sidney's work. Amadis has come to live among the shepherds, but he remains Amadis, as valiant and as ready as ever to draw his sword. To please his sister the better, Sidney mingles thus the two kinds of affectations in fashion, the affectation of pastoral and of chivalry, taking in this as his example the famous "Diana" of George de Montemayor, which was then the talk not only of Spain, but of all the reading public in Europe.[1] As for the shepherds, are we to pity them because their domain is invaded by foreign knights, by whom they are dispossessed of the high rank belonging to them, of all places, in Arcady? There is no need for pity; a time will come when they will repay their invaders, and the end of their piping has not come yet. Leaving their country, where their place has been taken by British noblemen, we shall see them some day invade the land of their conquerors, and, sitting in

[1] The "Diana" was turned into English by B. Yong, London, 1598, fol. Shakespeare derived from one of the stories in Montemayor's romance (the story of the shepherdess Felismena) a part of the plot of his "Two Gentlemen of Verona." See above p. 150.

their turn under the elms of Windsor Park, sing their songs at the call of Mr. Pope. They will look a little awry, no doubt, among the mists of an English landscape, with their loose tunics, bare limbs, and "in-folio" wigs; but they will prove none the less fine speakers, and they will for a time concentrate upon themselves the attention of the capital. Better still will be their treatment at the hands of a Frenchman, not a poet, but a painter, Gaspard Poussin, who will gain more permanent attention and sympathy for them than most poets when he will inscribe in his canvas, on the representation of a ruined tomb, his famous " Et in Arcadia ego."[1]

Sidney's heroes, in the meantime, Prince Musidorus and Prince Pyrocles, the latter disguised as a woman under the name of the amazon Zelmane, are in love with the Princesses Pamela and Philoclea, daughters of the King of Arcady. A great many crosses are in the way of the lovers' happiness. They have to fight helots, lions, bears, enemies from Corinth. They lose each other, find each other again, and relate their adventures. The masculine amazon especially does wonders, for she has to fight not only with the sword, but in argument. She is so pretty in woman's costume that the old king Basilius, until then wise and virtuous, falls distractedly in love with her, as imprudent as Fior-di-Spina in Ariosto; while the queen, whom the disguise does not deceive, feels an intense passion spring up in her heart for the false amazon and a terrible jealousy of her own daughter, Philoclea.

Disguises are numerous in this romance; they are

[1] Now in the Louvre.

also frequent in Shakespeare's plays and in most of the novels of the time. Parthenia gives herself out to her admirer, Argalus, as the Queen of Corinth, whom she resembles, and announces her own death. As pretended queen she offers her hand to Argalus, to prove him; but he refuses with horror; she then discovers herself to this paragon of lovers, and gives him his Parthenia alive and more loving than ever.

When we read now of such disguises, of princes Pyrocles dressed as women, of Rosalinds dressed as pages, we are tempted to smile at the vain fancies of the novelists of the Shakespearean era.[1] But it must not be forgotten that, after all, there was not so much invention in these fancies, and that living examples were not rare from which writers might copy. Disguises were abundantly used in fêtes and ceremonies, but they were also utilized in actual life. The manners of the time in this particular are well illustrated by the earnest entreaties of a certain ambassador to Her Majesty Queen Elizabeth, advising her to leave her palace secretly and travel over the country as his page. The Queen was in no way shocked, but rather pleased;

[1] The taste for these fancies had been handed down from the Middle Ages; ladies following as pages their own lovers, unknown to them, abound in the French mediæval literature; one, *e.g.*, is to be found in the "Très chevaleureux Comte d' Artois," a very old tale, of which we have only a version of the fifteenth century, but which existed long before, and supplied Boccaccio with the groundwork of his story of Giletta of Narbonne. From Boccaccio, this tale was transferred by Paynter to his "Palace of Pleasure," and from this work, by Shakespeare, to the stage, under the name of "All's well." Sidney's model Montemayor gives the same part to play, as we have seen, to his pretended shepherdess Felismena, who follows as his page her lover Don Felix.

she did not order the ambassador to be turned out of her palace, but heard him expound his plan, wishing she might have followed it. This happened in one of those curious conversations of which Melville, the ambassador of Mary Queen of Scots, has left us an account. Elizabeth was very desirous of seeing her " dear sister " of Scotland and of judging with her own eyes what truth there was in the reports concerning her beauty. " Then again," says Melville, " she wished that she might see the queen at some convenient place of meeting. I offered to convey her secretly to Scotland by post, clothed like a page, that under this disguise she might see the queen, as James the fifth had gone in disguise to France with his own Ambassadour, to see the Duke of Vendom's sister,[1] who should have been his wife. Telling her that her chamber might be kept in her absence, as though she were sick ; that none needed to be privy thereto except my Lady Strafford and one of the grooms of her chamber.

"She appeared to like that kind of language, only answered it with a sigh, saying : Alas, if I might do it thus."[2]

Surely ladies who " appeared to like that kind of language," and men who were wont to use it, would be certain to accept with much pleasure representations in plays and novels of he-Rosalinds and she-Pyrocles.

In the midst of battles, masques and eclogues, interludes are consecrated to fêtes of chivalry. As

[1] See "Les projets de mariage de Jacques V.," by Edmond Bapst, Secrétaire d'Ambassade, Paris, 1889, 8vo, ch. xxiv. p. 289.
[2] "Memoires of Sir James Melvil," London, 1683, fol., p. 51.

much as in Italy, France or England, the knights of Arcady challenge each other, and in brilliant tournaments break lances in honour of their mistresses. Sidney himself was very skilful at these sports; he proved it about this time in the festivities of May, 1581, by attacking with his companions, the Castle of perfect Beauty, which was reputed to contain the grace and attractions of the Queen, a treasure as may well be believed, most allegorical. His sonnets more than once refer to his prowess in the lists :

> "Having this day, my horse, my hand, my lance
> Guided so well that I obtain'd the prize,
> Both by the judgment of the English eyes,
> And of some sent from that sweet enemic France.
>
> Horsemen my skill in horsemanship advance;
> Towne-folks my strength; a daintier judge applies
> His praise to sleight, which from good use doth rise;
> Some luckie wits impute it but a chance . . .
> Stella lookt on. . . ."[1]

In his letters to his brother Robert, he is most particular as to the every-day exercise by which the young man should improve his fencing. He could not help giving his tastes to his Arcadian knights. They would, otherwise, have been considered by his lady-readers, uninteresting barbarians. He therefore allowed them good spurs and a ready lance; this meant civilization. On a certain day every knight appears in the vale of Arcady, with drawn sword, and carrying a portrait of his fair lady; the painting is to become the prey of the conqueror. The order of

[1] Sonnet 41. See also Sonnet 53.

merit of the various beauties is thus determined by blows of the lance. Pyrocles, who, dressed as a woman, cannot take part in the fighting, has the mortification of seeing the champion of Philoclea bite the dust and give up her portrait. He goes immediately and secretly puts on some wretched armour, lowers his visor, and like a brave hero of romance, runs into the lists, throws every one to the ground, regains the portrait, and all the others as well. He is proclaimed conqueror of the tourney, and the first of knights, while at the same time, Philoclea becomes again the most beautiful of women.

In this Arcadia of chivalry it must not be thought that only cottages and huts are to be found; sometimes the heroes sleep soundly in the open air, but seldom. In this country there are palaces like those of the rich English lords. The dwelling of the noble Kalander is of this number. The park is magnificent, and quite in the style of the Elizabethans, that style which is so minutely described in Bacon's "Essay on gardens." It did not differ much from the park at Kenilworth, a place well known to Sidney : " whearin, hard all along the castell wall iz reared a pleazaunt terres of a ten foot hy and a twelve brode, even under foot, and fresh of fyne grass : as iz allso the side thearof toward the gardein, in whiche by sundry equall distauncez, with obelisks, sphearz and white bearz [bears], all of stone, upon theyr curiouz basez, by goodly shew wear set ; too theez, too fine arbers redolent by sweete trees and floourz, at ech end one, the garden plot under that, with fayr alleyz green by grass." There were fountains with marble Tritons, with Neptune on his throne, and "Thetis on her chariot drawn by her Dollphins,"[1] with many other gods and goddesses.

Kalander's gardens in Arcady were of the same sort; their adornments were not very sober, and many eccentricities are presented as beauties; thus the fashion of the day would have it; Versailles in comparison is simplicity itself. Kalander and his guest go round the place, and "as soone as the descending of the staires had delivered them downe, they came into a place cunningly set with trees of the most taste-pleasing fruits: but scarcely they had taken that into consideration, but that they were suddenly stept into a delicate greene; of each side of the greene a thicket, and behind the thickets againe new beds of flowers, which being under the trees, the trees were to them a pavilion, and they to the trees a mosaicall floore. . . .

A SHEPHERD OF ARCADY, FROM THE TITLE-PAGE OF SIDNEY'S "ARCADIA."

"In the middest of all the place was a faire pond, whose shaking cristall was a perfect mirrour to all the other beauties, so that it bare shew of two gardens, one in deed, the other in shadowes. And in one of

[1] "Captain Cox his ballads . . . or Robert Laneham's Letter, 1575," ed. Furnivall, London, 1871, 8vo, p. 49.

the thickets was a fine fountaine made thus : a naked Venus of white marble, wherin the graver had used such cunning that the natural blue veins of the marble were framed in fit places to set forth the beautifull veines of her body. At her breast she had her babe Æneas, who seemed, having begun to sucke, to leave that, to look upon her faire eyes, which smiled at the babe's folly, meane while the breast running."[1] The effect produced must undoubtedly have been very pleasant, but scarcely more " natural " than the embellishments recommended by Bacon, who declares that hedges and arbours ought to be enlivened by the songs of birds ; and that to make such enlivening sure and permanent, the birds should be secured in cages. A good example of a garden in Sidney's time with beds of flowers,

A PRINCESS OF ARCADY, FROM THE TITLE-PAGE OF SIDNEY'S "ARCADIA."

arbours, pavilions, and covered galleries is to be seen in his own portrait by Isaac Oliver, of which we give a reproduction. It must be noticed that only the lower part of the long gallery at the back is built ;

[1] Book i. p. 8 (edition of 1633).

the vault-shaped upper portion is painted green, being supposed to be made of actual leaves and foliage. Except for such books as Sidney's it could not be said of those gardens that "they too were once in Arcady."

Costumes and furniture are of the same style, and accord with such gardens much more than with shepherd life. They are pure Renaissance, half Italian and half English. Musidorus disguised as a shepherd, dresses his hair in such a way as to look much more like one of the Renaissance Roman Emperors at Hampton Court than like a keeper of sheep : we see him while receiving a lesson on the use of the "sheep-hooke," wearing "a garland of laurell mixt with cypres leaves on his head."[1] The glowing descriptions of the private apartments of the heroes suit modern palaces better than Greek cottages ; while representations of ladies recumbent on their couches are obvious reminiscences of Tintoretto or Titian, whose newly painted works Sidney had admired in Italy. Here is a description of the beautiful Philoclea, resting in her bedroom ; it shows unmistakable signs of Sidney's acquaintance with the Italian painters : "She at that time lay, as the heate of that country did well suffer, upon the top of her bed, having her beauties eclipsed with nothing, but with her faire smocke, wrought all in flames of ash-colour silk and gold ; lying so upon her right side, that the left thigh down to the foot, yielded hir delightfull proportion to the full view, which was scene by the helpe of a rich lampe, which thorow the curtaines a little drawne cast forth a light upon her, as the moone doth when it shines into a thinne wood."[2]

[1] Book ii. p. 99.   [2] Book iii. p. 382.

Sidney, according to his friend Fulke Greville, Lord Brooke, had the highest moral and political purposes, in writing his "Arcadia" : " In all these creatures of his making, his interest and scope was, to turn the barren philosophy precepts into pregnant images of life ; and in them, first on the monarchs part, lively to represent the growth, state and declination of princes, changes of government and lawes... Then again in the subjects case, the state of favour, disfavour, prosperitie, adversity ... and all other moodes of private fortunes or misfortunes, in which traverses, I know, his purpose was to limn out such exact pictures of every posture in the minde, that any man might see how to set a good countenance upon all the discountenances of adversitie." [1] When Greville wrote thus, Sidney was dead, and in his retrospect of his friend's life he was with perfect good faith discovering high, not to say holy motives, for all his actions. Sidney's own explanation suits his work better ; he was delivering his " young head " of " many, many fancies," and their main object was not politics, but love. He described it as it was known and practised in his time. Most of the heroes in the "Arcadia," talk like Surrey, Wyatt, Watson, and all the "amourists" of the century, like Sidney himself when he addressed another than Stella. The modesty of their characters is equal to their tenderness ; valiant as lions before the enemy, they tremble like the leaf before their mistresses ; they feed on smiles and tender glances ; when they have to suffer a scarcity of this heavenly food they can only

[1] "Life of Sidney," London, 1652, 12mo, p. 18.

die: "Hee dieth: it is most true, hee dieth; and he in whom you live dieth. Whereof if though hee plaine, hee doth not complaine: for it is a harme but no wrong which hee hath received. He dies, because in wofull language all his senses tell him, that such is your pleasure." Fair Pamela feels deeply moved when reading this, and confesses her harshness; she denied him a look: "Two times I must confess," says she to her sister, not without a pretty touch of humour of a very modern sort, "I was about to take curtesie into mine eyes, but both times the former resolution stopt the entrie of it: so, that hee departed without obtaining any further kindenesse. But he was no sooner out of the doore, but that I looked to the doore kindly!" The poor lover who did not see this change in his lady's countenance went away fainting, "as if he had beene but the coffin that carried himselfe to his sepulchre!"[1]

Happiness produces the same effect on these heroes. Pyrocles-Zelmane when present in his false quality of woman at the bath of his mistress in the Ladon is on the point of swooning with admiration.[2] His friend, Prince Musidorus, in the ecstasies of his passion, falls "downe prostrate," uttering this prayer to the awful god who reigns paramount in Arcady: "O thou, celestiall or infernall spirit of Love, or what other heavenly or hellish title thou list to have (for effects of both I find in my selfe), have compassion of me, and let

---

[1] Book ii. p. 117.
[2] "Zelmane would have put to her helping hand, but she was taken with such a quivering, that she thought it was more wisdome to lean her selfe to a tree and look on" (book ii. p. 138).

thy glory be as great in pardoning of them that be submitted to thee as in conquering them that were rebellious." [1]

But Sidney painted also amours of another sort, and one of the great attractions of his book is the variety in the descriptions of this passion. Never had the like been seen before in any English novel, and as for France, it must be remembered, that d'Urfé's "Astrée," which has kept its place in literature for the very same quality, for its inconstant Hylas and its faithful Celadon, for its Astrée and its Madonte, was yet to be written. Sidney has, among several others, created one character which, forgotten as it is now, would be enough to give a permanent interest to this too much neglected romance; it is the Queen Gynecia, who is consumed by a guilty love, and who is the worthy contemporary of the strongly passionate heroes of Marlowe's plays. With her, and for the first time, the dramatic power of English genius leaves the stage and comes to light in the novel; it was destined to pass into it entirely.

Gynecia does not allow herself to be blinded by any subterfuge; love has taken possession of her; the rules of the world, the laws of blood, the precepts of virtue that she has observed all her life, are lost sight of; she is conscious of nothing but that she loves, and is ready, like Phædra of old, to trample everything under foot, to forsake everything, the domestic hearth, child, husband: and it is very interesting to see, about the time of Shakespeare, this purely dramatic character develop itself in a novel.

[1] Book i. p. 65.

"O vertue," she cries, in her torment, "where doest thou hide thy selfe? What hideous thing is this which doth eclipse thee? or is it true that thou wert never but a vaine name, and no essentiall thing; which hast thus left thy professed servant, when she had most neede of thy lovely presence? O imperfect proportion of reason, which can too much foresee, and too little prevent: Alas, alas, said she, if there were but one hope for all my paines, or but one excuse for all my faultinesse! But wretch that I am, my torment is beyond all succour, and my evill deserving doth exceed my evill fortune. For nothing else did my husband take this strange resolution to live so solitarily: for nothing else have the winds delivered this strange guest to my countrey: for nothing else have the destinies reserved my life to this time, but that onely I, most wretched I, should become a plague to my selfe and a shame to woman-kind. Yet if my desire, how unjust soever it be, might take effect, though a thousand deaths followed it, and every death were followed with a thousand shames, yet should not my sepulchre receive me without some contentment. But, alas, so sure I am, that Zelmane is such as can answer my love; yet as sure I am, that this disguising must needs come for some foretaken conceit: and then, wretched Gynecia, where canst thou find any small ground plot for hope to dwell upon? No, no, it is Philoclea his heart is set upon, it is my daughter I have borne to supplant me: but if it be so, the life I have given thee, ungratefull Philoclea, I will sooner with these hands bereave thee of, than my birth shall glory she hath bereaved me of my desires."[1]

We see with how little reason the "Arcadia" is sometimes placed in the category of bedizened pastorals, where the reader is reduced to regret the absence of a "little wolf," and whether Gynecia, in spite of the oblivion which has gathered over her, does not deserve a place by the side of the passionate heroines of Marlowe and Webster rather than in a gallery of Lancret-like characters.

Sidney, thus possesses the merit, unique at that time with prose writers, of varying his subjects by marking its *nuances* and by describing in his romance different kinds of love. Side by side with Gynecia's passion, he has set himself to paint the love of an old man in Basilius, of a young man in Pyrocles, of a young girl in Pamela. This last study led him to portray a scene which was to be represented again by one of the great novelists of the eighteenth century. Richardson borrowed from Sidney, with the name of Pamela, the idea of the adventure that shows her a prisoner of her enemies, imploring heaven that her virtue may be preserved. The wicked Cecropia who keeps Sidney's Pamela shut up, laughs heartily at her invocations : "To thinke," she says, "that those powers, if there be any such, above, are moved either by the eloquence of our prayers, or in a chafe at the folly of our actions, carries as much reason, as if flies should thinke that men take great care which of them hums sweetest, and

[1] Book ii. p. 95. The daughter's speeches though she believes Zelmane to be a woman and cannot understand her own feelings are scarcely less intemperate (book ii. p. 112).

which of them flies nimblest." Pamela, "whose cheeks were dyed in the beautifullest graine of vertuous anger," replies by speeches which yield in nothing as regards nobility and dignity, and length also, to those of her future sister, and which are followed as in Richardson, by an unexpected deliverance. These speeches are famous for yet another reason ; they are said to have been recited in one of the most terrible crises of the history of England and were not this time followed by a deliverance. Charles I., it is reported, had copied out, and recited a short time before his death, the eloquent prayers to God, of the young heroine of Sidney's novel. It seems that Pamela's prayer figured among the papers that he gave with his own hand, at the last moment, to the prelate who was attending him: and the Puritans, Milton especially, uttered loud cries, and saw in this reminiscence of the artist-prince, an insult to the divine majesty. "This King," writes the poet, "hath as it were unhallowed and unchristened the very duty of prayer itself, by borrowing to a Christian use prayers offered to a heathen god. Who would have imagined so little fear in him of the true all-seeing deity, so little reverence of the Holy Ghost, whose office is to dictate and present our Christian prayers, so little care of truth in his last words, or honour to himself or to his friends, or sense of his afflictions or of that sad hour which was upon him, as immediately before his death to pop into the hand of that grave bishop who attended him, for a special relique of his saintly exercises, a prayer stolen word for word from the mouth of a heathen woman, praying to a heathen god, and that in no serious book, but in the vain amatorious poem of Sir Philip Sidney's Arcadia."[1] Here is this prayer which is a very grave and eloquent one, and in no way justifies the bitter reproaches addressed to Charles by his enemies:

"Kneeling down, even where she stood, she thus said: O All-seeing Light, and eternall Life of all things, to whom nothing is either so great, that it may resist, or so small that it is contemned: looke upon my misery with thine eye of mercy, and let thine infinite power vouchsafe to limit out some proportion of deliverance unto mee, as to thee shall seeme most convenient. Let not injurie, O Lord, triumph over mee, and let my faults by thy hand bee corrected, and make not mine unjust enemy the minister of thy Justice. But yet, my God, if, in thy wisedome, this be the aptest chastisement for my unexcusable folly; if this low bondage be fittest for my over-high desires; if the pride of my not enough humble heart, be thus to be broken, O Lord, I yeeld unto thy will, and joyfully embrace what sorrow thou wilt have me suffer. Onely thus much let me crave of thee... let calamity be the exercise, but not the overthrow of my vertue: let their power prevaile, but not prevaile to destruction: let my greatnesse be their prey: let my paine be the sweetnesse of their revenge: let them, if so it seem good unto thee, vexe me with more and more punishment. But, O Lord, let never their wickednesse have such a hand, but that I may carry a pure minde in a pure

[1] And in order that no doubt may exist, Milton refers his reader to the page in Sidney and in Dr. Juxon's book of, "'Εικονοκλαστης," "Prose Works," London, 1806, 6 vols., 8vo, vol. i. p. 407.

body. And pausing a while : And, O most gracious Lord, said shee, what ever become of me, preserve the vertuous Musidorus." [1]

Thus incidents, showing much diversity, but little order, follow each other in great variety. There are touching episodes, ludicrous and, to our modern ideas, even shocking episodes, brilliant adventures, fine pastoral scenes, and much pleasant description ; Sidney had been perfectly frank and true when he had spoken of "his young head" and his "many many fancies." He allows his imagination to wander ; fancies are swarming in his mind, and he is no more capable of restraining or putting them into logical order than a man can restrain or introduce reason into a dream. Arcadia is sometimes in England and sometimes in Greece; Basilius' cottage sometimes becomes Hampton Court ; there are temples and churches also ; heroes are Christians, but they believe in Mars ; they act according to the Gospel and also according to the oracles ; they are before everything men of the Renaissance. Following his vein, Sidney, after innumerable adventures, pastoral and warlike scenes, disappearances, unexpected meetings, scenes of deep love, of criminal, sweet or foolish love, comes at last to a sort of conclusion. King Basilius drinks a soporific draught ; he is given up

[1] "Arcadia," book iii. p. 248. In the "Εἰκὼν βασιλική, the portraiture of his sacred majesty in his solitude and sufferings," 1648, 8vo, towards the end of the book, where are to be found "praiers used by his majestie in the time of his sufferings, delivered to Dr. Juxon, bishop of London, immediately before his death," the end of the prayer of course is altered : ". . . so that at the last, I may com to thy eternal kingdom through the merits of thy son our alone Saviour Jesus Christ. Amen."

as dead. Queen Gynecia is accused of being the author of the deed ; Zelmane, who has been found out to be a man is adjudged an accomplice ; both are about to be executed. At that point, fortunately, the dead king springs to his feet ; there are explanations, embracings, and a general pardon. Good Basilius, who alone seems to have understood nothing of all that happened, asks pardon of his wife and of the world at large for his silly love for Pyrocles-Zelmane, and proclaims, unasked, Queen Gynecia the most virtuous woman that ever was. The Queen blushes deeply and says nothing, but finding that the ties of her passion are now broken, she inwardly pledges herself to live in order to justify her husband's praise. She becomes the " example and glory of Greece : so uncertain are mortall judgements, the same person most infamous and most famous, and neither justly."

This might be taken as a sufficient conclusion in so loose a tale ; but in that case it would mean giving up many heroes whose fates are yet in suspense. In fact, an "Arcadia" of this sort might be continued till doomsday. Unless the hand of the writer grew tired, there is no reason why it should ever end. This is, in fact, the one and only reason Sidney puts forth as an excuse for taking his leave ; he makes no pretence of having finished, just the reverse ; for when he has married his princes he concludes thus : " But . . . the strange stories of Artaxia and Plexirtus, Erona and Plangus, Hellen and Amphialus, with the wonderfull chances that befell them ; the shepheardish loves of Menalcas with Kalodulus daughter ; the poore hopes of the poor Philisides," that is, Sidney himself, " in the pursuit of his affections; the strange continuance of Klaius and Strephons desire; lastly the sonne of Pyrocles named Pyrophilus, and Melidora the faire daughter of Pamela by Musidorus, who even at their birth entred into admirable fortunes, may awake some other spirit to exercise his pen in that wherwith mine is already dulled." From generation to generation the tale might as we see, have been continued for ages: so numerous were the wonderful adventures still to be told.

The style of the book is scarcely less fanciful than the stories it tells. It is only now and again that the charming prose of the "Apologie for Poetrie" is to be found in the "Arcadia." Sidney wished to remain faithful to his theories, and he believed it possible to write a poem in prose.[1] Here and there some speeches, passionate like those of Gynecia, or noble like Pamela's prayer, some brilliant repartee, a few observations of exquisite charm are lasting beauties, always in their place in all kinds of writing. Thus we meet the witty Sidney of the "Apologie" in the description of a spaniel, coming out of a river, who shakes off the water from his coat "as great men doe their friends;" Sidney, the poet and lover, appears in the description of Philoclea entering the water "with a prettie kind of shrugging . . . like the twinkling of the fairest among the fixed stars;" or in this expression in reference to the fair hair of one of his heroines: " her haire—alas too

---

[1] His contemporaries agreed in his belief: "Sir Philip Sidney writ his immortal poem 'The Countesse of Pembrokes Arcadia' in prose; and yet our rarest poet" (F. Meres "Paladis Tamia," 1598).

poore a word, why should I not rather call them her beams!"[1]

But, by the side of these graceful flowers, how many others are faded! What concessions to contemporary taste for tinsel and excessive ornament! Sidney forgets the rules of enduring beauty, and with the excuse that he will never be printed, he only seeks to please his one reader. To charm the Countess, his sister, like most women of his time, it was necessary to put his phrases in full dress, to place ruffs on his periods, and to make them walk according to the rules followed in courtly pageants. When, in spite of Sidney's earnest desire, his book was published after his death, people were enraptured with his ingeniously dressed out phrases. Lyly might shake with envy without having however the right to complain, for Sidney did not imitate him. Sidney never liked euphuism, quite the contrary, he formally condemns it in his "Apologie": "Now for similitudes in certain printed discourses I think all herberists, all stories of beasts, fowles and fishes, are rifled up, that they may come in multitudes to wait upon any of our conceits, which certainely is as absurd a surfet to the eares as is possible." But his own style is scarcely less artificial than that of Lyly, and consequently, its rules are quite as easy to discover.

They consist firstly in the antithetical and cadenced repetition of the same words in the sentences written merely for effect; secondly, in persistently ascribing life and feeling to inanimate objects. Sidney, it is true, as Lyly with his euphuism, happily only employs this style on particular occasions, when he intends to be especially

[1] Pp. 138 and 51.

attractive and brilliant. A few specimens will afford means of judging, and will show how difficult it was in Shakespeare's time, even for the best educated and most sensible men, for the sincerest admirers of the ancients, to keep within the bounds of good taste and reason. They might appeal to the Castalian virgins in their invocations, but William Rogers' Elizabeth was the Muse that rose before their eyes.

Here is an example of the first sort of embellishment: "Our Basilius being so publickly happy, as to be a prince, and so happy in that happiness, as to be a beloved prince; and so in his private estate blessed, as to have so excellent a wife, and so over-excellent children, hath of late taken a course which yet makes him more spoken of than all these blessings." In another passage Sidney wishes to describe the perfections of a woman; and "that which made her fairness much the fairer, was, that it was but a fair ambassador of a most fair mind." Musidorus considers it "a greater greatness to give a kingdome than get a kingdome."[1] Phalantus challenges his adversary to fight "either for the love of honour or honour of his love." In many of these sentences the same words are repeated like the rhymes of a song, taken up from strophe to strophe, and the sentence twists and turns, drawing and involving the readers in its spiral curves, so that he arrives at the

---

[1] On this and other occasions Sidney combines alliteration with the repetition of words. Here is another example: "Is it to be imagined that Gynecia, a woman, though wicked, yet witty, would have attempted and atchieved an enterprise no lesse hazzardous than horrible without having some counsellor in the beginning and some comforter in the performing?" (book v. p. 466).

end all bruised, and falls half stunned on the full stop.[1]

The other kind of elegance that Sidney affects is to be found in very many authors, and it is, so to say, of all time ; poets especially indulge in it without measure ; but Sidney surpasses them all in the frequent use he makes of it ; this peculiar language is more apparent and has still stranger effect in a prose writer than in a poet. In his Arcady, the valleys are consoled for their lowness by the silver streams which wind in the midst of them ; the ripples of the Ladon struggle with one another to reach the place where Philoclea is bathing, but those which surround her refuse to give up their fortunate position. A shepherdess embarks : "Did you not marke how the windes whistled, and the seas danced for joy ; how the sales did swell with pride, and all because they had Urania ? " Here is a description of a river : ". . . The banks of either side seeming armes of the loving earth, that faine would embrace it ; and the river a wanton nymph which hill would slip from it. . . There was . . . a goodly cypres, who bowing her faire head over the water, it seemed she looked into it and dressed her green locks by that running river." One of the heroines of the romance appears, and immediately the flowers and the fruits experience a surprising commotion ; the roses blush and the lilies grow pale for envy ;

---

[1] Pp. 10, 17, 129, 267, &c. The same curious repetition of words is sometimes to be noticed in Sidney's poetry :

"Nor faile my faith in my fayling fate ;
Nor change in change, though change change my state."

("The Smokes of melancholie.")

the apples perceiving her breast fall down from the trees out of vexation, unexpected vanity on the part of this modest fruit.[1]

Similar conceits were at that time the fashion not only in England, but also in Italy, in Spain, and in France. There might still be found in France, even in the seventeenth century, authors who described in these terms the appearance of flowers in spring : " There perhaps at the end of the combat, a pink all bleeding falls from fatigue ; there a rosebud, elated at the ill-success of her antagonist, blooms with joy ; there the lily, that colossus among the flowers, that giant of curdled cream, vain of seeing her image triumph at the Louvre, raises herself above her companions, and looks at them with contemptuous arrogance." The same author, who is Cyrano de Bergerac, calls ice " an hardened light, a petrified day, a solid nothing." [2] But contrary to what was the case in England, this style was in France, even before Boileau and in the preceding century, the style of bad authors. In England it is frequently adopted by the most eminent writers, since on many occasions it is even that of Shakespeare himself. Besides, the combinations of sound obtained by means of the repetition of words, added to the turgidness

---

[1] Pp. 2, 137, 51.

[2] " Là, possible au sortir du combat, un oeillet tout sanglant tombe de lassitude ; là un bouton de rose, enflé du mauvais succès de son antagoniste, s'épanouit de joie ; là le lys, ce colosse entre les fleurs, ce géant de lait caillé, glorieux de voir ses images triompher au Louvre, s'élève sur ses compagnes et les regarde de haut en bas." Ice is for Cyrano : " une lumière endurcie, un jour pétrifié, un solide néant " (" Lettre pour le printemps"; " Lettre à M. le Bret").

of the images, give to Sidney's language in the passages written for effect, a degree of pretension and bad taste that Cyrano himself, in spite of his natural disposition, could never have equalled. When both kinds of Sidney's favourite embellishments are combined in the same sentence, it becomes impossible to keep serious, and it is difficult to recognize the author of the "Apologie." Sidney thus describes wreckage floating on the water after a sea-fight: "Amidst the precious things were a number of dead bodies, which likewise did not onely testifie both elements violence, but that the chiefe violence was growne of humane inhumanity: for their bodies were full of grisly wounds, and their blood had, as it were, filled the wrinkles of the sea's visage; which it seemed the see would not wash away, that it might witnesse it is not always his fault, when we do condemne his cruelty."[1] There is indeed in French literature a dagger celebrated for having *rougi le traître!* but what is it in comparison, and ought it not in its turn to grow pale with envy at the thought of this sea that will not wash itself?

Thus men wrote in the time of Shakespeare, guilty himself of having made many a dagger blush and weep in his bloody dramas: "See how my sword weeps for the poor king's death!" says Gloucester in "Henry VI." When Brutus stabs Cæsar the blood followed the dagger

> "As rushing out of doors, to be resolv'd
> If Brutus so unkindly knocked or no."

Such was the irresistible power of fashion. Sidney who

[1] Book i. p. 4.

in his "Apologie" had laughed at these extravagances in the poets and dramatists, could not himself avoid them when he wrote his romance. When they concern themselves with criticism, nearly all, Shakespeare, Sidney, and their contemporaries, are to be admired for their moderation, wisdom, and good sense; but as soon as they take up the pen to write their imaginative works, intoxication overcomes their brain, a divine intoxication that sometimes transports them to heaven, an earthly intoxication that sometimes leads them into bogs and gutters.

III.

These surprising embellishments were in no way harmful, quite the contrary, to the success of the "Arcadia." From the first it was extremely popular and widely read; Sidney, who has kept his high repute as a knight and a poet to our day, was still more famous at first, and indeed for a long time, as a novelist. He was before all the author of the "Arcadia."[1] His influence as such was very great, if not always very beneficial; for his examples, as often happens, were more readily followed than his precepts. Until the practical Defoe worked his great reform in style, the language of the novel was encumbered with images and unexpected metaphors, or distorted by a pompous verbosity; romance writers mostly looked at life and realities

[1] Here is an example among many others. Sidney's portrait, now belonging to Earl Darnley, bears the following inscription painted on its canvas: "Sr Phillip Sidney, who writ the Arcadia" ('Tudor Exhibition, 1890).

through painted glass. For this, Sidney is in some degree responsible.

His book was, so to speak, a standard one; everybody had to read it; elegant ladies now began to talk "Arcadianism" as they had been before talking "Euphuism." Dekker, in 1609, advises gallants to go to the play to furnish their memories with fine sayings, in order to be able to discourse with such refined young persons: "To conclude, hoarde up the finest play-scraps you can get, upon which your leane wit may most savourly feede for want of other stuffe, when the *Arcadian* and *Euphuized* gentlewomen have their tongues sharpened to set upon you."[1] When he has to represent "a court-lady, whose weightiest praise is a light wit, admired by herself, and one more," her lover,. Ben Jonson, in his "Every man out of his humour," makes her talk "Arcadianism." Her lover, who is quite the man to appreciate these elegancies of speech, being "a neat, spruce, affecting courtier, one that wears clothes well and in fashion, practiseth by his glass how to salute . . . can post himself into credit with his merchant, only with the gingle of his spur and the jerk of his wand," thus describes the Arcadian music which falls from the lips of the lady Saviolina : "She has the most harmonious and musical strain of wit that ever tempted a true ear . . . oh ! it flows from her like nectar, and she doth give it that sweet quick grace and exornation in the composure, that by this good air, as I am an honest man, would I might never stir, sir, but —she does observe as pure a phrase and use as choice

[1] "The Guls Horne-booke," "Works," ed. Grosart, vol. ii. p. 254.

figures in her ordinary conference as any be in the
'Arcadia.'"¹

The demand for Sidney's book continued long
unabated. It was often reprinted during the seventeenth century,² and found imitators, abbreviators
and continuators. Among its early admirers it had
that indefatigable reader of novels, William Shakespeare, who took from it several hints, especially
from the story of the " Paphlagonian unkind king,"
which he made use of in his " King Lear."³ Books
were published under cover of Sidney's name, as
"Sir Philip Sydney's Ourania"; ⁴ others were given
away bearing as an epigraph an adaptation of two well-
known verses:

"Nec divinam *Sydneida* tenta
Sed longe sequere et vestigia semper adora," ⁵

no insignificant compliment, considering the word

---

¹ Act ii. sc. 1, performed 1599, printed 1600. See also in
" Bartholomew fair," performed in 1614, act iv. sc. 2, how
Quarlous chooses the word "Argalus" to try his luck in a love
affair.

² The British Museum, which does not possess a complete
collection, has editions of 1590, 1598, 1599, 1605, 1613, 1621,
1623, 1627, 1629, 1633, 1638, 1655, 1662, 1674.

³ From book ii. of the "Arcadia." It resembles the episode of
Gloucester and his sons, and shows the old King of Paphlagonia
dispossessed, become blind and led by his son Leonatus. See
"Shakespeare's Library," ed. Collier and Hazlitt, London, 1875,
6 vol. 8vo., "King Lear."

⁴ A philosophical and scientific poem by N. Baxter, dedicated
to the Countess of Pembroke, Lady Mary Wroth, &c., and published in 1606, 4to.

⁵ "Theophania or severall modern histories, represented by way
of Romance . . . by an English person of quality," London,
1655, 4to.

which had to make room for "Sydneida." Works without number were dedicated to the Countess of Pembroke, not only because she was what she was, and a poetess of some renown, but because she was the Mary Sidney of Arcadian fame.

As Sidney had stated that he did not consider his novel finished with the marriage of his heroes, and the reconciliation of his royal couple, continuations were not wanting; writers who did not consider their pen "dulled" as he had declared his own to be, volunteered to add a further batch of adventures to the "Sidneyd." Thus we have the "English Arcadia alluding his beginning to Sir Philip Sidnes ending," by Gervase Markham, 1607; a "Sixth booke to the Countesse of Pembrokes Arcadia, written by R[ichard] B[eling] of Lincolnes Inne," 1624; or again a "Continuation of Sir Philip Sydney's Arcadia: wherein is handled the loves of Amphialus and Helena . . . written by a young gentlewoman, Mrs. A. W.," 1651. Dramas were built upon incidents in the "Arcadia"; Shakespeare we have seen made use of it in his "King Lear"; John Day wrote after Sidney's tale, "The Ile of Guls," 1606, "the argument being a little string or rivolet drawne from the full streme of the right worthy gentleman, Sir Phillip Sydneys well knowne Archadea."[1] Some years later, in 1640, Shirley put Basilius and his court again on the stage in his "Pastorall called the Arcadia."[2]

---

[1] "The Ile of Guls, as it hath been often played in the blacke fryars by the children of the revels" (reprinted by Bullen, "Works of John Day," 1881, 4to.)

[2] "Works," ed. Dyce, vol. vi. All the main incidents of Sidney's

Authors of poems also took their plots from stories in Sidney's novel, one of the most popular among those stories was the adventures of Argalus and Parthenia; it was constantly reprinted in a separate form, and was the subject of a long poem by the well-known Francis Quarles, the author of the "Emblemes." "It was," says he in his preface, "a scion taken out of the orchard of Sir Philip Sidney of precious memory, which I have lately graffed upon a crab-stock in mine own.... This book differs from my former as a courtier from a churchman." Not less did it differ from his later books, among which the "Emblemes" were to figure; but the pious author eases his conscience about it by alleging "precedents for it." It cannot be denied that if Quarles' "churchman" was very devout his "courtier" was very worldly. He goes far beyond Sidney in his descriptions of love, of physical love especially, and uses in this matter a freedom of speech and a bantering tone which reminds us much more of the Reine de Navarre than of the author of the "Emblemes." Such as it is, however, this poem remains, so far as literary merit goes, one of the best Quarles ever wrote. He scarcely ever reached again this terseness and vivacity of style, and this *entrain*. Having for once shut himself out of the church, and not for long, he wanted it seems to do the best with his time, and if he was sinning, at least to enjoy his sin.

novel are reproduced by Shirley except the quarrel with Cecropia, and as the romance might very well have ended where Sidney left it, the dramatist did not go further and did not use any of the continuations. See also "Zelmane," by W. Mountfort, 1705, "Parthenia, an Arcadian Drama," 1764, &c.

ARGALUS AND PARTHENIA READING A BOOK IN THEIR GARDEN, 1656.

[*p.* 265.

His contemporaries enjoyed it greatly; "Argalus and Parthenia" went through an extraordinary number of editions;[1] some of them were very fine, and were even illustrated with cuts. We give an example of them showing the newly married couple sitting in their garden to read a story:

> "Upon a day as they were closely seated,
> Her ears attending whilst his lips repeated
> A story treating the renown'd adventures
> And famous acts of great Alcides, enters
> A messenger whose countenance did bewray
> A haste too serious to admit delay."

Is there any necessity for reminding the reader of the cause of the messenger's haste? Is it possible that such world-famous adventures can be now forgotten? The messenger was sent by King Basilius, who was sorely pressed by his arch-enemy Amphialus. The young hero rushes to the rescue of the Arcadian king, but he is piteously slain in a duel with Amphialus. Then Parthenia dresses herself as a knight, and fights her husband's conqueror. With more verisimilitude than is usually the case, she too is piteously slain. And this is the end of Argalus and Parthenia.

But there was still more than this, and like Lyly, Sidney had direct imitators who copied him in prose, and tried to fashion novels after his model. All the peculiarities of his style and of his way, or rather want,

[1] It was published in 1622. The British Museum possesses editions of the years 1629, 1632, 1647, 1651, 1656, 1677, 1684, 1687, 1700, 1708, 1726. Grosart (Quarles' "Complete Works," 1876) mentions one more of the year 1630.

of composition, are to be found minutely reproduced in : " The countesse of Mountgomeries Urania ; written by the Rt. Hon. the Lady Mary Wroath, daughter of the Rt. noble Robert earle of Leicester, and neece to the ever famous and renowned Sr Phillips Sidney Kt. and to ye most excelent Lady Mary Countesse of Pembroke late deceased." [1] This pedigree-shaped title is enough in itself to show what we may expect from the performance. It is a complete and pious imitation of Sidney's manner, especially of his defects, for they were more easily attained. Thus we have those repetitions of the same words which were so pleasant to Sidney's ear, and Lady Mary Wroth has a felicity of her own in twisting the idea into the words, screw-wise, with a perfection her model had scarcely ever attained : " All for others grieved ; pittie extended so, as all were carefull, but of themselves most carelesse : yet their mutual care made them all cared for." A very true and logical observation. Lady Mary is also fond of giving sense and feeling to inanimate objects, and scarcely, again, can Sidney, with his sea that will not wash, or Cyrano with his proud giant of curdled milk, suffer comparison with this description of a burning tower into which a woman throws the head of her enemy : " For her welcome [Dorileus] presented her with the head of her enemy, which he then cut off and gave unto her, who like Tomeris of Sithia, held it by the haire, but gave it quickly another conclusion, for she threw it into the midst of the flaming tower, which then, as being in it selfe enemy to good, because wasting good, yet hotly desiring to embrace as much

[1] London, 1621, fol. (a very curious engraved title).

ill, and so headlongly and hastily fell on it, either to grace it with the quickest and hottest kisses, or to conceale such a villanous and treacherous head from more and just punishments." [1]

As to the story, it is, like the "Arcadia," a tale of shepherds who are princes, and of shepherdesses with royal blood in their veins; there are eclogues, dialogues, and if not much poetry at least much verse. The events take place in Greece and in the Greek islands; people go to the temple of Diana and to the temple of Venus. In the last-named place they get married. These worshippers of the deities of old are dressed as follows. Here is the description of a man's costume: "Then changed he his armour taking one of azure colour, his plume crimson, and one fall of blew in it; the furniture to his horse being of those colours, and his device onely a cipher, which was made of all the letters of his misstrisses name, delicately composed within the compasse of one." Here is now a description of the costume women wore in Lady Mary's Greek land: "She was partly in greene too; as her upper garment, white buskins she had, the short sleeves which she wore upon her armes and came in sight from her shoulders were also white, and of a glistering stuffe, a little ruffe she had about her neck, from which came stripps which were fastned to the edges of her gowne, cut downe equally for length and breadth to make it square; the strips were of lace, so as the skinne came steallinglie through, as if desirous but afraide to bee seane, knowing that little joy would moove desire to have more." This clever young person had been

[1] Pp. 39 and 519.

"sworn a nymph," which prevented her getting married for some years. Waiting for that auspicious date a lover was offering his addresses to her, and as Lady Wroth's Arcadia is an Arcadia with a peerage, we are informed that this sworn nymph's lover was "the third sonne of an earle." [1]

No less a man than Ben Jonson proclaimed himself an admirer of Lady Mary; he dedicated one of his masterpieces, "the Alchemist," to "the lady most deserving her name and blood, Lady Mary Wroth," and in his "Epigrams" he addressed her as follows, his only but sufficient excuse being that the "Urania" was not yet written:

> "Madam, had all antiquity been lost,
> All history seal'd up and fables crost,
> That we had left us, nor by time nor place,
> Least mention of a Nymph, a Muse, a Grace,
> But even their names were to be made anew
> Who could not create them all from you?" [2]

The eighteenth century began, and Sidney's romance was not yet forgotten; his book was still alive, if one may say so, when the novel assumed its definite shape, style and compass with Defoe, Richardson and Fielding. Addison notices its presence in the fair Leonora's library, among "the some few which the lady had bought for her own use." [3] It continued

---

[1] Pp. 295, 298.
[2] In Jonson's "Masque of Blackness," 1605, Lady Mary Wroth played the part of Baryte, and Lady Rich, Sidney's Stella of many years before, personated Ocyte.
[3] "Spectator," April 12, 1711.

then to be fashionable, and a subject of conversation. No wonder, therefore, that between the date of "Robinson Crusoe" and the date of "Pamela" two more editions of the "Arcadia" were given to the public. One of them contained engravings after drawings by L. Chéron.[1] The other was "moderniz'd" and was published by subscription under the patronage of the Princess of Wales.[2] Sidney's novel continued to act on men's minds, and many proofs of its influence on eighteenth-century literature might be pointed out. That Sidney was Richardson's first teacher in the art of the novel is well known; that Cowper read the "Arcadia" with delight is well known too, and he confers no mean praise on our author when he speaks of

> "those golden times
> And those arcadian scenes that Maro sings
> And Sidney, warbler of poetic prose." [3]

Examples of Sidney's style are also to be found in several authors of that time. Consciously or not, Young

[1] "The Works of the honourable Sʳ Philip Sidney," London, 1725, 3 vols. 8vo.

[2] "Sir Philip Sidney's Arcadia," modernized by Mrs. [D.] Stanley, London, 1725, fol. It is a very fine volume with wide margins. One of the "improvements" due to Mrs. Stanley, is the suppression of all the verses. She did so, she says, at the invitation of her subscribers. The list of them which prefaces the book contains many Leonoras, who even at this late period desired to have a copy of the "Arcadia" for "their own use." In our century an abbreviated edition of the same work was published by Mr. Hain Friswell, London, 1867, 8vo.

[3] "The Task," bk. iii. l. 514.

sometimes adopts all the peculiarities of Sidney; for example, when he writes:

> "Sweet harmonist! and beautiful as sweet!
> And young as beautiful! and soft as young!
> And gay as soft! and innocent as gay!
> And happy (if aught happy here) as good!
> For fortune fond had built her nest on high." [1]

Sidney's popularity did not, of course, last so long without encountering some opposition. For Milton, and no wonder, the "Arcadia" was nothing but "a vain amatorious poem," though he is fair enough to add that it is "in that kind, full of worth and wit." [2] Horace Walpole was very hard upon our novelist: "We have a tedious, lamentable, pedantic pastoral romance," says he, in his "Royal and Noble Authors," "which the patience of a young virgin in love cannot now wade through." [3] It is sad to think that the once famous "Castle of Otranto," though twenty times shorter, requires now no smaller dose of patience.

None the less, the "Arcadia" was popular in the last century, and, at the same time as it attracted the attention of fair Leonoras, it also interested and delighted a much commoner sort of readers. It was several times printed in an abbreviated form, and circulated, with engravings, as a chap-book. Sometimes the whole of the "Arcadia" was compressed into a small volume, sometimes only an episode was given to the public. The story of Argalus and Parthenia was

---

[1] Night iii. "Narcissa."
[2] "Εἰκονοκλάστης," "Prose Works," 1806, vol. ii. p. 408.
[3] Ed. of 1806, 5 vols., 8vo, "Life of Fulke Greville," vol. ii. p. 231.

PHILIP SIDNEY AND PASTORAL ROMANCE. 273

especially popular.[1] The engravings, it is needless to say, were very coarse ; and if Sidney had taken little

" See the fond youth ! he burns, he loves, he dies,
He wishes as he pines and feeds his famish'd eyes."

[1] "The unfortunate lovers : the history of Argalus and Parthenia," London, 12mo. The date, 1700 (?), given for this edition in the British Museum catalogue, is obviously too early, as the publisher advertises at the beginning of this volume "Robinson Crusoe," "Jonathan Wild," &c. There were (not to mention earlier versions of "Argalus," *e.g.*, one of 1691) other editions of (about) 1710, 1715, 1750, 1770, 1780, 1788, &c. These little books had sometimes very long descriptive titles, such as those Defoe has made us familiar with : " The famous history of heroick acts of the honour of chivalry, being an abstract of Pembrokes' 'Arcadia,' with many strange and wonderful adventures, the whole being a compleat series interwoven with the heroick actions of many valiant men, as kings, princes, and knights, of undoubted fame, whose matchless deeds, . . . " &c., &c. London, 1701, 12mo, " Bound, 1s."

trouble to be historically or geographically accurate, the wood-block makers took even less, and they offer to our eyes an extraordinary medley of fifteenth-century knights, Roman soldiers, gentlemen in flowing wigs and court swords, all of them supposed to have at one time adorned with their presence the groves of Arcady. A few specimens of these engravers' art are here given; no doubt the reader will be pleased to know what the famous Argalus and Parthenia were supposed to have been like, how the bathing of Philoclea in the Ladon was represented, and the sorts of fêtes and courtly dances that enlivened the marriage of that princess.

More striking even than these tributes to Sidney's merits as a novelist is the treatment awarded him in France. The famous Du Bartas in his second "Week" names Sidney as one of the "three firm pillars of the English Speech." This speech, according to the French poet, is mainly supported by Thomas More and Bacon,

> "Et le milor Cydné qui cygne doux-chantant
> Va les flots orgueilleux de Tamise flatant;
> Ce fleuve gros d' honneur emporte sa faconde
> Dans le sein de Thétis et Thétis par le monde."[1]

Besides this, Sidney's romance received in France an

[1] Second day of the second Week, "Oeuvres," Paris, 1611, fol., p. 211. After Sidney, Du Bartas thus addresses the Queen:

> "Claire perle du nort, guerrière domte-Mars,
> Continue à chérir les muses et les arts,
> Et si jamais ces vers peuvent, d'une aile agile,
> Franchissant l' océan voler jusqu' à ton isle,
> Et tomber, fortunez, entre ces blanches mains
> Qui sous un juste frein régissent tant d'humains,
> Voy les d'un œil bénin et, favorable, pense
> Qu' il faut, pour te louer, avoir ton éloquence."

homage very rare at that epoch : it was translated. A Frenchman possessing a knowledge of the English language was then an extraordinary phenomenon. As late as the year 1665, no less a paper than the "Journal des Scavans" printed a statement to the following effect : "The Royal Society of London publishes constantly a number of excellent works But whereas most of them are written in the

"HOW THE TWO PRINCESSES PAMELA AND HER SISTER PHILOCLEA WENT TO BATH THEMSELVES . . . AND WHAT AFTER HAPNED."

English language, we have been unable till now to review them in our pages. But we have at last found an English interpreter through whose offices it will be henceforth possible for us to enrich our publication with the best things appearing in England." As for Sidney, not only was he translated, but what is not less strange, the fact provoked in France one of the most violent literary quarrels of the time. Two translations of the "Arcadia," now entirely forgotten, were published simultaneously, both in three volumes, both adorned with engravings.[1] As soon as a volume appeared, each of the translators profited by the occasion to write a new preface, and to repeat that his rival was a mere plagiarist and did not know a word of English. The other replied offering to prove such a rare knowledge ; had it been a question of Chinese or of Hindustani they could not have boasted more noisily of their unique acquaintance with so mysterious an idiom. Each appealed to his patroness, who was, in either case, no ordinary woman : the one had dedicated his work to Diane de Chateaumorand (D'Urfé's Diane), who had indeed the right to judge of Arcadias ; the other invoked the authority of the Queen-mother, Marie de Medicis, by whose express command he had carried on his work.

[1] " L'Arcadie de la Comtesse de Pembrok, mise en nostre langue," by J. Baudoin ; Paris, 1624, three vol. 8vo. It contains fancy portraits of Sidney and of his sister. The second translation appeared at the bookseller's, Robert Fouet, in 1625, in the same size ; it is ornamented with pretty engravings. Of its three parts the first was the work of " un brave gentilhomme," and the two others of Mdlle. Geneviève Chappelain. It is needless to observe that the great success of D'Urfé's "Astrée" had much to do with this zeal for translating Sidney's pastoral novel.
Baudoin, who died in 1650, was the translator of various other foreign works, among which part of the works of Bacon. Sir Kenelm Digby, whose fondness for romances was great, had in his library a copy of the "Arcadia" in French ; this was Baudoin's translation, and it is one of the items of the catalogue drawn in view of the sale of his library (" Bibliotheca Digbeiana," London, 1680, 4to). There was, a little later, a translation in German : "Arcadia . . . in unser Hochteutsche Sprach . . . ubersetzt," by Theocritus von Hirschberg [i.e., Martin Opitz], Francfort, 1629, 4to.

Baudoin, who had been the first to turn the "Arcadia" into French, published it in 1624, prefixing to it this remark, flattering to Sidney's memory, but which shows how very little his language was known in France: "Merely the desire of understanding so rare a book caused me to go to England, where I remained for two years in order to gain a knowledge of it."

"THE GLORIOUS ENTERTAINMENTS THAT GRACED THE HAPPY NUPTIALS."

Two years! immediately retorts the publisher of the other translation; we can do better than that: the author of the work that we publish is Mademoiselle Geneviève Chappelain, and what guarantees does she not offer! "She has the honour to have lived more than seven years at the court of the King of Great Britain, in the suite of the Countess of Salisbury, who esteemed her as no ordinary young girl, but as a very well-bred demoiselle who had been presented to her with good credentials, and who was descended from a race that has given us great men: verily, and women, too, that the muses have deigned to favour." This is a little like the argument of Scudéry, boasting, ten years later, of his noble birth in order to prove to poor Pierre Corneille that he is the better poet of the two, and that the "Cid" is worth nothing.

But something better still follows, and here the worthy publisher somewhat betrays himself: "If she has not been able to learn the language of the country in which she has lived for more than seven years, and nearly always with great ladies: how, I beg of you, could those who have only lived there two years, and among the common people, know the language? I do not wish to offend any one by this notice, which I thought it necessary to make only to defend a young lady *who is my near relation.*"

Baudoin maintains his statement, and defies his rivals to translate Sidney's verse, and he enumerates the precautions he himself has taken, precautions which certainly ought to satisfy the reader as regards his accuracy. Not only did he live for two years in England, but, he says, " I secured the assistance of a French gentleman of merit and learning, who has been good enough to explain to me the whole of the first book. I have acted in such a way as to procure two different versions of it in order to produce one good one." And he has done even something more : " I have always had near me one of my friends to whom this tongue was as familiar as our own; he has taken the trouble to elucidate for me any doubts I may have had." In truth, he could hardly have surrounded himself with more light, but then, what an arduous task to translate from English !

Baudoin's adversaries were in no way intimidated by this display; firstly, they had had the assistance of exactly the same gentleman; it appears that a second equally learned was not to be found; secondly, Mdlle. Chappelain also showed her translation to persons who knew both languages, and they found her work perfect; lastly, and what more can be required? she sends a challenge to Baudoin and his accomplices, and invites them to a decisive combat : "She is ready to show that she knows the English language better than they, and they would not dare to appear in order to speak it with her in the presence of persons capable of judging." Baudoin does not appear, indeed, to have accepted this challenge, but neither does it seem to have discouraged him. He closes the preface of his last volume with this poetical apostrophe to those who are envious of his reputation : " By the mouth of good wits—Apollo holds you in contempt,—Troop so ignorant and bold :—For you profane his beauteous gifts,—And cause thistles to spring up—In the midst of your Arcady." [1]

What astonishes us now, when we follow the vicissitudes of the long-forgotten dispute of these two writers is that so much passion should have been expended over Sidney's romance, however great might be its merit; while the attention of no one in France was attracted by Shakespeare and the inimitable group

[1] " Par la bouche des bons esprits
Apollon vous tient à mespris
Troupe ignorante et trop hardie,
Car vous prophanez ses beaux dons
Et faites naistre des chardons
Au milieu de vostre Arcadie."

of dramatists of his time. No Baudoin, no Geneviève Chappelain disputed the honour of translating "Hamlet," and a century was still to elapse before so much as Shakespeare's name should figure in a book printed in France.[1]

This double translation of the "Arcadia" did not, however, pass unnoticed, far from it; and from time to time we find the name of Sidney reappearing in French books, while the giants of English literature continued entirely unknown on the continent. When Charles Sorel satirized the long-winded romances of his time in his "Berger Extravagant," he did not forget Sidney, who figures among the authors alternately praised and criticized in the disputation between Clarimond and Philiris. The criticism is not very severe, and compared with the treatment inflicted on other authors, it would seem that Sorel wished to show courtesy to a foreigner who had been invited, so to say, as a visitor to France by his translators.[2] Copies of

---

[1] And then it was spelt *Chaksper*, "La critique du théâtre anglois," translated from the English of Collier, Paris, 1715, 8vo. In the "Journal des Scavans" for the year 1710 it appears under the shape "Shakees Pear," p. 110.

[2] Thus speaks Clarimond in his harangue against romances: "L'Angleterre n'a pas manqué d'avoir aussi son Arcadie, laquelle ne nous a esté montrée que depuis peu par la traduction qui en a esté faite. Je ne trouve point d'ordre là dedans et il y a beaucoup de choses qui ne me peuvent satisfaire. . . . Il est vrai que Sidney, étant mort jeune, a pu laisser son ouvrage imparfait." In his defence of romances, Philiris answers: "Quant a l'Arcadie de Sidney, après avoir passé la mer pour nous venir voir, je suis marry que Clarimond la reçoive avec un si mauvais compliment. S'il n'entend rien aux amours de Strephon et de Clajus, il faut qu'il s'en prenne a luy, non pas a l'autheur qui a rendu son livre l'un

Sidney's original "Arcadia" crept into France, and are to be found in rather unexpected places. Thus a copy of the edition of 1605 is to be seen in the National Library in Paris, with the Φ Φ of surintendant Fouquet on the cover. The way in which the letters are interlaced shows that the book did not come from Fouquet's own library, but from the library of the Jesuits,[1] to whom he had given a yearly income of 6,000 livres,

des plus beaux du monde. Il y a des discours d'amour et des discours d'estat si excellens et si délectables que je ne me lasserois jamais de les lire" ("Le Berger extravagant, où, parmy des fantaisies amoureuses, l'on void les impertinences des romans et de la poesie," vol. iii., Paris, 1628, pp. 70 and 134). Sorel's work was translated into English: "The extravagant shepherd. The antiromance, or the history of the shepherd Lysis," by John Davies, of Kidwelly; London, 1653, fol. The book has very curious plates; Davies in his preface is extremely hard upon Sidney, and heaps ridicule especially on the head of King Basilius. See *infra*, chap. vii.

[1] Fouquet, however, was very fond of foreign books; the catalogue (dated 1665) of his library, drawn up after his committal, shows that he had a fairly large number of English books. He was the earliest known French possessor of a Shakespeare. The catalogue, it is true, reveals the fact that he preserved it "in his garret":

"Livres in folio qui se trouvent dans le grenier :
Comédies de Jazon [*i.e.*, Ben Jonson] en anglois,
2 vol., London, 1640 ... ... 3*l*.
Idem, comédies angloises ... ... 10*s*.
Shakespeares comédies angloises ... ... 1*l*.
Fletcher commédies angloises ... ... 1*l*."

(MS. 9,438 français, in the Bibliothèque Nationale, Paris.)
The second in date of the French possessors of copies of Shakespeare was, strange to say, no less a person than the patron of Racine and Boileau, the Roi-Soleil himself. Looking over, some

and who, in memory of their benefactor, stamped thus books purchased from this fund.

In France, too, as well as in England, the "Arcadia" was turned into a play. Antoine Mareschal, a contemporary of Corneille and the author of such dramas as "La généreuse Allemande ou le triomphe de l'amour," 1631, the "Railleur ou la satyre du temps," 1638 the "Mauzolée," 1642, derived a tragi-comedy, in five acts, and in verse from the "Arcadia." The piece, which, if the author is to be believed, made a great sensation in Paris, was called the "Cour Bergère," and was dedicated to Robert Sidney, Earl of Leicester, ambassador of England to France, and brother to Sir Philip. It appeared in 1640; it was thus later than the "Cid." None the less, it exhibits the phenomenon of several deaths on the stage; but the ridiculous manner in which these deaths are introduced could only strengthen Corneille in his scruples. The wicked Cecropia, standing on a terrace at the back of the stage, moves without seeing the edge, and falls head foremost on the boards, exclaiming :

---

time ago, at the Bibliothèque Nationale, the original manuscript slips made in 1684 by the royal librarian, Nicolas Clément, for his catalogue of the books confided to his care, I found one inscribed : "Will. Shakspeare, poeta Anglicus. Opera poetica, continentia tragoedias, comoedias et historiolas, Anglice, Londres, Th. Cotes, 1632, fol." And to this, considering that he had to deal with a thoroughly unknown person, Clément was careful to add a note that people might be informed what was to be thought of the poet. This is (so far as now known) the earliest French allusion to Shakespeare : "Ce poète anglois a l'imagination assès belle, il pense naturellement ; mais ces belles qualitez sont obscurcies par les ordures qu'il mêle dans ses comédies."

"Ah ! je tombe, et l'enfer a mon corps entrainé . . .
Je déteste le ciel ! Ah ! je meurs enragée !"

In the following century Sidney was still remembered in France. In his "Mémoires pour servir à l'histoire de la République des lettres," Niceron mentions the "Arcadia" as "a romance full of intelligence and very well written in the author's language."[1] Florian knew him and held him in great honour ; he names him with D'Urfé, Montemayor, and Cervantes, as being, as it were, one of his literary ancestors,[2] and the fact is not without importance ; for Florian, continuing, as he did, Sidney's tradition, and trying in his turn to write poems in prose, stands as a link between the pastoral writers of the sixteenth century and the author who was the last to compose prose epics in our time : the author of "Les Martyrs," and of that American Arcadia called "Atala"—Chateaubriand.

[1] Vol. xv. published in 1731.
[2] "Essai sur la pastorale," prefacing "Estelle."

SAGITTARIUS.

AN INTERIOR VIEW OF A THEATRE IN THE TIME OF SHAKESPEARE.
THE SWAN THEATRE, 1596. [p. 286.

ELIZABETHAN GAIETIES. KEMP'S DANCE FROM LONDON TO NORWICH.

CHAPTER VI.

THOMAS NASH; THE PICARESQUE AND REALISTIC NOVEL.

I.

"THERE is nothing beside the goodnesse of God, that preserves health so much as honest mirth, especially mirth used at dinner and supper, and mirth toward bed. . . . Therefore, considering this matter, that mirth is so necessary a thing for man, I published this booke . . . to make men merrie. . . . Wherefore I doe advertise every man in avoiding pensivenesse, or too much study or melancholie, to be merrie with honesty in God and for God, whom I

humbly beseech to send us the mirth of heaven.
Amen." [1] Such was the advice attributed to a man
whose opinion should carry weight, for he had been
a "doctor of physicke" and had published with great
success a " Breviary of helth " which was a household
book in his time.

The pensive Sir Philip Sidney was, as we have seen,
of a very different turn of mind. He did not live
to read the above wise counsels, but he had had the
opinion of his friend Languet on this subject, and that
had been of no avail. His propensity to overthinking
is apparent in many places in his writings, especially
in his " Arcadia," where he made so little use of the
comical elements he had himself introduced into it.
The main incident in his book, the assignation given
by Zelmane to both Basilius and Gynecia and the
" mistakes of a night " which follow, would have been
from any other pen, only too comical. It is, in fact,
the character it bears in Shirley's drama, and it has
the same in the many modern plays founded on similar
mistakes, plays which serve to improve, according to
Andrew Borde's prescription, if not the morals, at least
the health of the " Palais Royal " audiences of to-day.
With Sidney, the comic is a vulgar style; he very

---

[1] "The first and best part of Scoggins Iests . . . being a preservative against melancholy, gathered by Andrew Boord," London, 1626, 8vo. Many of the jests, tricks, and pranks recounted here are to be found in other collections of such anecdotes, English as well as foreign. For example, the coarse story explaining "how the French king had Scogin into his house of office, and shewed him the King of England's picture" appears in Rabelais, where however the two kings play exactly opposite parts. Andrew Borde died in 1549.

rarely risks any jests, a portrait of a cowardly peasant, or of an injured husband.[1] One of his best attempts in this style is a character in his masque of the "Lady of May," the pedant Rombus, who gives quotations which are always wrong and like Rabelais' scholar, who belongs to "the alme, inclyte and celebrate academy, which is vocitated Lutetia," is careful to make use of nothing but quasi-Latin words. In order to relate how he has been unmercifully whipped by shepherds he declares: "Yet hath not the pulchritude of my vertues protected me from the contaminating hands of these Plebeians; for comming, *solummodo* to have parted their sanguinolent fray, they yeelded me no more reverence, than if I had beene some *pecorius asinus*."[2] But that is an easy way to amuse, and, even at that epoch, not very new. Rabelais had made a better use of it before Sidney, and after him, without mentioning Shakespeare, Cyrano de Bergerac furnished more laughable specimens. No phrase of Rombus equals the order given by the Pedant to his son when sending him to Venice to engage in commerce: "Since thou hast

---

[1] One of the few passages which would raise a laugh even to-day is the rapturous speech with which good Basilius greets the morning after his "mistakes of a night": "Should fancy of marriage keep me from this paradise? or opinion of I know not what promise bind me from paying the right duties to nature and affection? O who would have thought there could have been such difference betwixt women? Be jealous no more O Gynecia, but yield to the preheminence of more excellent gifts," &c. (bk. iv. p. 410). See also the ridiculous fight between Clinias and Dametas pp. 276 *et seq.;* and a story told in verse, bk. iii. p. 390. Molière built his "Ecole des maris" upon a similar plot.

[2] "Arcadia," ed. of 1633, p. 619.

never desired to drink of the pool engendered by the hoof of the feathered horse,[1] and as the lyric harmony of the learned murderer of Python has never inflated thy speech, try if in merchandise Mercury will lend thee his Caduceus. So may the turbulent Æolus be as affable to thee as to the peaceful nests of halcyons. In short, Charlot, thou must go." Sidney kept entirely to these ineffectual attempts, and had no desire to go further in his examination of the ridiculous side of ordinary men.

This study was undertaken by several of his contemporaries. One of the peculiarities of this first awakening of the novel in England, is that it was nearly complete and produced, if not standard masterpieces, at least curious examples of nearly all the different kinds of novel with which later writers have made us familiar. We have seen already how Lyly depicted courtly life, and tried to use the novel as a vehicle for wise and philosophical advice ; how Greene, Lodge and Sidney busied themselves with romantic tales ; how Greene tried to describe the realities of life in some of his autobiographical stories. There was something more to do in this line, and the Elizabethan drama offers innumerable examples of it ; but it is not so well known that in the time of Shakespeare, there were in circulation, besides romantic and

---

[1] That is to drink of the fountain of Hippocrene, to write verse. "Puis donc que tu n'as jamais voulu t'abreuver aux marais fils de l'ongle du cheval emplumé et que la lyrique harmonie du savant meurtrier de Python n'a jamais enflé ta parole, essaye si dans la marchandise Mercure te prêtera son Caducée. Ainsi le turbulent Éole te soit aussi affable qu'aux pacifiques nids des alcyons. Enfin, Charlot, il faut partir" ("Pédant joué," 1654).

chivalrous tales, regular realistic novels, the main object of which was to paint to the life ordinary men and characters. These are the least known, but not the least remarkable of the attempts made by Shakespeare's contemporaries in the direction of the novel as we understand it.

Works of this kind took for the most part the shape to which has been applied the name of *picaresque*. This was, like the pastoral, imported into England from abroad : in the sixteenth century it shone with particular brilliance in Spain. The incessant wars of that vast empire on whose frontiers the sun never set, had favoured the multiplication of adventurers, to-day great lords, to-morrow beggars ; one day dangerous, another day contemptible or ridiculous. " Such people there are living and flourishing in the world, Faithless, Hopeless, Charityless : let us have at them, dear friends, with might and main. Some there are, and very successful too, mere quacks and fools : and it was to combat and expose such as those, no doubt that *Laughter* was made." So wrote in our time William Thackeray,[1] who seems to have considered that the age of the *picaro* had not yet passed away, and that the novelist might still with advantage turn his attention to him. However that may be the great time for the rascal, the rogue, the knave, for all those persons of no particular class whom adventures had left poor and by no means peaceable, for the *picaro* in all his varieties, was the sixteenth century. A whole literature was devoted to describing the fortunes of these strange persons ; Spain gave it its name

[1] " Vanity Fair," chap. viii.

of *picaresque* and spread it abroad but did not altogether invent it. The rogue, who plays tricks which deserve a hanging, had already filled and enlivened tales in several languages. Master Reynard, in that romance of the Middle Ages of which he is the hero, is something like a *picaro*. Another of them is Til Eulenspiegel, whose adventures related in German furnished, in 1515, the subject of a very popular book;[1] even Panurge could at need be placed in this great family. Only, with Master Reynard we live in the world of animals and the romance is allegorical; with Til Eulenspiegel we find no truth, no probability, merely tricks for tricks' sake, and how coarse they are! With Panurge, we are distracted from the *picaro* by all the philosophic and fantastic digressions of an extensive tale in which he is not the principal hero. But with the Spaniards, with Lazarillo de Tormes, Guzman d'Alfarache [2] and the rest, the

[1] Many of his adventures are made up of old anecdotes which were current in Europe during the Middle Ages, and which the success of Eulenspiegel again put into circulation. The very coarse anecdote connected with the death of Til (chap. xcii.) is the subject of Chaucer's Sompnoures tale. The story in chapter lxxx. of the innkeeper who asks payment for the smell of his dishes, and who is paid with a tinkling of coins, is also very old, and was afterwards made use of by Rabelais. "Til" was very popular in France and in England. It was translated in both countries; in the latter one, under the title: "Here beginneth a merye Jest of a man that was called Howleglas," London, Copland, [1528?], 4to.

[2] "Guzman de Alfarache," by Mateo Aleman appeared in 1598 or 1599. The first edition of "Lazarillo de Tormes" was published a few years before the middle of the sixteenth century. All efforts to ascertain its authorship have proved fruitless. See Alfred Morel

picaro holds a place in literature which is peculiarly his own. Faithless, shameless, if not joyless, the plaything of fortune, by turn valet, gentleman, beggar, courtier, thief, we follow him into all societies. From hovel to palace he goes first, opens the doors and shows us the characters. There is no plot more simple or flexible, none that lends itself better to the study of manners, of abuses, of social eccentricities. The only defect is that, in order to abandon himself with necessary good will to the caprices of Fate, and in order to be able to penetrate everywhere, the hero has necessarily little conscience and still less heart; hence the barrenness of the greater part of the picaresque romances and the weak *rôle*, entirely incidental, reserved in these works for sentiment.

The success of these Spanish romances was immediate and lasting throughout Europe. " Lazarillo " and " Guzman " were translated into several languages, and were greatly appreciated here and abroad. " What ! sir," says the Burgundian lord in " Francion,"[1] " is it thus that you cruelly deprive me of the narration of your more amusing adventures? Do you not know that these commonplace actions are infinitely entertaining, and that we take delight in listening even to those of scoundrels and rascals like Guzman d'Alfarache

---

Fatio "Lazarille de Tormes," Paris, 1886, Introduction. As to the antiquity of some of the adventures in "Lazarillo," see *Athenæum*, Dec. 29, 1888, p. 883.

[1] "Histoire comique de Francion," par M. de Moulinet (*i.e.*, Charles Sorel), Paris, 1622 (?), 8vo. It was translated into English " by a person of honour," probably Robert Loveday : " The comical history of Francion," London, 1655, fol.

and Lazarillo de Tormes?" "Guzman" had in France several illustrious translators; the ponderous author of "La Pucelle" and famous academician, Chapelain, was one of them; another was Le Sage who, before penning this translation, had revived and doubled the popularity of the picaresque novel in publishing his "Gil Blas."[1] In Germany, Grimmelshausen, following the same models, wrote in the seventeenth century his "Simplicissimus." In England "Guzman" was several times translated; "Lazarillo" was continually reprinted during two centuries, and original romances of this kind were published here, among others, by Thomas Nash, in the sixteenth, by Richard Head in the seventeenth, by Defoe and Smollett, in the eighteenth century. The initiative of Nash and his group was all the more important and meritorious because before them the comic element was greatly wanting in the English prose romance; amusing stories in the manner of the French had found translators sometimes, but not imitators; the authors of Arcadias were especially concerned in depicting noble sentiments, and the gift of observation possessed by the English people ran the risk of being for a long time exercised nowhere but on the stage, or in metrical tales, or in moral essays.

[1] "Le Gueux ou la vie de Guzman d'Alfarache, image de la vie humaine," translated by J. Chapelain, Lyon, 1630. Le Sage published his "Gil Blas" in 1715, and his translation of "Guzman" in 1732. "Guzman" was several times translated into English, once by J. Mabbe: "The Rogue, or the Life of Guzman de Alfarache," London, 1623, fol.

II.

Thomas Nash made one of that group of young men, full of spirit, fire and imagination, who shone during the first part of Shakespeare's career, who fancied they could live by their pen, and who died prematurely and miserably. Nash was about thirty-three years old when he died in 1600 ; Marlowe was twenty-nine, Peele thirty, Greene thirty-two.

Nash was born at Lowestoft in 1567 :[1] "The head towne in that iland is Leystofe, in which, bee it knowne to all men, I was borne ; though my father sprung from the Nashes of Herefordshire ;" a family that could "vaunt longer petigrees than patrimonies." He studied at Cambridge, in St. John's College, "in which house once I tooke up my inne for seven yere together lacking a quarter, and yet love it still, for it is and ever was, the sweetest nurse of knowledge in all that university."[2] " Saint Johns in Cambridge," says he at another place, " at that time was an universitie within it selfe . . . having, as I have hearde grave men of credite report, more candles light in it everie winter morning before foure of the clocke than the foure of clocke bell gave stroakes."[3] Like Greene and Sidney, he

---

[1] He was baptized in November of that year. The discovery is due to Dr. Grosart. Memorial Introduction to the "Works" of Nash, vol. i. p. xii.
[2] "The Complete Works of Thomas Nashe . . . for the first time collected," ed. Grosart, London, 1883-4, 6 vol. 4to ; "Nashe's lenten stuffe," 1599, vol. v. p. 277 ; "Have with you to Saffron Walden," vol. ii. p. 256 ; "Lenten Stuffe," v. p. 241.
[3] Nash's letter "to the Gentlemen Students," prefacing his friend Greene's "Menaphon," 1589.

imbibed early a passionate taste for literature ; he learnt the classical languages and foreign ones too, at least French and Italian, and enjoyed much miscellaneous reading ; old English literature, Mandeville, Chaucer, Gower, Skelton, were not forgotten. Following then the usual course, he seems to have travelled on the continent, to have visited Italy and Germany,[1] and to have come home, also according to custom, to rush into literature : by which word was then habitually understood fame, poverty, quarrels, imprisonment, and an early death. Not one of these items was wanting in Nash's career. A prolific and easy writer, he tried his hand at all kinds of work, composing them rapidly and with visible pleasure, always ready to laugh at the follies of others, sometimes at his own, not melancholy like Sidney, nor downcast like Greene. He very rarely alludes to his miseries without a smile, though he could not help regretting the better things he might have done if Fortune had not been so adverse, "had I a ful-sayld gale of prosperity." But "my state is so tost and weather-beaten, that it hath nowe no anchor-holde left to cleave unto."[2] Having said thus much, he immediately resumes his cheerful countenance and in the best of spirits and in perfect good humour goes on

[1] This has been doubted, for the statement was considered mainly to rest upon the dedication of "An almond for a parrat," and Nash's authorship of this work is no longer accepted (Grosart, i. p. 4). But as good evidence, at least, for Nash's probable travels, is derived from his "Jack Wilton," in which more than one statement comes, to all appearance, from an actual eye-witness.

[2] "Lenten Stuffe," "Works," vol. v. p. 204. The first time he appeared in print was when he prefaced with the above-mentioned letter Greene's "Menaphon" in 1589.

describing the great city of Yarmouth, the metropolis of the Red Herring.

With this turn of mind and an inexhaustible fund of wit, satire, and gaiety, he published numerous pamphlets, threw himself impetuously into the Martin Marprelate controversy (in which another novelist, Lyly, was also taking part); sustained a rude warfare against Gabriel Harvey;[1] wrote a dissertation on social manners: the "Anatomie of absurditie," 1589; a disquisition with an autobiographical turn, which may be compared with those Greene has left; "Pierce Penilesse his supplication to the Divell," 1592 (it had great success, and was even translated into French, "maimedly translated," says Nash,[2] probably with great truth); a novel "The unfortunate traveller or the life of Jack Wilton," 1594, which has most undeservedly remained until now the least known of his works; a drama, "The Isle of dogs," 1597, which is lost, and for which the author was sent to prison; a curious and amusing discourse "in praise of the red herring," 1599; and many other books, pamphlets, and works of all kinds.[3]

[1] In his "Quip for an upstart courtier," 1592, Greene had spoken irreverently of Harvey's low extraction. Harvey heaped abuse upon Greene, being rather encouraged than stopped by the death of his opponent. In the same year, Nash, with great courage, rushed to the rescue of his friend and of his memory; when this was done he continued the war on his own account with great success, till the authorities interfered and stopped both combatants.

[2] "My Piers Penilesse . . . being above two yeres since maimedly translated into the French tongue." "Have with you to Saffron Walden," "Works," vol. iii. p. 47.

[3] His principal writings are distributed as follows in Dr.

Constantly entangled in quarrels, in such a way sometimes that the authorities had to interfere—for example, in his war with Gabriel Harvey, when the destruction of the books of both was ordered—he preserved to the last his good humour and his taste for people and authors who knew what it was to laugh. Curiously enough, he combined this taste with an intense fondness for pure literature and for lyrical poetry. Rabelais is among his masters, and so is Aretino, "one of the wittiest knaves that ever God made." Tarleton the jester is among his friends, and so is Kemp, the Dogberry of Shakespeare's "Much Ado," the Peter of "Romeo and Juliet," the famous dancer who performed a morris dance from London to Norwich. And at the same time he bestows with unbounded enthusiasm heartfelt praises upon Spenser, "heavenly

---

Grosart's edition :—I. "Anatomie of Absurditie," 1589; various Martin Marprelate tractates. II. "Pierce Penilesse," 1592; "Strange newes," 1593, and other writings against Harvey. III. "Have with you to Saffron Walden," 1596 (against Harvey); "The terrors of the night or a discourse of apparitions," 1594, in which Nash on many points anticipates Defoe. IV. "Christ's tears over Jerusalem," 1593, a long pious discourse. V. "The unfortunate traveller," 1594; "Lenten Stuffe," 1599. VI. "The tragedie of Dido," 1594 (in collaboration with Marlowe); "Summers last will and testament," a play by Nash alone.

His "Isle of dogs" is lost, having been suppressed as soon as performed. The troubles Nash got into on account of this unlucky play are thus commemorated by him: "The straunge turning of the Ile of Dogs from a commedie to a tragedie two summers past, with the troublesome stir which hapned about it is a general rumour that hath filled all England, and such a heavie crosse laide upon me as had well neere confounded mee" ("Lenten Stuffe," vol. v. p. 199).

Spenser"; upon "immortal" Sidney, whose "Astrophel and Stella" he himself published in 1591; and upon Marlowe, as the author of the exquisite Hero and Leander poem, " Leander and Hero of whome divine Musæus sung and a diviner muse then him, Kit Marlow."[1]

With all his fondness for merry authors, Nash can discern true poetry, and he adores it. If by chance, in the midst of an angry satirical disquisition, the word poetry comes to his pen, he is suddenly transformed, he smiles, he melts; nothing is left in him but human sympathies. " Nor is poetry an art where of there is no use in a man's whole life but to describe discontented thoughts and youthfull desires, for there is no study but it dooth illustrate and beautifie. . . . To them that demaund what fruites the poets of our time bring forth, or wherein they are able to approve themselves necessarie to the state, thus I answere: first and formost, they have cleansed our language from barbarisme, and made the vulgar sort, here in London, which is the fountaine whose rivers flowe round about England, to aspire to a richer puritie of speach than is communicated with the comminalty of any nation under heaven."[2] When a man like Nash could write in such a strain, with a passion for vernacular literature scarcely equalled at any time, there was obviously growing among that " vulgar sort, here in London," a public for any great man that might appear, a public for William Shakespeare himself, who was just then

[1] "The unfortunate Traveller," vol. v. p. 93; "Lenten Stuffe," vol. v. p. 262.
[2] "Pierce Penilesse," "Works," vol. ii. pp. 60, 61.

beginning to reach celebrity. Nash does not doubt that it is possible for English to become a classical language, however rude the garb it first bore. According to Nash, Surrey was "a prince in content because a poet without peere. Destinie never defames her selfe but when she lets an excellent poet die: if there bee any sparke of Adams paradized perfection yet emberd vp in the breasts of mortall men, certainely God hath bestowed that his perfectest image on poets." Differing from Francis Bacon and a few of the grave dignitaries of literature, he has faith in that group of artists in the first rank of whom he placed heavenly Spenser, who can well bear comparison with any author of France, Italy, or Spain. "Neither is he the only swallow of our summer."[1]

This fondness for pure literature, for musical verse and lyrical poetry, explains how, satirist as he was, Nash had numerous friends whose feelings towards him were nothing short of tenderness. "Sweet boy," "Sweet Tom," are not usual expressions towards a satirist; they are, however, applied to Nash both by Greene and by Francis Meres, because there was in Nash's mind something besides the customary rancour of born satirists. "The man," said Shakespeare,

> "The man that has no music in himself
> Nor is not mov'd with concord of sweet sounds,
> Is fit for treasons, stratagems and spoils;

---

[1] "The unfortunate Traveller, or the Life of Jack Wilton," "Works," vol. v. p. 60, and Prefatory letter to Greene's "Menaphon."

> The motions of his spirit arc as dull as night,
> And his affections dark as Erebus;
> Let no such man be trusted."[1]

A very different sort of a man was Nash; his friends found that he could be "mov'd with concord of sweet sounds," and that he could be trusted. As he survived Sidney at a time when a few years meant much for English literature, he could form a far more favourable judgment of the drama than the well-known one in the "Apologie." The ridiculous performances noticed by Sidney had not disappeared, but they were not the only ones to be seen on the stage; dramas of the highest order were being played; actors rendered them with becoming dignity, and, curiously enough to our ideas, Nash adds as a special praise that women were excluded from among their number: "Our players are not as the players beyond sea, a sort of squirting baudie comedians, that have whores and common curtezans to play womens parts, and forbeare no immodest speech or unchast action that may procure laughter; but our sceane is more stately furnisht than ever it was in the time of Roscius, our representations honorable and full of gallant resolution, not consisting like theirs of a Pantaloun, a whore and a Zanie, but of emperours, kings and princes whose true tragedies, *Sophocleo cothurno* they do vaunt."[2] In the next century, women were allowed to replace on the English stage the newly-shaven young fellows who used to play Juliet and Titania; we are happy to say that so indecent

---

[1] Greene's "Groats-worth," "Works," vol. i. p. 143; Mere's "Paladis Tamia"; "Merchant of Venice," act v. sc. 1.
[2] "Pierce Penilesse," "Works," vol. ii. p. 92.

a practice was due to foreign influence. We have Prynne's authority for believing that the first women who had the audacity to appear before a London audience were French. This happened in 1629 at the Blackfriars theatre. It is true that not long after, to make up, as it were, for lost time, plays were performed in England in which all the parts were taken by women; it is not known whether on that occasion they were French.[1]

Another very important characteristic in Nash is the high ideal he has shaped for himself of the art of writing, not only in verse, but in plain prose. At a time when English prose was scarcely acknowledged to be capable of artistic treatment, and when rules, regulations and theories had, as is generally believed, very little hold upon writers, it is interesting to notice that such an author as Nash, with his stirring style and unbridled pen, with his prison and tavern life, understood that words had a literary value of their own. They were not to be taken at random, but chosen with care. His theory may on some points be disputed, but it is certainly interesting to note that he had a theory at all. First, he desires that a man shall write in his own vein and not copy others, especially those who by their vogue and peculiarities, such as Lyly or Greene,

[1] "Histrio-mastix," 1633, 4to, p. 215. Coryat reports on hearsay (1608) that women had already appeared at that date on the English stage; but he is careful to note that he had never personally witnessed this extraordinary phenomenon; and he adds that he was greatly astonished to see in Italy women perform their parts in a play "with as good a grace, action and gesture and whatsoever convenient for a player as ever I saw any masculine actor" ("Crudities," London, 1776, vol. ii. p. 16).

were easiest of reach and the most tempting to imitate. He strongly defends himself from having ever done anything of this sort ; on the contrary, more than once appeals were made to him to give judgment in literary matters :

"Is my style like Greenes, or my jeasts like Tarletons? "Do I talke of any counterfeit birds, or hearbes or stones? ... This I will proudly boast ... that the vaine which I have ... is of my own begetting and cals no man father in England but myselfe, neither Euphues, nor Tarlton, nor Greene.

"Not Tarlton nor Greene but have beene contented to let my simple judgment overrule them in some matters of wit. Euphues I read when I was a little ape in Cambridge, and I then thought it was *ipse ille:* it may be excellent still for ought I know, but I lookt not on it this ten yeare : but to imitate it I abhorre."[1]

His vocabulary is very rich ; he has always a variety of words at his disposal and uses often two or three the better to impress our minds with the idea in his own. He coins at need new words or fetches them from classical or foreign languages. He does not do this in an off-hand way, but on purpose and wilfully ; he possessed much of that curious care for and delight in words which is one of the characteristics of the men of the Renaissance. To deal with words was in itself a pleasure for them ; they liked to mould, to adopt, to combine, to invent them. Word painting delighted them ; Nash has an extreme fondness

[1] "Strange newes of the intercepting certaine letters," 1592, "Works," vol ii. p. 267.

for it, and satirical and comical as he is, he often astonishes us by the poetic gracefulness of his combinations of words. In this as in many other particulars he imitates, *longe sequens*, the master he seems to have admired above others, Rabelais, who, in the tempestuous roll of his diverse waters, sometimes washes up on to the sand pearls fit to adorn the crown of any lyrical poet. Fishes appear in Nash's otherwise unpoetical prose as "the sea's finny freeholders;" the inhabitants of a port town do not sow corn, "their whole harvest is by sea;" they plough "the glassy fieldes of Thetis." He has an instinctive hatred for abstract terms; he wants expressive words, words that shine, that breathe, that live. Instead of saying that Henry III. *granted* a charter and certain privileges in a particular year of his *reign*, he will write that "he *cheard up their blouds* with two charters more, and in Anno 1262 and forty-five of his *courte keeping*, he permitted them to wall in their towne."[1] The pleasure of replacing stale, common-place expressions by rare, picturesque, live ones, and in lieu of a plain sentence to give an allegorical substitute, has so much attraction for Nash, that clear-sighted as he is, he cannot always avoid the ordinary defects of this particular style, defects which he has in common with many of his contemporaries, not excluding Shakespeare himself, namely, obscurity and sometimes bad taste.

Another of Nash's tendencies, which he has most decidedly in common with Rabelais, consists in the use of a number of expressions in the same sentence for the same idea. Of course one carefully chosen

[1] "Lenten Stuffe," vol. v. pp. 226, 244, 216.

word would be enough ; such a man as Mérimée, to take an example at the other extremity of the line, picks out the one term he wants, puts it in its place ; word and place fit exactly ; there is nothing to add or desire. Not so Rabelais ; not so either his admirer Nash ; the newly-awakened curiosities of the Renaissance were too young as yet, too fresh and strong upon them, to be easily kept down by rule and reflection. Literature too was young then, and young things are endowed with eyes that stare and admire more easily than old ones. When entering their word-shop, writers of the sixteenth century were fain to take this word, and this other too, and yet that one more ; and when on the threshold, about to go, they would turn and take two or three again. There are pages in Rabelais and pages in Nash where most of the important words are supplemented and fortified with a number of others placed there at our disposal as alternatives or substitutes, for the pleasure of our ears and eyes, in case we might like them better. Nash has to express this very simple idea : Look at Yarmouth, what a fine town it is ! Well, it owes all it is to the red herring. This he formulates in the following manner with quite a Rabelaisian mixture of native and half Latin words and iterations for most terms of importance : " Doe but convert, said hee, the slenderest twinckling reflexe of your eyesight to this flinty ringe that engirtes it, these towred walles, port-cullizd gates, and gorgeous architectures that condecorate and adorne it, and then perponder of the red herringes priority and prevalence, who is the onely inexhaustible mine that hath raised and begot all this, and, minutely, to riper maturity, fosters and cherisheth it." [1]

[1] "Works," vol. v. p. 231.

Some critics of his time abused Nash for the liberties he took with the vocabulary, especially for his foreign and compound words. He was ready with this half-serious, half-jocose answer: "To the second rancke of reprehenders, that complain of my boystrous compound wordes, and ending my Italionate coyned verbes all in *ize*," such as "tympanize; tirannize," says he elsewhere; "thus I replie : That no winde that blowes strong but is boystrous; no speech or wordes of any power or force to confute or perswade, but must be swelling and boystrous. For the compounding of my wordes, therein I imitate rich men, who having gathered store of white single money together, convert a number of those small little scutes into great peeces of gold, such as double Pistoles and Portugues. Our English tongue of all languages, most swarmeth with the single money of monosillables, which are the onely scandall of it. Bookes written in them and no other seeme like shopkeepers' bookes, that containe nothing else save halfepence, three-farthings, and two-pences. Therefore what did me I, but having a huge heape of those worth lesse shreds of small English in my *pia maters* purse, to make the royaller shew with them to men's eye, had them to the compounders immediately, and exchanged them foure into one, and others into more, according to the Greek, French, Spanish, and Italian." [1]

Nash had a particular literary hatred for mere empty bombast. His love for high-sounding words with a meaning was not greater than his aversion for big sounds without one. Even his friend Marlowe

[1] Preface to "Christ's teares," edition of 1594, "Works," vol. iv. p. 6.

does not escape his censure for having trespassed in this particular beyond the limits of good taste. Nash wonders " how eloquent our gowned age is growen of late," and he has nothing but contempt for those "vain-glorious tragoedians who contend not so seriously to excel in action, as to embowell the clowdes in a speach of comparison ; thinking themselves more than initiated in poets immortalitie, if they but once get Boreas by the beard and the heavenlie bull by the deaw-lap." [1]

His ideas regarding the art of novel writing are very liberal, and he accepts as belonging to literature many specimens we should sternly reject. The one point to remember, however, is that he does not accept them all ; he draws the line somewhere, and in that age when the novel was in its infancy, there was merit in doing even no more than this. He is very hard upon the old mediæval romances, which it is true he seems to have known only through the abridged and degenerate texts circulated in his time, for the amusement of idle readers. He readily endorses the moral views of Ascham about them, adding however, what is more interesting for us, some literary criticism : "What els I pray you, doe these bable booke-mungers endevor but to repaire the ruinous wals of Venus court, to restore to the worlde that forgotten legendary licence of lying, to imitate a fresh the fantasticall dreames of those exiled Abbie-lubbers [*i.e.*, the monks] from whose idle pens proceeded those worne out impressions of the feigned no where acts of Arthur of the rounde table, Arthur of litle Brittaine, Sir Tristram, Hewon of Bur-

[1] Prefatory letter to Greene's " Menaphon."

deaux, the Squire of low degree, the four sons of Amon, with infinite others. . . . Who is it that reding Bevis of Hampton, can forbeare laughing, if he marke what scambling shyft he makes to end his verses a like? I will propound three or foure payre by the way for the readers recreation :

>The porter said : By my snout,
>It was Sir Bevis that I let out."[1]

Every reader will agree with Nash, I suppose, in condemning this as balderdash.

Endowed thus with artistic theories of his own, with an intense love of literature, with an inborn gaiety and faculty of observation, Nash added to the collection of novels of the Shakespearean era, not another Bevis of Hampton, but his "Jack Wilton,"[2] the best specimen of the picaresque tale in English literature anterior to Defoe. His romance, written in the form of memoirs, according to the usual rule of the picaresque, is dedicated to the Earl of Southampton, under whose patronage Shakespeare had already placed his "Venus and Adonis." It has the defect of all the romances of the time, in England as elsewhere : it is incoherent and badly put together. But it contains excellent fragments, two or three capital portraits of individuals which show careful observation, and a few solidly constructed scenes like the vengeance of Cutwolfe which allow us to foresee that one day the dramatic power of the English genius, worn out doubtless by a too long career on the

---

[1] "Anatomie of Absurditie," 1589, "Works," vol. i. p. 37.
[2] "The unfortunate Traveller, or the Life of Jack Wilton," 1594, "Works," vol. v.

stage, instead of dying altogether, will be revived in the novel.

Nash, after the manner employed by More in his "Utopia," by Greene in his "Ciceronis amor," and in our age, with a splendour of fame to which several generations have already borne testimony, by Sir Walter Scott, introduces historical personages in his fiction. The page Jack Wilton, the hero of the tale, a little superior by his rank to the ordinary *picaro* has, like Gil Blas, little money in his pocket and a few odds and ends of Latin in his head; he distributes in his conversation the trite quotations that have remained by him, skilfully enough to persuade the vulgar that he does not belong to their tribe. "Tendit ad sidera virtus—Paulo majora canamus—Secundum formam statuti," &c., and from time to time, when he is greatly elated and wishes to show himself in all his magnificence, he adopts the elegances and similes proper to the euphuistic style : "The sparrow for his lecherie liveth but a yeere," &c.[1]

Wilton is present first with the royal court of England at the siege of Tournay, under Henry VIII. What my credit was at this court "a number of my creditors that I coosned can testifie." He lives on the resources of his wits, playing tricks worthy a whipping if not a hanging on respectable persons of limited

[1] In these cases, Nash, or rather his hero (for Nash does not himself make use of this language which he in no way admired, but only puts it into the mouth of his self-confident good-for-nothing as the finishing touch to his portrait), adopts Lyly's style entirely, alliteration and all : "The sparrow for his lecherie liveth but a yeere, he for his trecherie was turned on the toe."

capacity. His most notable victim is the purveyor of drink or victualler to the camp, a tun-bellied coward, proud of his pretended noble descent, a Falstaff grown old, whose wit has been blunted, who has ended by marrying Mistress Quickly, and has himself become tavern keeper in partnership with her. In old days he drank on credit : now the good fellows tipple at his expense. Such is the end of all the Falstaffs and all the Scapins. "This great Lorde, this worthie Lord," relates the wicked page, "thought no scorne, Lord have mercy upon us, to have his great velvet breeches larded with the droppings of this dainty liquor," that is, the cider that he sold ; "and yet he was an olde servitor, a cavelier of an ancient house, as it might appear by the armes of his ancestrie, drawen very amiably in chalk, on the in side of his tent doore." [1]

The scene between the fat, ruddy host, open-mouthed, blear-eyed, and the frolicking slender page, who delights in his tricks and covers his victim with jesting compliments, is extremely well described. Wilton finds his man "counting his barrels, and setting the price in chalke on the head of everie one of them." He addresses him his "duty verie devoutly," and tells him he has matters of some secrecy to impart to him for which a private audience is necessary :

"With me, young Wilton ? quoth he, marie and shalt. Bring us a pint of syder of a fresh tap into the 'Three Cups' [2] here ; wash the pot !

"So into a backe roome he lead mee, where after hee had spit on his finger, and picked off two or three

[1] "Works," vol. v. pp. 15 *et seq.* [2] Name of a room in the tavern.

moats of his olde moth eaten velvet cap, . . . he badde me declare my minde, and there upon he dranke to me on the same."

Jack is careful not to touch at once on the matter in his head : he knows his man and attacks him first by that vanity of a noble descent which he possesses in common with Falstaff. Jack has always borne him affection, " partly for the high discent and linage from whence he sprung, and partly for the tender care and provident respect he had of poore soldiers . . . he vouchsafed in his own person to be a victualer to the campe : a rare example of magnificence and courtesie ; and diligently provided, that without farre travel, every man might have for his money syder and cheese his bellyfull. Nor did he sell his cheese by the way onely, or his syder by the great, but abast himselfe with his owne hands to take a shoomakers knife : a homely instrument for such a high personage to touch, and cut it out equally like a true justiciarie in little pennyworthes that it would doo a man good for to looke upon. So likewise of his syder, the pore man might have his moderate draught of it (as there is moderation in all things) as well for his doit or his dandiprat as the rich man for his halfe souse or his denier . . . "

Jack goes on irrepressible, overflowing ; it is his best moment ; he does not want the sport to end too quickly : " Why, you are everie childs felow : any man that comes under the name of a souldier and a good fellowe, you will sitte and beare companie to the last pot, yea, and you take in as good part the homely phrase of : ' Mine host heeres to you,' as if one saluted you by all the titles of your baronie. These considerations, I saie, which the world suffers to slip by in the channell of carelesnes, have moved me in ardent zeale of your welfare, to forewarne you of some dangers that have beset you and your barrels.

"At the name of dangers hee start up, and bounst with his fist on the boord so hard, that his tapster overhearing him cried : 'Anon ! anon ! sir,' and entering with a bow askt him what he wanted.

"Hee was readie to have stricken his tapster for interrupting him in attention of this his so much desired relation, but for feare of displeasing me he moderated his furie, and onely sending him for the other fresh pint, wild him looke to the barre, and come when he is cald with a devilles name.

"Well, at his earnest importunitie, after I had moistned my lips, to make my lie run glib to his journies end, forward I went as followeth . . ." And the good apostle stops again ; the cider and his own words have moved him ; he is a little fuddled, so is mine host ; they both fall to weeping. The innkeeper is ready to believe anything, and at this moment, which is the right one, the page at length determines to inform him that in an assembly where he was present, he heard mine host, the purveyor of the camp, accused of connivance with the enemy, by giving information to the besieged through letters hidden in his empty barrels. High treason is suspected ! How are these dangerous rumours to be dissipated ? There is only one way of doing it, that is in becoming popular in the army, very popular ; he must make himself beloved by all ; he must distribute cider freely and for a time suppress in his shop the unbecoming custom of paying.

The victualler follows this advice, but soon the trick is discovered; the page is roundly whipped, but being to the core a true picaroon, Wilton does not for all that feel his spirit in any way lessened: "Here let me triumph a while, and ruminate a line or two on the excellence of my wit!" This is all the sorrow and repentance the whip extracts from him.

Shakespeare, two years later, fused the two characters into one, caused the wit of the page to enter the brain of the fat man, and the blending, animated by his genius, produced the inimitable customer of the "Boar's Head" tavern.

After various adventures, Wilton returns to London, and struts about in fine clothes, whose originality he describes with an amusing rush of language: "I had my feather in my cap as big as a flag in the fore-top; ... my cape cloake of blacke cloth, over-spreading my backe like a thornbacke or an elephantes eares, ... and in consummation of my curiositie my hands without gloves, all a mode French." The sense of the picturesque, the careful observation of the effect of a pose, of a fold of a garment, were, before Nash, entirely unknown to English novel writers, and it was not until the eighteenth century, until the time of Defoe, Fielding, and, above all, Sterne, that the author of "Jack Wilton" was excelled in this special talent.

Soon the page takes up the course of his adventures again, and travels anew on the continent. He visits Venice, Florence, Rome, refraining with a care for which he is to be thanked from trite descriptions. What's the good of describing the monuments of Rome? he says; everybody knows them: "he that

hath but once drunke with a traveller, talkes of them."
Sir Thomas More contemplating his "Utopia," John
of Leyden dragged to the scaffold, the Earl of Surrey
jousting for the fair Geraldine "against all commers,"
Francis I., conqueror at Marignan, Erasmus, Aretino,
"one of the wittiest knaves that ever God made," and
other personages of the Renaissance, figure in the narrative. Faithful to the picaresque plot, Nash conducts
his reader into all societies, from the tavern to the
palace, from the haunt of robbers to the papal court,
and makes his hero no better than he should be. At
Marignan, Wilton occupies himself especially in discovering quickly who is likely to be the strongest, in
order to attach himself ardently to the winner. At
Venice he runs away with an Italian lady, deserts his
master, the Earl of Surrey, and passes himself off as
the Earl.

All this is too much at length for honest Nash, and
feeling not less displeased than ourselves with the wicked
actions of his hero, he himself interposes at times, not
without disadvantage to his plot, and, in spite of the
improbability of placing such remarks in Wilton's
mouth, introduces his own opinions on the persons and
incidents of the romance. This is an effect of the
impetuosity of his temperament, blameable undoubtedly
from an artistic point of view. We shall be indulgent
to him if we remember that no author of the time was
entirely master of himself and faithful to his plot.
Even Shakespeare rarely resists like temptation, and
when a poetic image comes into his mind, little matters
it to him what character is on the stage; he makes of
him a dreamer, a poet, and lends to him the exquisite

language of his own emotion. Let us remember how the murderers hired to assassinate Edward's children describe the scene of the murder. They saw "the gentle babes . . . girdling one another

> Within their alabaster innocent arms:
> Their lips were four red roses on a stalk,
> And, in their summer beauty, kiss'd each other."

A very improbable remark, it will be admitted, on the part of the murderers. But, then, it is Shakespeare who talks aloud, forgetting that he is supposed not to be there.

Nash, with like heedlessness, often interposes in his own person, and takes the words out of his page's mouth; and his bold, characteristic and concise opinions are very curious in the history of manners and literature. For example, when he describes the war of the Anabaptists and the execution of John of Leyden, he sums up thus in a short pithy sentence the current opinion of his day among literary people and men of the world, on the already formidable sect of the Puritans: "Heare what it is to be Anabaptists, to bee puritans, to be villaines: you may be counted illuminate botchers for a while, but your end wil be: Good people pray for me."

His open admiration of the charity of the Catholics at Rome reveals in him great independence of mind and much courage: "Yet this I must say to the shame of us Protestants, if good workes may merit heaven they doo them, we talke of them. Whether superstition or no makes them unprofitable servants, that let pulpets decide: but there, you shall have the bravest Ladies in

gownes of beaten gold, washing pilgrimes and poore souldiours feete, and dooing nothing they and their wayting mayds all the yeare long, but making shirts and bandes for them against they come by in distresse."
At Wittenberg, Wilton sees "Acolastus" performed, an old play that was as popular in England as on the continent,[1] and Nash's severe criticism on the actors shows how well the difference between good comedians and common players was understood in London. Nash shared Shakespeare's opinion of the actors who "out-heroded Herod," and he would have been of Molière's way of thinking about the performances at the Hôtel de Bourgogne : "One as if he had beene playning a clay floore, stampingly troade the stage so harde with his feete, that I thought verily he had resolved to doe the carpenter that sette it uppe some utter shame. Another floung his armes lyke cudgelles at a peare tree, insomuch as it was mightily dreaded that hee woulde strike the candles that hung above theyr heades out of their sockets, and leave them all darke." This severe criticism may serve to reassure us about the way in which the great English dramas were interpreted at that period.[2] And indeed they deserved that some trouble

[1] It was translated into English from the Latin by John Palsgrave : "Acolastus," London, 1540, 4to. As to this play and its author, Gulielmus Gnapheus (Fullonius) of the Hague, who had it represented in 1529, see C. H. Herford, "Studies in the Literary Relations of England and Germany in the Sixteenth Century," Cambridge, 1886, 8vo, pp. 84 *et seq.*, 108 *et seq.*

[2] *Ibid.* p. 71. *Cf.* "Returne from Parnassus," 1601, ed. Macray, Oxford, 1886, act iv. sc. 3, pp. 138 *et seq.*, where the rules of good acting are also under discussion. Shakespeare's opinions on the same are well known ("Hamlet," act iii. sc. 2, A.D. 1602).

should be taken with them, for in London it was the time of "Romeo and Juliet," of "Midsummer Night's Dream," of "Richard III."

In fact, Nash does not only possess the merit of knowing how to observe the ridiculous side of human nature, and of pourtraying in a full light picturesque figures now worthy of Teniers and now of Callot; some fat and greasy, others lean and lank; he possesses a thing very rare with the picaresque school, the faculty of being moved. He seems to have foreseen the immense field of study which was to be opened later to the novelist. A distant ancestor of Fielding, as Lyly and Sidney appear to us to be distant ancestors of Richardson, he understands that a picture of active life, reproducing only, in the Spanish fashion, scenes of comedy, is incomplete and departs from reality. The greatest jesters, the most arrogant, the most venturesome have their days of anguish; no brow has ever remained unfurrowed from the cradle to the grave, and no one has been able to live an impassive spectator and not feel his heart sometimes beat the quicker, nor bow his head in sorrow. Nash caught a glimpse of this, and therefore mingled serious scenes with his pictures of comedy, in order that his romance might the more closely resemble life. Sometimes they are love scenes as when the Earl of Surrey describes to us his awakening passion for Geraldine, and how he met her at Hampton Court: "Oh thrice emperiall Hampton Court, Cupids inchaunted castle, the place where I first sawe *the perfect omnipotence of the Almightie expressed in mortalitie!*" Sometimes they are tragic scenes full of blood and tortures. It is true that Nash then falls into melodrama and conducts his Wilton to a sort of Tour de Nesles where the Countess Juliana, the Pope's mistress, gives herself up to excesses, by the side of which those of Margaret of Burgundy are but child's play. Murders, rapes, and scenes of robbery multiply under cover of the plague that rages at Rome, and the horrors resulting from the pestilence are described with a vigour that reminds us of Defoe, without however equalling him. Carts containing the dead go up and down the streets, and lugubrious cries resound : " Have you anie dead to burie ? Have you anie dead to burie ? " The carts " had manie times of one house their whole loading."

Wilton is accused of murders committed in his house ; the rope almost about his neck, he is saved by an English earl, in exile, who seems to have been imbued with Ascham's teaching, and who reproaches him for travelling, especially in Italy, where morals are so corrupt and where immorality is so dangerous. " Take care," said the earl, " if thou doest but lend halfe a looke to a Romans or Italians wife, thy porredge shall bee prepared for thee, and cost thee nothing but thy life." The earl, who proves to be a rather pedantic nobleman, passes in review all nations, and proves that they are not worth the trouble of going to see. Wilton, whose personal experience does not justify such unfavourable prognostications, especially now that he is out of danger, is wearied by this talk, and, pretending important business, gives his chattering benefactor the slip. He is soon punished ; he is captured by the Jews of Rome ; his adventures become more and more mysterious and alarming, and more and more does melodrama invade the story.

Sometimes, however, in the midst of these abominations, Nash's tone rises; his language becomes eloquent and his emotion infectious; he shudders himself, horror penetrates him and seizes us; the jests of the picaroon are very far from our mind, the drama is then as terrible as with the most passionate romanticists of our century in their best moments.

Few stories of our day are better contrived to give the sense of the horrible than the story of the vengeance of Cutwolfe related by himself just as he is going to be tortured. After a prolonged search, Cutwolfe at last finds his enemy, Esdras of Granada, alone, in his shirt, and far from all help. The unfortunate man implores Cutwolfe, whose brother he had killed, to make it impossible for him to do any more harm, to mutilate him, but to spare his life. His enemy replies: "Though I knewe God would never have mercie on mee except I had mercie on thee, yet of thee no mercie would I have. . . . I tell thee, I would not have undertooke so much toyle to gaine heaven, as I have done in pursuing thee for revenge. Divine revenge, of which, as one of the joies above, there is no fulnes or satietie. Looke how my feete are blistered with following thee from place to place. I have riven my throat with overstraining it to curse thee. I have ground my teeth to powder with grating and grinding them together for anger, when anie hath nam'd thee. My tongue with vaine threates is bolne, and waxen too big for my mouth. . . . Entreate not, a miracle maye not reprive thee."

The scene is prolonged. Esdras continues to beg for his life; he will become the slave, the chattel of his enemy. An idea comes into the mind of the latter: Sell thy soul to the devil, and I will pardon thee. Esdras immediately utters horrible blasphemies.

"My joints trembled and quakt," continues Cutwolfe, "with attending them, my haire stood upright, and my hart was turned wholly to fire. . . . The veyne in his left hand that is derived from his heart with no faint blow he pierst, and with the bloud that flowd from it, writ a ful obligation of his soule to the divell: yea more earnestly he praied unto God never to forgive his soule than manie Christians doo to save theyr soules. These fearfull ceremonies brought to an end, I bad him ope his mouth and gape wide. He did so: as what wil not slaves doo for feare? Therwith made I no more adoo, but shot him ful into the throat with my pistol: no more spake he after; so did I shoote him that hee might never speak after, or repent him. His body being dead lookd as black as a toad."[1]

This conversation and the sight of Cutwolfe's horrible punishment, recall Jack Wilton to himself. He regrets his irregular life, but not to the point of refunding the money stolen from the Countess Juliana; rich as Gil Blas, he can now, like him, take rank among peaceable and settled folk; he marries his Venetian lady, and returns to the king of England's army, occupied in giving a grand reception to Francis I. at the Field of the Cloth of Gold. There ends the most complete career furnished in England, before Defoe, by a character of fiction.

The primary if not only result of the publication of "Jack Wilton" was, so far as the author himself was

[1] "Works," vol. v. p. 183.

concerned, to place him in new difficulties. His well-known satirical vein, his constant use and abuse of allusions, which often render him obscure, were so well known that it was considered improbable that he had been writing this time with a merely artistic aim. He had been careful to state in his dedication that readers would merely find in his book "some reasonable conveyance of historie and varietie of mirth," and that he was attempting a kind of writing new to him; it was to no purpose. Readers were on the look-out for allusions; they took his historical heroes for living people but thinly disguised, and lined Nash's story with another of their own invention. The author, who well knew the dangers of such interpretations, never ceased to protest that, in this work at least, there was no place for them. When once the public is started upon such a track, it is no easy matter to make them turn round. Nash had recourse to his usual revenge, that is, to laugh at his interpreters. "I am informed," he wrote, shortly after his "Wilton" was printed, "there be certaine busie wits abrode that seeke to anagrammatize the name of Wittenberge to one of the Universities of England; that scorn to be counted honest, plaine meaning men, like their neighbours, for not so much as out of mutton and potage, but they will construe a meaning of kings and princes. Let one but name bread, but they will interpret it to be the town of Bredan in the Low countreyes; if of beere he talkes, then straight he mockes the countie Beroune in France; if of foule weather or a shower of raine, he hath relation to some that shall raigne next."[1]

[1] "Christs teares" (preface of the edition of 1594), "Works,"

His remonstrances seem to have had very indifferent success, and Nash, to our great loss, did not again attempt novel writing. But the vein was in him, and it constantly reappears in the variety of pamphlets he has left behind him. Fine scenes of comedy, good portraits of ridiculous characters to be met in everyday life, amusing anecdotes, nearly all the elements of a sound comic novel are scattered through his writings. The familiar portraits of the upstart, of the false politician, of the inventor of new sects, portraits at which many observers of human nature in the time of Shakespeare tried their hand, are to be seen in the gallery Nash painted in his "Pierce Penilesse."[1] Conformably to the fitness of things, Nash described himself under the name of Pierce,[2] as Sidney had given his high moral tone, his melancholy and loving soul to the shepherd Philisides, as Greene had told his own miseries under the name of poor Roberto. Here is Nash's portrait of the upstart who has travelled abroad and has brought back from his journey nothing more valuable than scorn for his own country : " Hee will bee humorous forsooth and have a broode of fashions by himselfe. Somtimes, because Love commonly wears the liverie of wit, hee will be an *Inamorato poeta*, and sonnet a whole quire of paper in praise of Ladie Manibetter, his yeolowfac'd mistres. . . .

vol. iv. p. 5. He recurs again to the same topic in his " Lenten Stuffe " (1599), and complains that when he talks of rushes it is taken to mean Russia, &c.

[1] " Pierce Penilesse his supplication to the Divell" (1592), "Works," vol. ii.

[2] Nash speaks of himself as being Pierce : "'This is a predestinate fit place for Pierse Pennilesse to set up his staff on." " Lenten Stuffe " " Works," vol. v p. 201.

All *Italionato* is his talke, and his spade peake [*i.e.*, his beard] is as sharpe as if he had been a pioner before the walls of Roan. Hee will dispise the barbarisme of his owne countrey, and tell a whole legend of lyes of his travayles unto Constantinople. If he be challenged to fight . . . hee objects that it is not the custome of the Spaniard or the Germaine to looke backe to everie dog that barks. You shall see a dapper Jacke that hath beene but once at Deepe, wring his face round about, as a man would stirre up a mustard pot and talke English through the teeth, like Jaques Scabdhams, or Monsieur Mingo de Moustrapo ; when, poore slave, he hath but dipt his bread in wylde boares greace and come home againe, or been bitten by the shinnes by a wolfe ; and saith he hath adventured uppon barricadoes of Gurney or Guingan, and fought with the yong Guise hand to hand."

Like Ben Jonson, Nash met on his way some Politick Would-Bes that "thinke to be counted rare politicians and statesmen, by beeing solitarie : as who should say, I am a wise man," [1]—"and when I ope my lips," would have added Shakespeare, "let no dog bark !" He has met inventors of sects, and has heard of pre-Darwinian "mathematicians" who doubt the fact that there were no men before Adam and are inclined to think there are no devils at all. Nash strongly con-

[1] "Works," vol. ii. *Cf.* Ben Jonson : "Sir Politick (speaking to Peregrine) :

"First for your garb, it must be grave and serious,
Very reserv'd and lock'd ; not tell a secret
On any terms, not to your father ; scarce
A fable, but with caution " ("The Fox," act iv. sc. 1).

demns these inventors and mathematicians, drawing at the same time a curious picture of the state of confusion in religious matters which was then so conspicuous in England: "They will set their self love to study to invent new sects of singularitie, thinking to live when they are dead, by having their sect called after their names: as Donatists of Donatus, Arrian[s] of Arrius, and a number more of new faith founders, that have made England the exchange of innovations and almost as much confusion of religion in everie quarter, as there was of tongues at the building of the Tower of Babel...

"Hence atheists triumph and rejoyce and talke as prophanely of the Bible as of Bevis of Hampton. I heare say there are mathematicians abroad that will proove men before Adam; and they are harboured in high places, who will maintayne to the death that there are no divells." [1]

Scenes of light comedy abound in Nash; they are especially numerous in his "Lenten Stuff," [2] a queer little book, his last work, and one which he seems to have written *con amore*. Never was he in better humour than when, the year before his death, he betook himself to singing "the praise of the red herring," Monsieur Herring, Solyman Herring, Sacrapant Herring, Red Herring of Red Herring hall, Pater Patriæ, as he is fond of calling him, inventing on each page a new title for his hero. There is no event in ancient or modern history where he does not discover that

[1] "Works," vol. ii.
[2] "Nashe's Lenten Stuffe, containing the description ... of Great Yarmouth ... with a ... praise of the Red Herring," 1599, "Works," vol. v.

"Cæsarean Charlemaine Herring" has had a part to play; no person of however mean or exalted rank who has not had to deal with "Gentleman Jacke Herring." The fishes made him their king, and the Pope made him a saint. The first time he appeared at the Pope's court was a great event in Christendom. An English sailor had sold him for three hundred ducats to the purveyor of the papal kitchen, and "delivered him the king of fishes, teaching hym to geremumble it, sauce it, and dresse it, and so sent him away a glad man. All the Pope's cookes in their white sleeves and linnen aprons met him middle way to entertaine and receyve the king of fishes, and together by the eares they went, who shoulde first handle him or touch him. But the clarke of the kitchin appeased that strife, and would admit none but him selfe to have the scorching and carbonadoing of it, and he kissed his hands thrice, and made as many *humblessos* before he woulde finger it; and, such obeysances performed, he drest it as he was enjoyned, kneeling on his knes, and mumbling twenty *Ave Maryes* to hymselfe, in the sacrifizing of it on the coales, that his diligent service in the broyling and combustion of it, both to his kingship and to his fatherhood might not seeme unmeritorious." [1]

However careful Thomas Nash had been to act according to the views attributed to Dr. Andrew Borde concerning the cultivation of mirth as a preservative of health, he reached what this authority calls "the mirth of heaven," with much more rapidity than might have been expected. His mirth diet was obviously adulterated and mingled with wrath and sorrow. He

[1] "Lenten Stuffe," vol. v. p. 280.

had been born in 1567, and we read about him in a comedy performed at Cambridge in 1601, these verses which are friendly if not very poetical:

"TOM NASH HIS GHOST."

"Let all his faultes sleepe with his mournfull chest,
And there for ever with his ashes rest,
His style was wittie, though it had some gall,
Some things he might have mended, so may all,
Yet this I say, that for a mother witt,
Few men have ever seen the like of it."[1]

---

[1] "The Returne from Pernassus," ed. W. D. Macray, Oxford, 1886, p. 87.

The manner in which his friend Dekker represents him, shortly after, reaching the Elysian fields, leaves little doubt that his life was shortened not only by his angry passions, but by sheer want : "Marlow, Greene and Peele had got under the shades of a large vyne, laughing to see Nash, that was but newly come to their colledge, still haunted with the sharpe and satyricall spirit that followed him heere upon earthe : for Nash inveyed bitterly, as he had wont to do against dryfisted patrons, accusing them of his untimely death, because if they had given his Muse that cherishment which she most worthily deserved, hee had fed to his dying day on fat capons, burnt sack and sugar, and not so desperately have venturde his life and shortned his dayes by keeping company with pickle herrings."[1]

III.

Some of Shakespeare's contemporaries attempted to give their readers " the like " of Nash's wit, and tried their hand either at the picaresque novel or at the reproduction of scenes taken from ordinary life, of which Greene also had left some examples. The comic school was far from equalling the fecundity of its romantic rival; it existed however, and though absolutely forgotten now, it helped to keep up and improve the natural gift of observation which belonged to the English race.

One of the most extraordinary ventures ever at-

[1] "A Knights Conjuring," 1607, "Works," ed. Grosart, vol. v. p. xx.

tempted in the picaresque style was made by Henry
Chettle, another member of the group to which Greene,
Nash, and the others belonged. He was, like Nash
himself, a personal friend of Greene, and published after
his death his " Groats-worth of wit," 1592, for which,
as we have seen, he had to offer in his next pamphlet
explanations and apologies, among others, to Shakespeare. Chettle seems to have followed the literary
career usual in his time; he composed many dramas
alone[1] or in collaboration; he was perpetually borrowing money from the notorious Henslowe, and he was
occasionally lodged in Her Majesty's prisons. In 1595
he published his " Piers Plainnes seaven yeres pren-
tiship,"[2] in which we find, mingled together, Sidney's
Arcady, Greene's romantic heroes, and the customary
incidents of picaresque novels. The scene is laid in
Tempe; there are Menalcas and Corydons; there are
sheep who are poetically invited by their keeper to eat
their grass:

> "Sport on faire flocke at pleasure
> Nip Vestaes flouring treasure."

There is too Piers Plain, now a shepherd but
formerly nothing short of a picaro, who has seen much
and has followed many trades, and served many masters.
His companions asked for his story, and he very
willingly agreed to tell them what he had been, "and

---

[1] Only one of this sort has been preserved: "The tragedy of Hoffman or a revenge for a father," published in 1631. Chettle died about 1607.

[2] London, 1595, 4to. It has never been reprinted; only one copy belonging to the Bodleian Library is known to exist.

what the world is," no mean subject to be sure, and no wonder that he " cravde pardon to sit because the taske was long, which they willingly graunted." Piers, according to the picaresque traditions, had been the servant of many masters; he tells his experience of them in the first person, following also in this the rules of the picaresque tale. He first introduces us to a swaggering and cowardly courtier, and plays his part in intrigues and conspiracies. Then he describes the " vertuous and famous virgin Æliana," Queen of Crete, who delighted in hunting, and went to the woods " Diana-like." To be " Diana-like," she dressed as follows :

" On her head she wore a coronet of orientall pearle ; on it a chaplet of variable flowers perfuming the ayre with their divers odors, thence carelessly descended her amber coloured hair . . . Her buskins were richly wrought like the Delphins spangled cabazines ; her quiver was of unicornes horne, her darts of yvorie ; in one hand she helde a boare speare, the other guided her Barbary jennet, proud by nature, but nowe more proude in that he carried natures fairest worke, the Easterne worlds chiefe wonder." In a somewhat similar style Zucchero painted the Queen, not of Crete, but of England, and when dressed in this fashion, Her Majesty too, was supposed to be represented " Diana-like."

Of the misrule in Crete, and of the dangers Æliana runs from the incestuous passions of her uncle, and of her escape through the providential intervention of Prince Æmilius, we shall say nothing ; nor of the " frolicke common-wealth " established in Thrace, feeling as we do some sympathy with Corydon, who interrupts the speaker, saying: "Reach hither thy bottle that we may drinke round; I am sure thou must needes be dry with talking when I am so a thirst with hearing." Piers passes from the court to the shop of a dealer in old clothes and an usurer. He leads a very miserable life, and we have sordid descriptions of scenes in low life with which Chettle was better acquainted than with the loves of Æmilius and Æliana. Princes and princesses come in again; there are revolutions, awful dangers and marvellous deliverances. All ends happily, and Piers and his hearers agree to meet "at theyr ploughman's holidaye. Where what happened, if Piers Plainnes please, shall per adventure be published." This "adventure" never took place. The incoherent mixture of the picaresque, romantic, and Arcadian tale resulted in such an unpalatable compound that even novel-readers of Shakespeare's time objected to a narration of this kind, and did not trouble Chettle with a demand for its continuation.

His reputation therefore rests mainly on his dramas. One of his most frequent associates in writing them, and one of the most prolific and gifted, Thomas Dekker, was also something of a novelist. He has left, besides a great quantity of plays, a number of pamphlets written very much in Nash's vein,[1] in which there is some excellent realism, together with the

---

[1] Some also are in Greene's and Harman's vein; for example, his "Belman of London," 1608, and his "Lanthorne and candle-light," 1608, in which he describes, with no less success than his predecessors, "the most notorious villanies that are now practised in the kingdome."

most amusing and whimsical fancies.[1] His biography is a mere repetition of his friend's life, and the words: Henslowe, drama, penury, pamphlets, prison, quarrels, put together, will give a sufficient idea of the sort of existence led by him as well as by so many of his associates.[2] He wrote some of his plays alone, many others with numberless collaborators, such as Chettle, Drayton, Wilson, Ben Jonson (with whom he afterwards had a violent quarrel), Haughton, Day, Munday, Hathaway, Middleton, Webster, Heywood, Wentworth Smith, Massinger, Ford, Rowley, and even others, for

[1] "Dramatic Works, now first collected," London (Pearson), 1873, 4 vol. 8vo.; "Non-Dramatic Works," ed. Grosart, London, 1884, 5 vol. 4to, which non-dramatic works are the following:
I. "Canaans Calamite, Jerusalem's misery," 1611 (a poem on the siege and destruction of Jerusalem by the Romans); "The wonderfull yeare 1603" (on the plague of London); "The Batchelars banquet," 1603 (an adaptation of the "Quinze joyes de mariage"). II. "The seven deadly sinnes of London ... bringing the plague with them," 1606; "Newes from Hell," 1606, shortly after reprinted as "A Knights conjuring"; "The double P.P., a papist in armes," 1606 (in verse); "The Guls Hornebooke," 1609; "Jests to make you merie," 1607. III. "Dekker his dreame," 1620 (in verse); "The Belman of London," 1608; "Lanthorne and candle-light," 1609; "A strange horse race, at the end of which comes in the catch-poles masque," 1613. IV. "The dead tearme or ... a dialogue betweene the two cityes of London and Westminster," 1608; "Worke for armourers ... open warres likely to happin," 1609; "The ravens Almanacke, foretelling of a plague," &c., 1609; "A rod for run-awayes, in which ... they may behold many fearefull Judgements of God ... expressed in many dreadfull examples of sudden death," 1625. V. "Foure birdes of Noahs Arke," 1613; "The pleasant comodie of Patient Grissil," 1603 (with Chettle and Haughton).

[2] Only there was this notable difference, he died old, at about seventy years of age, probably in 1641.

the dramatic faculty was then so very common that any one, so to say, was good enough to act as a collaborator in writing plays.

He had many traits in common with Nash: the same excellent faculty of observation, the same gaiety and *entrain*, with powers of his own to associate it with the most exquisite tenderness and pathos; the same love for literature and for the poets, for Chaucer, for Spenser, whose arrival in the Elysian fields he describes in a way to tempt the pencil of a painter: " Grave Spenser was no sooner entred into this chappell of Apollo, but these elder fathers of the divine furie gave him a lawrer and sung his welcome; Chaucer call'd him his sonne and plac'd him at his right hand. All of them, at a signe given by the whole quire of the Muses that brought him thither, closing up their lippes in silence, and turning all their eares for attention to heare him sing out the rest of Fayrie Queenes prayses."[1]

But a marked difference between Dekker and Nash resulted from the fact that Dekker had not only a love of poetry, but a poetical faculty of a high order. He went far beyond the picturesqueness of Nash's word-painting, and reached in his prose as well as in his verse true lyrical emotion and pathos; he had, said Lamb, " poetry enough for anything;"[2] and while

---

[1] "A Knights conjuring," 1607. In the same happy retreat Dekker, gives a place to Watson, Kyd, Marlowe, Greene, Peele, Nash, Chettle, who comes in "sweating and blowing, by reason of his fatness" ("Non-Dramatic Works," vol. v. p. xx.).

[2] "Notes on the Elizabethan Dramatists"; "Philip Massinger; Thomas Dekker."

Nash's gaiety, true and hearty as it is, takes often and naturally a bitter satirical turn, Dekker's gaiety though sometimes bitter, more usually takes a pretty, graceful, and fanciful turn. " Come, strew apace, strew, strew:

"DEKKER HIS DREAM."

in good troth tis a pitty that these flowers must be trodden under feete as they are like to be anon . . .

" Pitty? come foole, fling them about lustily; flowers never dye a sweeter death than when they are smother'd to death in a Lovers bosome, or else pave the high wayes over which these pretty, simpering, setting things call'd brides must trippe." [1]

Intimate literary ties, however, existed between Nash and Dekker; many passages in the one remind us of similar things in the other, the result sometimes of actual imitation, sometimes of involuntary reminiscences. Dekker was well aware of the family likeness between the two, so much so that we see him once calling Nash's ghost to his assistance, as one from whom he might most naturally gain help: "And thou into whose soule . . . the raptures of that fierie and inconfinable Italian spirit were bounteously and boundlesly infused; thou sometimes secretary to Pierce Pennylesse and master of his requests, ingenious, ingenuous, fluent, facetious T. Nash, from whose aboundant pen hony flow'd to thy friends, and mortall aconite to thy enemies; thou that madest the doctor a flat dunce [2] . . . sharpest satyre, luculent poet, elegant orator, get leave for thy ghost to come from her abiding and to dwell with me awhile." [3]

Nash's ghost was most certainly hovering about Dekker when he was writing the pamphlet from which this apostrophe is taken; it taught him how to disrobe for our amusement the heroes of antique legends of their dignified looks and dresses, and place their haloed selves in the open daylight of the street below our

[1] "Satiro-mastix or the untrussing of the humorous poet," 1602. "Dramatic Works" vol. i. p. 186. This is the play Dekker wrote as a revenge for Ben Jonson's "Poetaster," 1601, in which he was himself ridiculed under the name of Demetrius.

[2] *I.e.*, Gabriel Harvey, Nash's obstinate adversary.

[3] "Newes from Hell," "Non-Dramatic Works," vol. ii. pp. 102–103.

window. With all his admiration for Marlowe's performance Nash had told, in very ludicrous fashion indeed, the story of Hero and Leander, associating in a manner unwarranted by ancient historians their fate with the vicissitudes of Great Yarmouth and the red herring. In the same way Dekker makes choice of that exquisite tale of Orpheus which reads so pathetically in the prose of King Alfred, and he tells it thus:

"Assist mee therefore, thou genius of that ventrous but zealous musicion of Thrace, Euridice's husband, who being besotted on his wife, of whiche sin none but . . . should be guiltie, went alive with his fiddle at's backe, to see if he could bail her out of that adamantine prison. The fees he was to pay for her were jigs and countrey-daunces: he paid them; the forfeits if he put on yellow stockings and lookt back upon her, was her everlasting lying there, without bayle or mayne-prize. The loving coxcomb could not choose but look backe, and so lost her: perhaps hee did it because he would be rid of her. The morall of which is, that if a man leave his owne busines and have an eie to his wives dooings, sheele give him the slip though she runne to the divell for her labour."[1]

Dekker did not write novels properly so called, but his prose works abound with scenes that seem detached from novels, and that were so well fitted for that kind of writing that we find them again in the works of professional novelists of his or of a later time. His "Wonderfull yeare 1603," from which Defoe seems to have taken several hints, abounds in scenes of this

[1] "Newes from Hell," "Non-Dramatic Works," vol. ii. p. 101.

sort.[1] It is a book "wherein is shewed the picture of London lying sicke of the plague. At the ende of all, like a mery epilogue to a dull play sundry tales are cut out in sundry fashions of purpose to shorten the lives of long winters nights that lye watching in the darke for us." Some of these tales are extremely well told, for Dekker is more successful in describing the humours than the terrors of the plague. In one of them we find another copy of the fat hostler so well described already by Nash and, as it seems, inspired by a reminiscence of the picture in "Jack Wilton." Dekker's man is not thinner, cleaner, nor braver than Nash's victualler. He is a country innkeeper : "a goodly fat burger he was, with a belly arching out like a beere-barrell, which made his legges, that were thicke and short like two piles driven under London bridge. . . . In some corners of [his nose] there were blewish holes that shone like shelles of mother of pearle . . . . other were richly garnisht with rubies, chrisolites, and carbunckles, which glistered so oriently, that the Hamburgers offered I know not how many dollars for his companie in an East-Indian voyage, to have stoode a nightes in the poope of their Admirall, onely to save the charge of candles.

"In conclusion he was an host to be ledde before an Emperour, and though he were one of the greatest men in all the shire, his bignes made him not proude, but he humbled himself to speake the base language of a tapster, and uppon the Londoners first arrival, cried : 'Welcome! a cloth for this gentleman !' The

[1] "Non-Dramatic Works," vol. i. Cf. Defoe's "Journal of the plague year . . . 1665," London, 1722.

linnen was spread and furnisht presently with a new cake and a can, the roome voided, and the guest left, like a French Lord, attended by no bodie." [1]

This new-comer, freshly arrived from London was flying on account of the plague; but it so happened that he had himself already contracted the disease; he was scarcely seated before it grew upon him and he fell dead. Great was the terror in the inn. The host, the maids, all the inmates ran from the corpse and left the house; the terror spread in the borough; no one would even walk near the place.

"At last a tinker came sounding through the towne, mine hosts being the auncient watring place where he did use to cast anchor. You must understand he was none of those base rascally tinkers that with a bandog and a drab at their tayles and a picke staffe at their necks will take a purse sooner then stop a kettle. No this was a devout tinker, he did honor God Pan; a musicall tinker, that upon his kettle-drum could play any countrey-dance you cald for, and upon Holly-dayes had earned money by it, when no fidler could be heard of. Hee was onely feared when he stalkt through some towns where bees were, for he strucke so sweetely on the bottome of his copper instrument that he would emptie whole hives and leade the swarmes after him, only by the sound."

These two beings, the host and tinker, depicted as vividly by Dekker as Callot would have drawn them, meet in the open air, and the former offers the tinker a crown if he undertakes to bury the dead man. The tinker haggles for better payment and they agree for

[1] "Non-Dramatic Works," vol. i. pp. 138 *et seq.*

ten shillings. "The whole parish had warning of this presently . . . therefore ten shillings were leveyed out of hand, put into a rag, which was tyed to the ende of a long pole and delivered, in sight of all the parish, who stood aloofe stopping their noses, by the head boroughs owne selfe in proper person." Nothing dismayed by this awful array, the tinker sits at table, drinks deep, takes the corpse on his back and carries it to a field. Before committing it to the earth he carefully searches its pockets and empties them ; he then makes a parcel of the clothes "and carrying that at the end of his staffe on his shoulder, with the purse of seven pounds in his hand, backe againe comes he through the towne, crying aloud : ' Have you any more Londoners to bury ; Hey downe a downe dery ; Have you any more Londoners to bury ?' The Hobbinolls running away from him as if he had beene the dead citizens ghost, and he marching away from them in all the hast he could, with that song still in his mouth."

Another sort of writing congenial to Dekker's temperament, and which novelists of a later date continued to cultivate after him, are those series of counsels or praises in which, with due seriousness, the thing is recommended or praised which ought to be avoided. An example of this kind of satirical composition is the famous "Quinze joyes de mariage," in which the pleasant humours of a young wife are described in such a way as to deter even a Panurge from marrying. Another example is the "Grobianus"[1]

---

[1] "Grobianus. De morum simplicitate, libri duo. In gratiam omnium rusticitatem amantium conscripti," Francfort, 1549,

Latin poem of the German F. Dedekind, which enjoyed
an immense reputation throughout Europe in the sixteenth century; it contains ironical advice to a gallant
with regard to his behaviour so that in any given
circumstances he may be as objectionable and improper
as possible.

Dekker translated both works into English, but
with many alterations, so numerous indeed, especially
in the last, that his book may be considered almost
original.[1] He called it "The Guls Horne-booke," or
alphabet. He gives in it a lively description of the
humours of gallants in the time of Shakespeare, of the
places they used to frequent, and the company they
liked to meet. Grobianism differs from the picaresque
tale by the absence of a story connecting the various
scenes, but it resembles it in the opportunity it affords
for describing a variety of characters, humours, and
places. In the same way as we follow the picaro in
the houses of his several masters, we here follow the
gallant from his rooms to his ordinary, and from St.

8vo. It was translated into English by "R. F.," a little before
Dekker adapted it: "The schoole of slovenrie : or Cato turned
wrong side outward . . . to the use of all English Christendome,"
London, 1605, 4to. In the same category of works may be
placed Erasmus's famous: "Moriae Encomium," Antwerp, 1512,
4to, translated by Sir T. Chaloner: "The Praise of Folie,"
London, 1549, 4to. Many scenes in the comedies of the period
are written in a style akin to Grobianism. They are especially
to be found in Ben Jonson; see, for example, his satire of courtiers in "Cynthia's revels," act iii. sc. 1 and 3, &c.; note how
their elegancies of speech are mostly derived from plays and novels.

[1] "The Bachelars banquet . . . pleasantly discoursing the
various humours of women," 1603; "The Guls Horne-booke,'
1609; "Non-Dramatic Works," vols. i. and ii.

Paul's to the play. We climb with him to the top of the cathedral, we show our new garments in the walks, meet courtiers, soldiers and poets at dinner, stroll at night in the dark streets of the city and fall in with the watch. Here, again, Dekker paints from life scenes with which he was familiar, and we have but to follow his footsteps to become acquainted with the haunts of the Bohemians of his time, and of the great men too, of Jonson and Shakespeare themselves.

The scene at the theatre is the most original and lively of all. The serio-comic advice to the gallant how he "should behave himself in a playhouse"[1] is a perfect picture of what was daily taking place, be the play Shakespeare's "Hamlet" or Dekker's "Patient Grissil."[2] Of course the gallant must sit on the stage and " on the very rushes," which in the theatre, and also in palaces and houses, continued as in the Middle Ages to serve for carpets;[3] he will not care for the disapprobation of the groundlings, but must plant himself valiantly, " beating downe the mewes and hisses of opposed rascality.

"For do but cast up a reckoning; what large commings-in are pursd up by sitting on the stage? First a conspicuous eminence is gotten; by which meanes, the best and most essencial parts of a gallant (good cloathes, a proportionable legge, white

[1] "Non-Dramatic Works," vol. ii. pp. 246 *et seq*.
[2] 1603; with Chettle and Haughton.
[3] A scene at court. "*Amorphus* (to the prentice courtier Asotus): If you had but so far gathered your spirits to you as to have taken up a rush when you were out, and wagged it thus, or cleansed your teeth with it; or but turn'd aside . . ." &c. Ben Jonson, "Cynthia's Revels," act iii. sc. 1.

hand, the Persian lock, and a tollerable beard), are perfectly revealed."

Of course you must choose with the greatest care your time to come in. "Present not your selfe on the stage especially at a new play until the quaking Prologue hath, by rubbing, got [colour] into his cheekes and is ready to give the trumpets their cue that hees upon point to enter; for then it is time, as though you were one of the properties, or that you dropt out of ye hangings, to creepe from behind the arras, with your tripos or three-footed stoole in one hand and a teston (*i.e.*, six pence) mounted betweene a forefinger and a thumbe in the other; for if you should bestow your person upon the vulgar when the belly of the house is but halfe full, your apparell is quite eaten up, the fashion lost . . ."[1]

When the play is well begun, there is also a special behaviour to observe: "It shall crowne you with rich commendation to laugh alowd in the middest of the most serious and saddest scene of the terriblest tragedy; and to let that clapper your tongue, be tost so high that all the house may ring of it: your lords use it; your knights are apes to the lords, and do so too . . . be thou a beagle to them all. . . . [At] first, all the eyes in the galleries will leave walking after the players and onely follow you; the simplest dolt in the house snatches up your name, and when he meetes you in

[1] *Cf.* Ben Jonson: "Why, throw yourself in state on the stage, as other gentlemen use, sir."—"Away, wag; what, would'st thou make an implement of me? 'Slid, the boy takes me for a piece of perspective, I hold my life, or some silk curtain, come to hang the stage here" ("Cynthia's Revels," Induction).

the streetes, . . . heele cry : ' hees such a gallant.' . . . Secondly you publish your temperance to the world, in that you seeme not to resort thither to taste vaine pleasures with a hungrie appetite ; but only as a gentleman to spend a foolish houre or two, because you can doe nothing else ; thirdly you mightily disrelish the audience and disgrace the author." Perhaps the next time he will be wise enough to offer you a dedication sonnet " onely to stop your mouth."

The getting away must not be less carefully performed than the getting in. If you owe the author a particular grudge, mind you leave just in the middle of his play : " bee it Pastoral or Comedy, Morall or Tragedie, you rise with a screwd and discontented face from your stoole to be gone : no matter whether the scenes be good or no ; the better they are, the worse you distast them. And being on your feet, sneake not away like a coward ; but salute all your gentle acquaintance, that are spred either on the rushes or on stooles about you ; and draw what troope you can from the stage after you. The mimicks are beholden to you for allowing them elbow roome ; their poet cries perhaps, 'A pox go with you'; but care not for that ; there is no musick without frets."

But the rain outside may deprive you of the benefits of this carefully laid plan. In that case, and this is the last piece of advice, here is what you must do : " If either the company or indisposition of the weather binde you to sit it out, my counsell is then that you turne plain ape : take up a rush, and tickle the earnest eares of your fellow gallants to make other fooles fall a laughing; mewe at passionate speeches; blare at merrie; find fault with the musicke; whew at the children's action, whistle at the songs."

Dekker knew only too well such gallants as those he describes, and if his picture of a theatre in Shakespeare's time seems now somewhat exaggerated, if we cannot conceive "Hamlet" or "Romeo" performed while gallants on the stage tickle each other's ears with rushes picked from the stage boards, let us remember as a confirmation of his accuracy that such customs were prevalent, not only in England, but in Europe. In France especially, even in the time of the Grand Roi, when Molière and Corneille were shining in all their glory, we have Molière's corroborating evidence that these customs had not been abolished. Molière was annoyed by the same malpractices as Shakespeare, only he did not, like Shakespeare, who never complained of anything or anybody, keep his displeasure to himself. He recurs in more than one of his plays to the indecent behaviour of marquesses sitting on the stage, and there is scarcely one of the particulars mentioned by Dekker which does not find place in Molière's angry pictures of ill-bred gallants:

"The actors began; every one kept silence; when ... a man with large rolls entered abruptly crying out: 'Hulloa, there, a seat directly!' and disturbing the audience with his uproar, interrupted the play in its finest passage. ...

"Whilst I was shrugging my shoulders, the actors attempted to continue their parts. But the man made a fresh disturbance in seating himself, and again crossing the stage with long strides, although he might have been quite comfortable at the wings, he planted his chair full in front, and, defying the audience with his broad back, hid the actors from three-fourths of the pit.

"A murmur arose, at which any one else would have felt ashamed; but he, firm and resolute, took no notice of it, and would have remained just as he had placed himself if, to my misfortune, he had not cast his eyes on me. . . .

"He began asking me a hundred frivolous questions, raising his voice higher than the actors. Every one was cursing him; and in order to check him, I said, 'I should like to listen to the play.'

"'Hast thou not seen it, marquis? Oh! on my soul I think it very funny, and I am no fool in those matters. I know the canons of perfection and Corneille reads me all that he writes.'

"Thereupon he gave me a summary of the piece informing me, scene after scene, of what was about to happen; and when we came to any lines which he knew by heart, he recited them aloud before the actor could say them. It was in vain for me to resist; he continued his recitations, and towards the end rose a good while before the rest. For those fashionable fellows, in order to behave gallantly, especially avoid to listen to the conclusion."[1]

Grobianism and the picaresque novel, long survived both Nash and Dekker. English, Spanish, and French rogues, invented or imitated, swarmed in the

[1] "Les Fâcheux," act i. sc. 1 (Van Laun's translation, vol. ii. p. 97); cf. "Critique de l'Ecole des Femmes," sc. vi.

English literature of the seventeenth century, without, however, in any case reaching the level attained by "Jack Wilton." Both kinds of writing had to wait for the time of Swift and Defoe to reach their highest point. Defoe has left the best examples of the picaresque tale extant in English literature, and Swift revived Grobianism with unparalleled excellence in his "Directions to Servants" and his "Complete Collection of genteel and ingenious conversation, according to the most polite mode and method now used at court and in the best companies of England."[1]

As for the "Quinze joyes," turned also into English by Dekker, its popularity was equally great in England; a new and different translation was published in the seventeenth century and had several editions. It was prefaced with a note " to the Reader," in which the satirical aims of the author in this study of woman's foibles is accentuated by a tone of pretended praise, savouring of Grobianism and anticipating the sort of ridicule which was to be relished by Pope and the critics of Queen Anne's time. " This treatise . . . will at least shake, if not totally explode, that common opinion, viz., that women are the worst piece of the Hexameron creation. . . . This is the composition of some amorous person, who, animated with the same

[1] The connection of Swift with Grobianism was noticed in his time, and a new translation of Dedekind's poem, " Grobianus or the compleat Booby," 1739, was dedicated by Roger Bull " to the Rev. Dr. Jonathan Swift, . . . who first introduced into these kingdoms . . . an ironical manner of writing, to the discouragement of vice, ill-manners and folly." To come to even nearer times, Flaubert's "Bouvart et Pecuchet" may be taken as a branch of Grobianism.

spirit and affection as I am, hath undertaken, and judged it his duty too, to satisfie you, and he hopes so far as to work upon you a persuasion that the modesty, bashfulness, debonaireté and civility, together with all qualifications that adorn and beautifie the soul, are as exemplarily eminent in women of this age as ever they were in any of the former ; and instruct you to set a value on their actions as the best creatures in the worst of times, whose vertue must needs shine with the greater lustre, being subject to the vain assaults and ineffectual temptations of men grown old, like the times, in wickednes, malice and revenge." [1]

[1] "The fifteen comforts of rash and inconsiderate marriage . . . done out of French," London, 1694, 12mo, fourth edition.

CAPRICORNUS.

HEROICAL DEEDS IN A HEROICAL NOVEL, 1665.

CHAPTER VII.

AFTER SHAKESPEARE.

I.

IN the works of Nash and his imitators, the different parts are badly dovetailed; the novelist is incoherent and incomplete; the fault lies in some degree with the picaresque form itself. Nash, however, pointed out the right road, the road that was to lead to the true novel. He was the first among his compatriots to endeavour to relate in prose a long-sustained story, having for its chief concern: the truth. He leaves to his real heroes, Surrey, More, Erasmus, Aretino, their historical character, and he gives to his fictitious ones caprices and qualities which make of them distinct and living beings like those of every-day life. He gives us no more languid shepherds, no more romantic disguises, no more pretended warriors whose helmets cover, as in Ariosto, a woman's fair locks. His style is flexible, animated, suited to the circumstances, free from those ornaments of language so sought after in his time; no one, Ben Jonson excepted, possessed at that epoch, in so great a degree as himself, a love of the honest truth. With Nash, then, the novel of real life, whose invention in England is generally attributed to Defoe, begins. To connect Defoe with the past of English literature, we must get over the whole of the seventeenth century and go back to "Jack Wilton," the worthy brother of "Roxana," "Moll Flanders," and "Colonel Jack."

But shepherds were not yet silenced, nor had romantic heroes spoken their last. On the contrary, their best time was still to come; in the seventeenth century they resumed their hardly interrupted speeches, conversations, correspondence, exploits and adventures, and flourished mightily in the world. We come to the time of the heroic romance and heroic drama. The main originality of the romance literature in England during this century was the ncrease and over-refinement of heroism in works of fiction. For many among the reading public of that age, Shakespeare was barbarous and Racine tame; but Scudéry was the "greatest wit" that ever lived.

This kind of writing was thus partially renovated

through certain superadded characteristics, the part
allotted to "heroism" being the foremost; but the
groundwork was as old as the very origin of the nation.
For this new species of novel was mainly a development
of the old chivalrous romances of early and mediæval
times. These romances, as we know, had continued in
Elizabethan times to enjoy some reputation, and under
an altered shape to have a public of their own. Even
in the seventeenth century they had not passed entirely
out of sight. Palmerins, Dons Belianis and Esplandians
continued to be written, translated, adapted, para-
phrased, printed, purchased, and read. There was still
a brisk trade in this sort of literature. People continued to read "the auncient, famous and honourable
history of Amadis de Gaule, discoursing the adventures
loves and fortunes of many princes;"[1] or again "the
famous history of Hercules of Greece, with the manner
of his encountering and overcoming serpents, lyons,
monsters, giants, tyrants and powerful armies."[2] Guy
of Warwick, our friend of former chapters, still carried
on, with undaunted energy, his manifold exploits
throughout the world. Only, as time passes, we find
that he has become civilized; he has taken trouble
to improve his mind, he has read books; he has even
gone to the play. And his choice shows him a man
of taste and feeling; a man with a memory too; for
reaching a cemetery somewhere in his travels he "took

[1] London, 1619, fol., translated by Anthony Munday (first
edition of first part, 1590, 4to). Another translation of the same
romance was made by F. Kirkman, and published in 1652, 4to.

[2] Advertised by Ch. Bates at the end of "the history of Guy
earl of Warwick," London, 1680 (?), 4to (illustrated).

up a worm-eaten skull, which he thus addressed: Perhaps thou wert a prince or a mighty monarch, a King, a Duke or a Lord. But the King and the beggar must all return to the earth; and therefore man hath need to remember his dying hour. Perhaps thou mightest have been a Queen or a Dutchess, or a Lady varnished with much beauty; but now thou art worms meat, lying in the grave, the sepolchre of all creatures." We are only surprised that "Alas poor

SIR GUY OF WARWICK ADDRESSING A SKULL.

Yorick" does not come in. The page is beautifully adorned with an engraving representing Sir Guy in cocked hat, addressing a skull he carries in his hand.[1]

The same phenomenon was taking place in France, and from France were to come the first examples of the regular heroic romance. "I have read [Lancelot]" says Sarasin, in a conversation reported by the well-known Jean Chapelain, the author of "La Pucelle," and "I have not found it too unpleasant. Among the things that have pleased me in it I found that it was

[1] From a chap-book of the eighteenth century: "History of Guy earl of Warwick," 1750 (?)

the source of all the romances which for four or five centuries have been the noblest entertainment of all the courts of Europe and have prevented barbarism from encompassing the whole world."[1] But as well as Guy of Warwick, Lancelot wanted some "rajeunissement." His valour was still the fashion, but his manners, after so many centuries, and his dress too, were a little out of date. The new heroism was to pervade the whole man, and, in order to make him acceptable, to influence his costume as well as his mind.

BURIAL OF SIR GUY OF WARWICK.

There was to be something Roman in him, and something French; he was to be represented in the style of Louis the Fourteenth's statues, where the monarch appears in a Roman tunic and a French wig.

The transformation occurred first in France, and was received with great applause. The times indeed were most propitious for a display, not of the barbaric heroism of olden times, but of courtly heroism; of an

[1] "De la Lecture des vieux romans," by Jean Chapelain, ed. Feillet, Paris, 1870, 8vo.

heroism which plumes, wigs and ribbons well fitted, and which, with scarcely any change, could be transferred from the battle field to the drawing-room, from Rocroy to the Hôtel de Rambouillet : no mean heroism, however, for all its ribbons. At this period, in France, manly and lofty virtues, as well as worldly ones, were worshipped in life, in literature and in art. From the commencement to the end of the century, examples of undoubted heroes were not lacking ; Henri IV., Richelieu, Mme. de Longueville, Condé, Louis XIV., Turenne, now by their good qualities, now by their caprices, now by their deeds and now by their looks, resembled heroes of romance, and popularized in France an ideal of nobleness and greatness. In order to please and to be admired, it was necessary to show a lofty character ; men must be superior to fortune, and women must appear superior to the allurements of passion ; the hero made a display of magnanimity, the heroine of chastity. The hero won the battle of Fribourg, and the heroine had Montausier to pay court to her for thirteen years before she consented to be united to him in the bonds of wedlock. Such were the persons most admired in real life ; such were the characters of romance and tragedy whom the public liked best, without, however, distinguishing between them. The Cid, Alceste, Artaban, Nicomède, as well as Julie d'Angennes, Montausier and Condé, were all members of the same family, and not any one of them more than another appeared comic or ridiculous : that is why Montausier was very far from being offended that traits of the character of Alceste were thought to be found in him, and that is why Mme. de

Sévigné, a passionate admirer of Corneille, becomes as honestly enthusiastic over the extravagant heroes of the new romances as over those of the great Cornelian tragedies. "I am mad for Corneille ; everything must yield to his genius ... My daughter, let us take good care not to compare Racine with him. Let us feel the difference!"[1] She writes elsewhere with regard to the heroes of La Calprenède: "The beauty of the sentiments, the violence of the emotions, the grandeur of the incidents and the miraculous success of their invincible swords, all that delights me like a young girl."[2] This change, which consisted, not of course in the introduction of heroism into novels, where it had in all times found place, but in the magnifying, to an extraordinary degree, of this source of interest, and in a transformation of costume and of tone of speech, appeared not only in romances, but in the drama also, and even in history. Everything worthy of attention was for many years to be heroical. Heroes defy earth and heaven ; they do not, like Aucassin, with a temper of ironical submission, give up Paradise in the hope of joining Nicolete in the

[1] Edition of the "Grands Ecrivains de la France," vol. ii. pp. 529 and 535.
[2] 12th July, 1671, "Grands Ecrivains," vol. ii. p. 277. A few days before, on the 5th, she had been writing : " Je suis revenue à 'Cléopatre'... et par le bonheur que j'ai de n'avoir point de mémoire, cette lecture me divertit encore. Cela est épouvantable, mais vous savez que je ne m'accommode guere bien de toutes les pruderies qui ne me sont pas naturelles, et comme celle de ne pas aimer ces livres là ne m'est pas encore entièrement arrivée, je me laisse divertir sous le pretexte de mon fils qui m'a mise en train."

nether world; they make the nether world itself tremble on its foundations: for nothing can resist them. Even in serious historical works the old rulers of the French nation appear under an heroical garb. King Clovis is thus described by Scipion Dupleix, historiographer royal, in his "Histoire Générale de France," 1634: "The hour of Easter-eve at which the King was to receive the baptism at the hands of St. Remy having come, he appeared with a proud countenance, a dignified gait, a majestic port, very richly dressed, musked and powdered; his flowing wig was curiously combed, curled, frizzed, undulated and perfumed, according to the custom of the old french Kings;"[1] but much more it seems according to the custom of less ancient sovereigns; and there is at the Louvre, a portrait of Louis XIII. bare-legged, periwigged, ermine-cloaked, which corresponds far better to this description than anything we know of Clovis.

The same characteristics appear in the epic and the drama. Antoine de Montchrestien, besides having written the earliest treatise of political economy, and thus having stood, if nothing more, godfather to a new science,[2] wrote a number of plays, flavoured most of them with a grandiloquence and heroism which give us a foretaste of Dryden. In his "Aman ou

[1] "L'heure de la veille de Pasques, à laquelle le Roy devoit recevoir le baptesme de la main de S. Remy estant venue, il s'y présenta avec une contenance relevée, une démarche grave, un port majestueux, très richement vestu, musqué, poudré, la perruque pendante, curieusement peignée, gauffrée, ondoiante, crespée et parfumée, selon la coustume des anciens rois François" ("Histoire Générale de France," Paris, 1634, vol. i. p. 58).

[2] "Traicté de l'Economie politique," Rouen, 1615, 4to.

la vanité," he treats the same subject as Racine in his "Esther," but he has nothing in common with his successor, and much with the dramatists of the heroical school. In order, doubtless, to justify from the first the title of the play, Aman indulges his " vanité" in an opening monologue to the following effect :

"Whether fair Phœbus coming out of the hollow waters brings back colour to the face of the world, whether with his warmer rays he sets day ablaze or departs to take his rest in his watery bower, he cannot see in all the inhabited world a single man to be compared with me for successes of any sort. My glory is without peer, and if any of the gods were to exchange heaven for earth and dwell under the lunar disc, he would content himself with such a brilliant fortune as mine."[1]

Nearly all the dramas of Scudéry are made up of such speeches, and they were the rage in Paris before Corneille arose, Corneille in whom something of this style yet lingers. Each of Scudéry's heroes, be it in his dramas, in his epics, in his romances, is like his

---

[1] "Soit que le blond Phœbus, sortant du creux de l'onde
Vienne recolorer le visage du monde ;
Soit que de rays plus chauds il enflame le jour,
Ou qu'il s'aille coucher en l'humide séjour,
Il ne void un seul homme en ce monde habitable
Qui soit en tout bon-heur avec moi comparable :
Ma gloire est sans pareille, et si quelqu'un des Dieux
Vouloit faire à la terre un eschange des cieux,
Et venir habiter sous le rond de la lune,
Il se contenteroit de ma belle fortune."

"Aman ou la vanité"; "Tragédies d'Antoine de Mont chrestien," Rouen, 1601, 8vo.

Alaric, nothing less than " le vainqueur des vainqueurs de la terre "; and having conquered all the world is in his turn conquered by Love. To write thus was supposed to be following the noble impulse given by the Renaissance, to be Roman, to outdo Seneca.[1]

In the novel especially this style shone in all its lustre and beauty. All the heroes of the interminable romances of the time, by Gomberville, George and Madeleine de Scudéry, La Calprenède and many others, be they Greek, Roman, Turk or French, are all of them the conquerors of the world and the captives of Love. "I can scarcely believe," wrote wise censors, "that the Cyrus and the Alexanders have suddenly become, as I hear it reported, so many Thyrsis and Celadons."[2] But their protests were of no avail, for a time, and romance heroes continued to reign in France, having had from the first for their palace and chief place of resort the famous Hôtel de Rambouillet.

[1] "Outre qu'on m'a vu naistre avec une couronne,
La fortune qui m'aime est celle qui les donne,
Et sans prendre la leur, ce bras a le pouvoir
De m'en acquérir cent, si je les veux avoir.
Mais souffrez mon discours, il est pour votre gloire ;
Je suy, je suy l'Amour et non pas la Victoire."
("L'amour tirannique," 1640. Speech by Tiridate.)

"Je tiens en mon pouvoir les sceptres et la mort ;
Je t'arracherais l'un, je te donnerais l'autre . . .
Mais j'ay cette faiblesse," &c. ("Ibrahim," 1645.)

[2] Boileau, "Les héros de romans, dialogue à la manière de Lucien," written in 1664, published 1713, but well known before in literary drawing-rooms, where Boileau used himself to read it aloud.

This hotel had been building from 1610 to 1617 in the Rue St.Thomas-du-Louvre. Polite society began to gather there soon after its completion, and began to desert it only thirty years later. The heroic romances of the period were among the chief topics of conversation ; and this is easily understood : they were meant as copies of this same polite society, and of its chiefs ; under feigned names people recognized in Cyrus the Grand Condé ; in Mandane, Madame de Longueville ; in Sapho, the authoress herself, Mdlle. de Scudéry ; in Aristhée, the poet Jean Chapelain. Persons thus designated often continued in real life to be called by their romance appellations ; thus Madame de Sévigné is wont to subscribe herself "the very humble servant of the adorable Amalthée."[1] Men and women considered it a great honour to have their portraits in a romance ; they felt sure then of going down to the remotest posterity, a fond belief to which posterity has already given the lie. Much intrigue went on to obtain such a valuable favour. While we are scarcely able now to plod on for a few chapters along the winding road which led Cyrus to his victories, these volumes were awaited with intense interest and discussed with passion as soon as published. Neither the expectation of the next number of the "Revue des deux Mondes," when it contains some important new study of actual life, nor the discussion about the last play of Dumas, can give us now an adequate idea of the amount of interest concentrated in Paris at that

---

[1] *I.e.*, Mme. du Plessis Guénégaud, who figures in "Clélie" under this name. "Letter to Pompone, Nov. 18, 1664."

time upon those heroical, grandiloquent, periwigged figures.

And sometimes it was a very long time before the end of the adventures, and the answers of the lovers were known. These books were not written without care and thought and some attention to rules and style. In the preface to his "Ibrahim" Scudéry gives us a sort of "Ars poetica" for heroic romance writers; he states what precepts it is necessary to follow, and those which may sometimes be dispensed with; he informs us that attention is to be paid to the truth of history, and that manners must be observed. For example, in "Ibrahim" he has thought fit to use some Turkish words, such as "Alla, Stambol"; these he calls "historical marks," and they correspond to what goes now under the name of local colour; according to his way of thinking they give a realistic appearance to his story. His heroes in this particular romance are not kings, he confesses; his excuse is that they are worthy to be such, and that besides they belong to very good families. He has been careful to use an easy, flowing style, and to avoid bombast "except in speeches." He has something to say about the unities, which have their part to play even in romances. Nothing must be left to chance in those works; and as for himself, he would have refused, he declares, the praise bestowed upon the Greek painter who, by throwing his brush against his work, obtained thus the finest effect in his picture. In Scudéry's picture everything is drawn with a will and a purpose, everything is the result of thought and calculation, and, if we are to believe him, much art was thus spent by the gallant

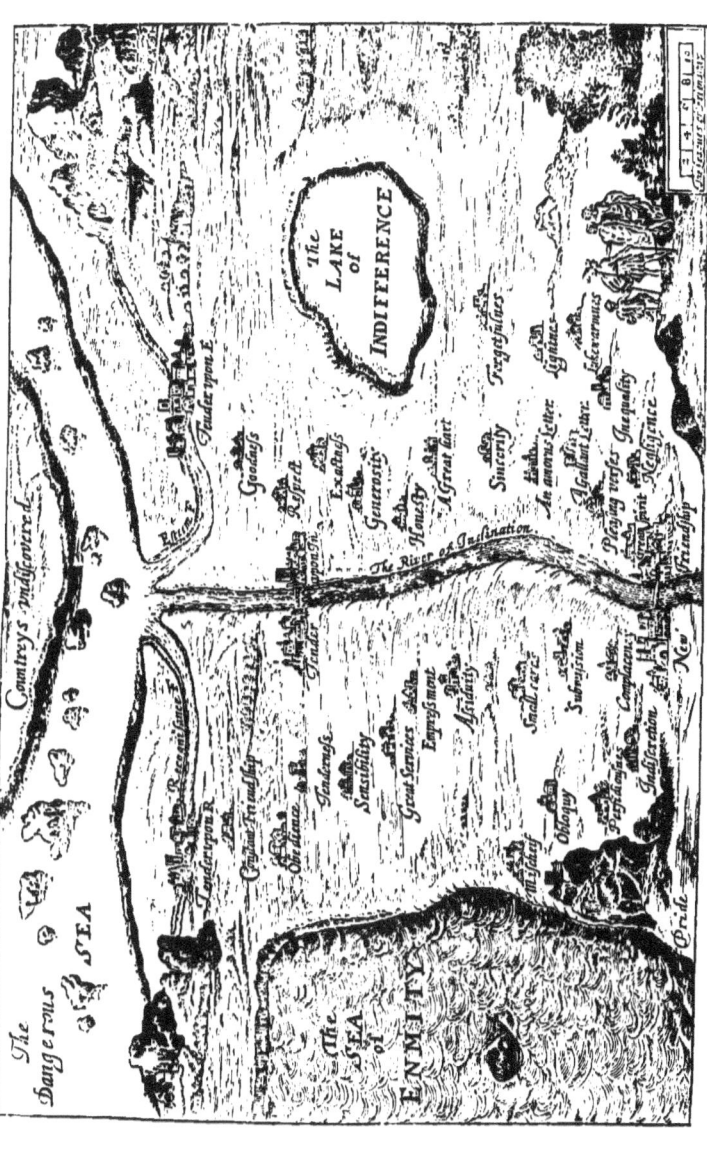

A MAP OF THE "TENDRE" COUNTRY.
(*From an English translation of "Clélie."*)

Gouverneur de Nostre Dame ; much art that is now entirely concealed from the dim eyes of posterity.[1]

Speeches, with descriptions, letters (which are always given in full as if they were documents of state), conversations and incidental anecdotic stories, were among the most usual means employed to fill up the many volumes of an ordinary heroical romance. For the volumes were many : "There never shone such a fine day as the one which was to be the eve of the nuptials between the illustrious Aronce and the admirable Clélie." Such is the beginning of the first volume of "Clélie, histoire romaine," by Madeleine de Scudéry, published in January, 1649. It happens that the marriage thus announced is delayed by certain little incidents, and is only celebrated towards the end of the tenth and last volume published in September, 1654. Volume I. contained the famous " Carte du Tendre," to show the route from " Nouvelle amitié " to " Tendre," with its various rivers, its villages of " Tendre-sur-Inclination," " Tendre-sur-Estime," with the ever-to-be-avoided hamlets of Indiscretion and Perfidy, the Lake of Indifference and other frightful countries. Let us turn away from them and go back to our heroes.

One of their chief pleasures was to tell their own stories. Of this neither they nor their listeners were ever tired. Whenever in the course of the tale a new person is introduced, the first thing he is expected to do is to tell us who he is and what he has seen of the world. Sometimes stories are included in his own, and when the first are finished, instead of taking up again

[1] Scudéry's preface to " Ibrahim, or the illustrious bassa .. englished by Henry Cogan," London, 1652, fol.

the thread of the main tale, we merely resume the hearing of the speaker's own adventures: a custom which sometimes proves very puzzling to the inattentive frivolous reader of to-day. As for the supposed listeners in the tale itself, the men or women the hero has secured for his audience, they well knew what to expect, and took their precautions accordingly. We sometimes see them go to bed in order to listen more comfortably. In "Cassandre," the eunuch Tireus has a story to tell to Prince Oroontades: "The prince went to his bedroom and put himself to bed; he then had Tireus called to him, and having seats placed in the *ruelle*, he commanded us to sit," and then the story begins; and it goes on for pages; and when it is finished we observe that it was included in another story told by Araxe; wherefore, instead of finding ourselves back among the actors of the principal tale, we alight only among those in Araxe's narrative.[1] These stories are thus enclosed in one another like Chinese boxes.

II.

This literature as soon as imported into England realized there the most complete success. To find a parallel for it we must go back to the time when mediæval Lancelot and Tristan were sung of by French singers, and afterwards by singers of all countries. Cyrus and Mandane, Oroontades and Tireus, Grand Scipio and Illustrious Bassa, Astrée and Céladon, our heroes and our shepherds once more began

[1] 'Cassandre,' vol. i book v.

the invasion and conquest of the great northern island. As was to be expected from such unparalleled conquerors, they accomplished this feat easily, and their work had consequences in England for which France can scarcely offer any perfect equivalent. Through their exertions there arose in this country a dramatic literature in the heroical style which, thanks especially to Dryden, has still a literary interest. But in France our heroes of fiction were curtailed of much of their glory by the inexorable Boileau. They left, it is true, some trace of their influence in the works of Corneille and even of Racine, but the heroic drama, properly so called, was restricted to the works of the Scudérys and Montchrestiens, which is saying enough to imply that it was not meant to survive very long.

During the greater part of the century French romances were in England the main reading of people who had leisure. They were read in the original, for French was a current language in society at that time, and they were read in translations both by society and by the ordinary public. Most of them were rendered into English, and so important were these works considered that sometimes several translators tried their skill at the same romance, and published independently the result of their labours, as if their author had been Virgil or Ariosto, or any classical writer. French ideas in the matter of novels were adopted so cordially that not only under Charles I., but even during the civil war and under Cromwell this rage for reading and translating did not abate. The contrary, it is true, has often been asserted, without inquiry, and as a matter of course; but this erroneous statement was due to a mere *a priori* argument, and had no other ground than the improbability of the same fashion predominating in the London of the Roundheads and the Paris of the Précieuses. What likelihood was there of any popularity being bestowed upon heroes who were nothing if not befeathered heroes, heroes *à panaches* at a time when Puritans reigned supreme, staunch adversaries as we know of *panaches*, curls, vain talk, and every sort of worldly vanity? Was it not the time when books were published on "The unlovelinesse of Love-lockes," being "a summarie discourse prooving the wearing and nourishing of a locke or love-locke to be altogether unseemely, and unlawfull unto Christians. In which there are likewise some passages collected out of Fathers, Councells and sundry authors and historians against face-painting, the wearing of supposititious, poudred, frizled or extraordinary long haire, the inordinate affectation of corporall beautie, and womens mannish, unnaturall, impudent, and unchristian cutting of their haire"?[1] So early in the century as 1628 it was thus discovered that women's short hair and men's long wigs were equally unchristian. What was to be the fate of our well-curled heroes? They were received with open arms. "Polexandre," for example, was published in English in 1647; "Ibrahim ou l'illustre Bassa," "Cassandre," and "Cléopatre" in 1652; "Le Grand Cyrus" in 1653, the very year in which Cromwell became Protector; the first part of "Clélie" in 1656; "Astrée" in 1657; "Scipion" in 1660, &c.

The English prefaces to these French novels plainly

[1] By William Prynne, London, 1628, 4to.

showed that, notwithstanding the puritanical taunts of the party in power, publishers felt no doubt as to the success of their undertaking. These works were not spread timidly among the public ; they were announced noisily in the most pompous terms :

"I shall waste no time to tell you how this book hath sold in France where it was born : since nothing falls from Monsieur de Scudéry's hand, but is receiv'd there as an unquestionable piece, by all that have a taste of wit or honour. The translator hath inserted no false stitches of his own, having only turn'd the wrong side of the Arras towards us, for all translations, you know, are no other." [1]

The translator of "Astrée" was fain to inform his readers of a judgment passed, as he pretends, on this work by "the late famous Cardinall of Richelieu. That he was not to be admitted in the Academy of wit who had not been before well read in Astrea." And he claims for his author a highly beneficial purpose, that could be condemned by none except obdurate Puritans : " These are the true designs and ends of works of this nature : these are academies for the lover, schools of war for the soldier, and cabinets for the statesman ; they are the correctives of passion, the restoratives of conversation, . . . in a word, the most delightful accommodations of civill life." [2]

---

[1] Preface to "Artamenes, or the Grand Cyrus," London, 1653-1654, five vols. fol.
[2] "Astrea . . . translated by a person of quality," *i.e.*, J. D[avies ?], London, 1657-8, 3 vols. fol. ; prefaces to vols. i and ii. Dramas with their plots taken from "Astrée" were written in England and in France, such as "Tragi-comédie pastorale ou les

Another goes so far as to give the lie direct to the Puritans, to "those morose persons" who condemn novels; in truth, "delight is the least advantage redounding from such compositions." French romances (which seem to have altered somewhat in this respect) are nothing but a school of morality, generosity, and self-restraint: "Not to say anything concerning the ground work which is generally some excellent piece of ancient history accurately collected out of the records of the most eminent writers of old, . . . the addition of fictitious adventures is so ingenious, the incident discourses so handsome, free and fitted for the improvement of conversation (which is not undeservedly accounted of great importance to the contentment of human life), the descriptions of the passions so lively and naturally set forth; yea the idea of virtue, generosity and all the qualifications requisite to accomplish great persons so exquisitely delineated that . . . I must speak it, though I believe with the envy and regret of many, that [the French] have approv'd themselves the best teachers of a noble and generous morality that are to be met with."[1]

Sometimes both the engravings and the story were imported from France. As the illustrations to Harington's translation of "Ariosto" had been originally made by an Italian artist, so now French engravings began to be popularized in England. For example,

amours d'Astrée . . . par le Sieur de Rayssiguier," Paris, 1632, 8vo; "Astrea, or true love's mirrour, a pastoral," by Leonard Willan, London, 1651, 8vo.

[1] "'The Grand Scipio . . . by Monsieur de Vaumoriere, rendered into English by G. H.," London, 1660, fol.

ENDYMION PLUNGED INTO THE RIVER IN THE PRESENCE OF DIANA.
(*French Engraving used in an English book.*) [*p.* 367.

when a translation appeared of "Endimion," the curious mythological novel of Gombauld, with its pleasant descriptions and incidents, half dreamy, half real, the plates from drawings by C. de Pas were sent over to England and used in the English edition. Sometimes, too, the English copies had original plates or engraved titles; but even in these the French style was usually apparent. Robert Loveday, who translated La Calprenède's "Cléopatre," prefaces his book with one such plate; and it is curious to notice when reading his published correspondence that the engraving was made according to his own minute directions. The bookseller "offer'd to be at the charge of cutting my own face for the frontispiece, but I refused his offer." As, however, the publisher insisted on having something, "I design'd him this which is now a-cutting: Upon an altar dedicated to Love, divers hearts transfix'd with arrows and darts are to lye broiling upon the coals ; and upon the steps of it, Hymen . . . in a posture as if he were going to light [his taper] to the altar ; when Cupid is to come behind him and pull him by the saffron sleeve, with these words proceeding from his mouth : Nondum peracta sunt præludia"; [1] a statement that is only too true and in which Loveday summarizes unawares the truest criticism levelled at these romances. You may read volume after volume, and still "nondum peracta sunt præludia," you have not yet done with preliminaries.

But this constant delaying of an event, sometimes

[1] "Loveday's letters, domestick and foreign," seventh impression. London, 1684, 8vo, p. 146 (first edition 1659).

announced, as in "Clélie," at the top of the first page, was not in the least displeasing to seventeenth-century readers. The lengthy episodes, the protracted conversations, enchanted them; it was an age when conversation was at its height in France, and from France the taste spread to other countries. Translators, as we have seen, expressly mentioned as an attraction in their books the help they would give to conversation. Numberless examples of this polite pastime are provided in the heroic romances; in "Almahide, or the Captive Queen,"[1] among others, we read discussions as to whether it is better for a man to court a lady in verse or in prose, whether an illiterate lover is better than a learned one, &c., &c.

Such topics, and many more of a higher order, which were the subject of persistent debate in the drawing-rooms of the Hôtel de Rambouillet, were also discussed in England; there was, it is true, no Hôtel de Rambouillet, but there was the house of the Philips at Cardigan. There was no Marquise, but there was Catherine Philips, the "matchless Orinda," who did much to acclimatize in England the refinements, elegancies, and heroism *à panache* of her French neigh-

[1] By Scudéry, translated by J. Philips, London, 1677, fol. part ii. bk. ii. p. 166. Books entirely made up of "conversations" were published by Mdlle. de Scudéry, treating of pleasures, of passions, of the knowledge of others and of ourselves, &c. They read very much like dialogued essays; and it is interesting to compare them with Addison's essays which treat sometimes of the same subjects. They were received with great applause; Madame de Sévigné highly praises them. They were translated into English: "Conversations upon several subjects, . . . done into English by F. Spence," London, 1683, 2 vol. 12mo.

"HYMEN'S PRÆLUDIA."
(*Frontispiece of the translation of La Calprenède's "Cléopatre."*)

bours. With the help of her friends she translated some of the plays of Corneille, not without adding something to the original to make it look more heroical. The little society gathered round her imitated the feigned names bestowed upon the habitués of the Parisian hotel. While she went by the name of Orinda, plain Mr. Philips, her husband, was re-baptized Antenor; her friend Sir Charles Cotterel, translator of "Cassandre," was Poliarchus; a lady friend, Miss Owen, was Lucasia;[1] fine names, to be sure, which unfortunately will remind many a reader not only of matchless Arthenice, of the Hôtel de Rambouillet, but of Molière's Cathos and Madelon, who, too, had chosen to imitate the Marquise, and insisted on being called Aminte and Polixène, to the astonishment of their honest father.[2]

The high morality and delicacy, both of the "Hôtel," and, alas, of Molière's "Précieuses," were also imitated at Cardigan. To get married was a thing so coarse and vulgar that people with refined souls were to slip into that only at the last extremity. "A fine thing it would be," says the Madelon of the "Précieuses," "if from the first Cyrus were to marry Mandane and if Aronce were all at once wedded to Clelia!" We have seen that such is not the case, and that ten volumes of adventures interpose between their love and their marriage. In the same way an eternal

[1] About this curious little society see Mr. Gosse's "Seventeenth Century Studies," 1883, pp. 205 *et seq.*
[2] "*Cathos*: Le nom de Polixène que ma cousine a choisi et celui d'Aminte que je me suis donné ont une grâce dont il faut que vous demeuriez d'accord" ("Précieuses Ridicules," sc. v.).

friendship, a marriage of soul to soul, having been sworn between Orinda and Lucasia, it was a matter of great sorrow, shame and despair for the first when the second, after thirteen years of this refined intercourse proved frail and commonplace enough to marry a lover of appropriate age, fortune and position.

Another centre for heroic thoughts and refined morality was the country house of the pedantic but pretty Duchess of Newcastle, a prolific writer of essays, letters, plays, poems, tales, and works of all kinds. To her, literature was a compensation for the impossibility, through want of opportunity, of performing with her own hand heroical deeds : " I dare not examine," says she, " the former times, for fear I should meet with such of my sex that have out-done all the glory I can aime at or hope to attaine ; for I confess my ambition is restless, and not ordinary ; because it would have an extraordinary fame. And since all heroick actions, publick employments, powerfull governments and eloquent pleadings are denyed our sex in this age or at least would be condemned for want of custome, is the cause I write so much." [1]

She wrote a great deal, and not without feeling a somewhat deep and naïvely expressed admiration for her own performances. The epithet "restless" which she applies to her ambition, well fits her whole mind ; there is restlessness about everything she did and wrote. She is never satisfied with one epistle to the reader ; she must have ten or twelve prefaces and under-prefaces, which forcibly remind us of her contemporary, Oronte, in his famous sonnet scene with Alceste. Her

[1] "Natures pictures," London, 1656, fol., preface No. 2.

A FASHIONABLE CONVERSATION. [*p*. 375.

'Natures pictures drawn by Fancies pencil to the life" is preceded by several copies of commendatory verses and a succession of preambles, entitled : " To the reader— An epistle to my readers—To the reader—To the reader—To my readers—To my readers"; each being duly signed " M. Newcastle." It seems as if the sight of her own name was a pleasure to her. These prefaces are full of expostulations, explanations and apologies, quite in the Oronte style : " The design of these my feigned stories, is to present virtue, the muses leading her and the graces attending her. . . . Perchance my feigned stories are not so lively described as they might have been. . . . As for those tales I name romancicall, I would not have my readers think I write them either to please or to make foolish whining lovers. . . . I must entreat my readers to understand, that though my naturall genius is to write fancy, yet . . . Although I hope every piece or discourse in my book will delight my readers or at least some one, and some another . . . yet I do recommend two as the most solid and edifying." Great is the temptation to answer with Alceste : " Nous verrons bien !"[1] But how could one say so when she was so pretty? The best preface to her volumes is in fact the charming engraving representing a party meeting at her house to tell and hear tales round the fire, and of which we give a reproduction. The only pity is that the figure meant as her portrait, though laurel-crowned, looks much more plain and commonplace than we might have expected.

[1] Her "Playes," 1662, are preceded by two dedications, one prologue, and *eleven* prefaces.

She wrote then abundantly "romancicall" tales, as she called them, with a touch of heroism; edifying tales in which she prescribes "that all young men should be kept to their studies so long as their effeminate beauties doth last;" dialogues "of the wise lady, the learned lady and the witty lady," the three being only too wise; plays in which she depicts herself under the names of Lady Sanspareile, of Lady Chastity, &c., unpardonable sins, no doubt, to give oneself such names; but it is reported she was so beautiful!

Among the mass of her writings, it must be added, ideas are scattered here and there which were destined to live, and through which she anticipated men of true and real genius. To give only one example, she too may be credited with having anticipated Richardson in her "Sociable Letters," in which she tries to imitate real life, to describe scenes, very nearly to write an actual novel: "The truth is," she writes, "they are rather scenes than letters, for I have endeavoured under cover of letters to express the humors of mankind, and the actions of man's life by the correspondence of two ladies, living at some short distance from each other, which make it not only their chief delight and pastime, but their tye in friendship, to discourse by letters as they would do if they were personally together."[1] Many collections of imaginary letters had, as we have seen, been published before, but never had the use to which they could be put been better foreseen by any predecessor of Richardson.

The Duchess lived till 1674, surrounded by an ever-

[1] "CCXI. Sociable Letters." London, 1664, fol.

CONVERSATION AND TELLING OF STORIES AT THE HOUSE OF THE DUCHESS OF NEWCASTLE, 1656. [*p.* 379.

increasing group of admirers, deaf to the jokes of courtly people concerning her old-fashioned chastity; more than consoled by the firm belief she had as to the strength of her mind and genius. In this persuasion "she kept," wrote Theophilus Cibber, "a great many young ladies about her person, who occasionally wrote what she dictated. Some of them slept in a room contiguous to that in which Her Grace lay, and were ready at the call of her bell to rise any hour of the night to write down her conceptions, lest they should escape her memory. The young ladies no doubt often dreaded Her Grace's conceptions, which were frequent."[1] Here, again, her restless spirit was in some manner anticipating unawares another great writer, namely, Pope.

Thus, in spite of Cromwell and the Puritans on the one side, and Charles II. and his courtiers on the other, French ideas as to the possible dignity and purity of lives in which the worldly element was not wanting grew to some extent on the English soil, though, it is true, with less success, being as we see mainly relegated at that time to the country. The true hour for virtues not the less real because sociable, virtues such as they were understood by Madame de Sévigné or Madame de Rambouillet, had not yet come. They were to be thoroughly acclimatized only in the next century, principally through the exertions of Steele and Addison.

But the strictly heroical part of French tastes was accepted immediately and with great enthusiasm. The extraordinary number of folio heroical romances still

[1] "Lives of the Poets ... to the time of Dean Swift," London, 1753, 5 vols. 12mo; vol. ii. p. 164.

to be seen in old English country houses testifies at the present day to their extraordinary hold upon the polite society of the time. The King gave the example. Charles I. had been a reader of such novels; on the eve of his death he distributed a few souvenirs to his most faithful friends, and we see him give away, besides Hooker's "Ecclesiastical Polity" and Dr. Andrews' sermons, the romance of "Cassandre," which he left to the Earl of Lindsey. During the troublous times of the civil war, Dorothy Osborne constantly alludes, in her letters to Sir William Temple, to the books she reads, and they are mostly these same French novels. While troops are marching to and fro; while rebellions and counter-rebellions are preparing or breaking out, the volumes of "Cléopatre" and "Grand Cyrus" go to and fro between the lovers and are the subject of their epistolary discussions. "Have you read 'Cléopatre'? I have six tomes on't here that I can lend you if you have not; there are some stories in't you will like, I believe."—"Since you are at leisure to consider the moon, you may be enough to read 'Cléopatre,' therefore I have sent you three volumes. ... There is a story of Artimise that I will recommend to you; her disposition I like extremely, it has a great deal of practical wit; and if you meet with one Brittomart, pray send me word how you like him."—"I have a third tome here [of "Cyrus"] against you have done with that second; and to encourage you, let me assure you that the more you read of them, you will like them still better,"[1] and so on.

[1] "Letters from Dorothy Osborne to Sir William Temple, 1652-4," ed. Parry, London, 1888, 8vo. Letter ix. p. 60; Letter x. p. 64; Letter xxiv. p. 124. year 1653.

The wife of Mr. Pepys was not less fond of French romances than Dorothy Osborne, and we sometimes find her husband purchasing copies at his bookseller's to bring home as presents. But he himself did not like them very much; he seems to have been deterred from this kind of literature by his wife's habit of reciting stories to him out of these works; some quarrel even took place between the couple about "Cyrus," though it seems that "Cyrus" was in this case more the pretext than the reason of the discussion, as honest Pepys with his usual frankness gives us to understand: "At noon home, where I find my wife troubled still at my checking her last night in the coach in her long stories out of 'Grand Cyrus,' which she would tell, though nothing to the purpose, nor in any good manner. This she took unkindly, and I think I was to blame indeed; but she do find with reason that in the company of Pierce, Knipp, or other women that I love I do not value her as I ought. However very good friends by and by." As a penance doubtless we see him buying for her later "L'Illustre Bassa in four volumes" and "Cassandra and some other French books."[1]

III.

But reading and translating was not enough for a society so enamoured of heroical romances; some original ones were to be composed for English readers and the composing of them became a fashionable pastime. "My lord Broghill," writes again Dorothy

[1] May 13, 1666; Feb. 24, 1667-8; Nov. 16, 1668.

Osborne to her future husband, Sir William Temple, the patron hereafter of the yet unborn Jonathan Swift, "sure will give us something worth the reading. My Lord Saye, I am told, has writ a romance since his retirement in the isle of Lundy, and Mr. Waller they say is making one of our wars, which if he does not mingle with a great deal of pleasing fiction, cannot be very diverting, sure, the subject is so sad." [1]

The following year, that is 1654, the English public received, according to Dorothy's previsions, the first instalment of the most noticeable heroical romance composed in their language. It was called "Parthenissa," [2] and had for its author Roger Boyle, Lord Broghill, afterwards Earl of Orrery, one of the matchless Orinda's great friends.[3]

In this heroic romance, the imitation of France is as exact as possible; the few literary qualities perceptible in the vast compositions of Mdlle. de Scudéry and of La Calprenède, do not shine with any brighter lustre in "Parthenissa." As in France ancient history is put to the torture, though Scudéry, as we have seen, had set up as a rule that the truth of history was to be respected in romances; of observation of nature there is little or none, and the conversations of the characters are interminable. "Turning over the leaves of the large folio," wrote

---

[1] Letter xxxiv. p. 162. Year 1653.
[2] "Parthenissa, that most fam'd romance," London, 1654.
[3] He assisted her in getting her translation of Corneille's "Pompée" represented at Dublin with embellishments, consisting in dances, music, songs, &c. He was born in 1621 and was held in great esteem both by Cromwell and by the Stuarts. He left dramas and other works and died in 1679.

one of the last critics who busied themselves with this work, "I perceived that ... the story some-how or other brought in Hannibal, Massinissa, Mithridates, Spartacus, and other persons equally well known. . . . How they came into the story or what the story is I cannot tell you; nor will any mortal know any more than I do, between this and doomsday; but there they all are, lively though invisible, like carp in a pond."[1] We must make bold, though doomsday has not yet come, to draw forth some of these carp out of the water, and, after all, this is not the darkest pond in which we shall have fished.

At the commencement, Boyle introduces us to a young and handsome stranger who comes to Syria in order to consult the oracle of Venus. The priest Callimachus appears before him, and quite suddenly asks for his history. The stranger is very willing to tell it. His name is Artabanes and he is the son of the King of Parthia; he is in love with the Princess Parthenissa and has proved his affection for her in the manner of Sidney's heroes: he met on one occasion an Arab prince, who was travelling with a collection of twenty-four pictures, representing the mistresses of twenty-four famous champions overthrown by him. Artabanes in his turn measured swords with the Arab and got possession of the twenty-four paintings, and one in addition, which represented the mistress of his adversary: whence it results that Parthenissa is the most beautiful woman in the world, exactly what the hero intended to prove.

[1] "British Novelists," by David Masson, Cambridge, 1859, 8vo. p. 72.

Artabanes has a rival, Surena; he fancies that Surena is the happy man, leaves Parthenissa and goes to live in solitude. Pirates carry him off, and sell him at Rome for a slave. Then under the name of Spartacus, he stirs up a revolt and accomplishes exploits attributed by ancient writers to that rebel; however he does not die as in history, but returns to Asia. There, Parthenissa, rather than surrender to a lover, swallows a drug and dies; but hers is only an apparent death and she returns to life. Artabanes, in the same way, stabs himself, but he is cured; and then it is that he comes to consult the oracle.

Callimachus thanks him for his interesting but somewhat lengthy story, and revenges himself by relating his own. Unfortunately he is interrupted: they see a lady who looks exactly like Parthenissa herself enter a neighbouring grove; she is accompanied by a young cavalier; they embrace and disappear among the trees. Artabanes' anguish at this sight cannot be described. But here Roger Boyle found that he was tired and wrote no more. His romance, which already comprised five parts, was published by him in this unfinished form.

For a long time the public was left in suspense. The Protector was dead, his son had fallen, the Stuarts had again ascended the throne, and no one knew the end of the loves of Prince Artabanes. The continuation of the romance is due to the charming Henrietta of England, Duchess of Orleans. Ten or twelve years after the appearance of the first volume, she was curious to know what Parthenissa was doing in the wood, and begged Roger Boyle to bring her out of it. He wrote a sixth part in four books and dedicated it to her.

Are we to imagine that the author is now going to lead his impatient readers in search of the heroine? Not at all. Callimachus, who was unfairly interrupted in his tale, proposes to his companions to leave one of them, Symander, on guard, and to go and refresh themselves. When they were rested, " they conjur'd him to prosecute his story, though what they had seen and heard gave them impatiences which nothing but their desires of knowing so generous a friend's fortunes could have dispensed with." The four books of the sixth part are devoted to this narrative; Boyle, as he said in his preface, had thought at first of concluding everything in this supplement; but he was forced to recognize that it was impossible to "confine it within so narrow a compass." This statement will be found on page 808 of his folio volume. Why Parthenissa entered the grove was never to be known nor what she had to say in her justification. Boyle, who had taken up his pen again at the instance of the young duchess, had very soon no reason to continue: Bossuet was calling on the court of the Grand Roi to weep with him for the loss of this charming woman, whose beauty and grace had only blossomed " for one morning."

As soon as the book was out, Dorothy Osborne had a copy sent to her, but she did not like it so much as the French models. She writes to Temple : "I'll . . . tell you that ' Parthenissa ' is now my company. My brother sent it down and I have almost read it. 'Tis handsome language; you would know it to be writ by a person of good quality though you were not told it; but on the whole I am not very much taken with it. All the stories have too near a resemblance with those of other romances; there is nothing new and *surprenant* in them; the ladies are all so kind they make no sport." [1]

Boyle, it is said, besides his dramas and other works, again tried his fortune as a novel writer, and published in 1676 " English Adventures by a person of honour." It is in a style so absolutely different from his former romance that it is scarcely credible that both came from the same pen. " English Adventures " tell the story of the amours of King Henry VIII., of Brandon, and others. All the reserve in " Parthenissa " has entirely disappeared, and scenes are presented to the eye which, except at the time of the Restoration, have usually been veiled. Love is in this novel the subject of many discussions, and so it was in heroic romances, but while it was spoken of there with decency and dignity, it is never mentioned in " English Adventures " but in a tone of banter and raillery. The discourses about this passion recall Suckling's ideas much more than those of Madeleine de Scudéry. " Pardon me, madam, Wilmore reply'd, if I think you mistake the case, for I never said I was for a siege in Love: that is the dull method of those countries whose discipline in amours I abominate. I am for the French mode, where the first day, I either conquer my mistress or my passion." Whether or not this be according to " the French mode," we are obviously very far from the Montausier ideal. The author continues : " Nor indeed did I ever

[1] Letter LI. p. 236, year 1654.

see any woman (I mean in France) cry up constancy, but she was decaying ; for when any thing but love is to maintain love 'tis a proof Beauty cannot do it, and then, alas, nothing else can."[1] If this and the very licentious adventures which follow are really Boyle's, it must be conceded that the change worked upon him by the new Restoration manners was indeed vast and comprehensive.

Other original attempts at the heroical romance were made in England at this period. It will be enough to mention one more. The two main defects of the heroical dramas of Dryden and his contemporaries are bombast in the ideas and bad taste in the expressions. In Crowne's heroical novel of "Pandion and Amphigenia,"[2] both defects are pushed to an extreme which, incredible as it may seem to the readers of Dryden, was never at any time reached by the laureate.

The story is the usual heroical story of valorous deeds and peerless loves; the author is careful to assert that he is perfectly original: "All . . . is genuine, nothing stole, nothing strained." He has been especially careful to avoid imitating the French and the elegancies of "that ceremonious nation." After such a declaration we are rather surprised to hear Periander thus answer a lady who, in the usual way, had asked him for his inevitable story : " Madam," said he, " your expressions speak you no less rich in virtue than beauty. . . .

[1] P. 54. Part of the tale, viz.: the adventures of Brandon, supplied Otway with the plot of his "Orphan" (performed 1680).
[2] "Pandion and Amphigenia, or the history of the coy lady of Thessalia adorned with sculptures," London, 1665, 8vo. Crowne died about 1703 ; his dramatic works have been published in four vols., 1873.

I should be more savage then the beasts that Orpheus charmed into civility, should I remain inexorable to the intreaties of so sweet an orator, whose perfections are such that I cannot but account it as great a glory to obey you, as it would make me sensible of shame to refuse any thing you should command, though it were to sacrifice my life and honour, which are the only jewels I ever prized in my prosperity, and which is all that Fortune hath left to my disposal in my adversity." Then he tells his story, which we had better not listen to, for it begins : " Know you then that in the city of Corinth, there dwelt a gentleman called Eleutherius . . .," and we know full well what such beginnings threaten. The romance goes on describing bloody feuds and matchless beauties. Here is in characteristic style a portrait of a matchless beauty :

"The pillow blest with a kiss from her cheeks, as pregnant with delight, swelled on either side. . . . A lock that had stollen from its sweet prison, folded in cloudy curls, lay dallying with her breath, sometimes striving to get a kiss, and then repulsed flew back, sometimes obtaining its desired bliss, and then as rapt with joy, retreated in wanton caperings. . . . Her breasts at liberty displayed were of so pure a whiteness as if one's eye through the transparent skin, had viewed the milky treasures they inclosed."

Oh ! for a Boileau, shall we exclaim, to cut off the flowers of such paper gardens ! for a Defoe to show how prose fiction should be written ! But Boileau is abroad and Defoe's time is yet to come. Wait, besides, for this is nothing and we have better in store ; that was love, here is war :

" The signal for the battail being given, there began such a terrible conflict, as that within a short time thousands lay dead in the place, both sides maintaining their assaults with such impetuous rage as if the Gyants had been come to heap mountains of carcasses to assail heaven and besiege the gods ; nothing but fury reigned in every breast, some that were thrust through with lances would yet run themselves farther on to reach their enemies and requite that mortal wound ... the earth grew of a sanguine complexion, being covered with blood, as if every soldier had been Death's herald, and had come to emblazon Mars's arms with a sword Argent on a field Gules.... In one place, lay heads deposed from their sovereignties, yawning and staring as if they looked for their bodies."[1] One refreshing thought is the remembrance of the pure, deep pleasure Crowne must have found in fastening together such an unparalleled series of conceits. " Peste," is he sure to have said with Sosie :

" Peste ! où prend mon esprit toutes ces gentillesses ? "

As for the final result of these wars and love-makings, it is a very airy one ; for Crowne seems to have entertained a higher ideal of purity than even Montausier and Orinda. His ladies bestow upon their lovers nothing at all, not even marriage, and the author, after having been at some trouble to re-establish order in Thessaly and other countries, gives up all idea of getting Pandion and Amphigenia wedded, this lady, she of the pillow above described, being as he says so very " coy."

[1] Pp. 140, 141.

Though not quite a match for Crowne's it must be conceded that neither is Dryden's bombast of a mean order. The following passage which very nearly bears comparison with the above, will show how heroism appeared when transferred to the stage. In one of the dramas, the plot of which Dryden took from the French romances, Almanzor thus addresses a rival :

> " If from thy hands alone my death can be,
> I am immortal and a god to thee,
> If I would kill thee now, thy fate's so low
> That I must stoop ere I can give the blow :
> But mine is fixed so far above thy crown,
> That all thy men,
> Piled on thy back, can never pull it down :
> But at my ease, thy destiny I send,
> By ceasing from this hour to be thy friend.
> Like heaven, I need but only to stand still,
> And not concurring to thy life, I kill." [1]

Any number of speeches of this sort are to be found in the heroical dramas of Dryden, Settle, Lee, and their contemporaries. Roman, Arab, Turk, Greek or Moorish heroes, pirates or princes, when they mean to set anything at defiance, choose nothing less than heaven and earth as their object ; they divide the world between them as if it were an orange ; they rush to the fight or stop for a speech with a fine shake of the head which sends a majestic undulation round the wig worn by them, even by the Moors, as we may see in one of the very rare dramas then published with

---

[1] "Almanzor and Almahide, or the Conquest of Granada," performed (with great success) in the winter, 1669-70, act iii. sc. 1.

HEROES (MOORISH ONES) AS THEY APPEARED ON THE STAGE, FROM SETTLE'S "EMPRESS OF MOROCCO," 1673.   [*p.* 393.

engravings. They are represented there with embroidered justaucorps, wigs and ribbons.[1]

Crowne besides his romance wrote several dramas that secured him a wide, if temporary, popularity. He also adapted Racine's "Andromaque" for the English stage, but he was very much disgusted with this work; the French original, though not "the worst" of French plays, was after all so mean and tame! "If the play be barren of fancy, you must blame the original author. I am as much inclined to be civil to strangers as any man; but then they must be strangers of merit. I would no more be at the pains to bestow wit (if I had any) on a French play, than I would be at the cost to bestow cloaths on every shabby Frenchman that comes over." Here we have Racine put in his proper place; what claim had he to be considered "a stranger of merit"? True, some crabbed English critics seem to have taken his part against the translator, and, incredible as it may seem, they have expressed a thought that "this suffered much in the translation.—I cannot tell in what," answers Crowne, "except in not bestowing verse upon it, which I thought it did not deserve. For otherwise, there is all that is in the French play, verbatim, and something more, as may be seen in the last act, where what is dully recited in the French play is there represented, which is no small advantage."[2] And true, it is, Pyrrhus is slain

[1] Settle's "Empress of Morocco," London, 1673, 4to. The engraving we reproduce represents the interior of a Moorish prison, with Muley Labas, son of the Emperor of Morocco, and the Princess Morena.

[2] "Andromache, a tragedy, as it is acted at the Dukes Theatre," London, 1675, 4to.

before our eyes ; there are " alarums " and other lively, if customary, ornaments.

In this age obviously Racine could not please. Nor would Shakespeare have pleased a French audience, but as we know no attempt in that direction was made in Paris. The two nations lent one another, if anything, their defects. "Alaric" was named with praise by Dryden ; Scudéry and La Calprenède continued to be most popular French authors during the century. Even in the next we find something remaining of their fame. Among the books in the library of the fashionable Leonora, Addison notices : "'Cassandra,' 'Cleopatra,' 'Astræa' ... the 'Grand Cyrus,' with a pin stuck in one of the middle leaves ... 'Clelia,' which opened of it self in the place that describes two lovers in a bower," [1] &c. The passions in them which seem to us now so incredibly frigid, had not yet cooled down ; their warmth was still felt : so much so that in one of Farquhar's plays, " Cassandra " is mentioned as greatly responsible for Lady Lurewell's first and greatest fault, the beginning of many others : " After supper I went to my chamber and read ' Cassandra,' then went to bed and dreamt of it all night, rose in the morning and made verses ... "[2] We cannot follow her in her account of the consequences.

All that was truly noble and simple in French literature was known, but at the same time generally misunderstood in England. To make French authors acceptable, grossness was added to Molière, bombast to Racine ;

---

[1] *Spectator*, April 12, 1711.
[2] "The Constant Couple, or a trip to the Jubilee," 1700, act iii., last scene.

even Otway, when translating "Bérénice," transformed
Racine's "Titus" into a bully of romance who, in order
to assuage his grief, goes to overrun "the Universe"
and make "the worlds" as wretched as he is.[1] Madame
de la Fayette had shown how it was possible to copy
from life, in a novel, true heroism and true tenderness
without exaggeration; her exquisite masterpiece was
translated of course as was everything then that was
French; but oblivion soon gathered round the
"Princess of Cleve," and the only proof we have
that it did not pass unnoticed is a clumsy play by
Lee, in which this best of old French novels is merci-
lessly caricatured.[2] There was no attempt to imitate
the Comtesse's pure and perfect style and high train of
thought.

IV.

Reaction against the heroical romances did not wait,
however, till the eighteenth century to assert itself in
England; it set in early and very amusingly: but it
remained powerless. As the evil had chiefly come from

[1] "Titus and Berenice; a tragedy," 1677.
[2] "The Princess of Montpensier," 1666; "The Princess of
Cleve . . . written by the greatest wits of France, rendred
into English by a person of quality at the request of some friends,"
1688: "Zayde," 1688. Nat. Lee's play is entitled, "The Princess
of Cleve," London, 1689, 4to. As to the popularity of this novel
in France, it will be enough to notice Madame de Sévigné's
allusion to "ce chien de Barbin," who does not fulfil her orders
when she wants books, because she does not write "des Princesses
de Clèves."

France, so did the remedy ; but the remedy in France proved sufficient for a cure. In that country at all times the tale had flourished, and at all times in the tale, to the detriment of chivalry and heroism, writers had prided themselves on seeking mere truth. Thus, in the charming preface of the Reine de Navarre's "Heptaméron," Dame Parlamente establishes the theory of these narratives, and relates how, at the court, it had been decided to write a series of them, but to exclude from the number of their authors " those who should have studied and be men of letters ; for Monseigneur the Dauphin did not wish their artifice to be introduced into them, and was also afraid lest the beauty of rhetoric should in some place injure the truth of the tale."

In the seventeenth century, the tradition of the old story-tellers is carried on in France in more developed writings, in actual novels, such as the " Baron de Fœneste " of D'Aubigné, 1617 ; the " Francion " of Charles Sorel, 1622 (?) ; the " Berger extravagant " of the same, 1628 ; the " Roman Comique " of Scarron, 1651 ; the " Roman bourgeois " of Furetière, 1666, and many others. Scarron, who had travestied Virgil, was not the man to spare La Calprenède, and he does not lose his opportunity. " I cannot exactly tell you," he writes of one of his characters, " whether he had sup'd that night, or went to bed empty, as some Romance-mongers use to do, who regulate all their heroes' actions, making them rise early, and tell on their story till dinner time, then dine lightly, and after their meal proceed in the discourse ; or else retire to some shady grove to talk by themselves, unless they have something to discover to the rocks and trees."

Furetière, writing in the same spirit, declares that he wishes to concern himself with "persons who are neither heroes nor heroines, who will neither raise armies nor overturn kingdoms; but who will be good people of middling rank who quietly go on their usual way, of whom some are handsome and others plain, some wise and others foolish; and the latter have the appearance indeed of forming the greatest number."[1]

Without speaking of the more important works of Cervantes and Rabelais,[2] most of these novels were translated into English, and in the same spirit as they had been written, that is, to be used as engines of war against heroes and heroism. "The French themselves," writes one of the translators, "our first romantique masters . . . have given over making the world otherwise than it was; are now come to represent it to us as

---

[1] "Je ne vous dirai pas exactement s'il avait soupé et s'il se coucha sans manger comme font quelques faiseurs de romans qui règlent toutes les heures du jour de leurs héros, les font se lever de bon matin, conter leur histoire jusqu'à l'heure du dîner, reprendre leur histoire ou s'enfoncer dans un bois pour y aller parler tout seuls, si ce n'est quand ils ont quelque chose à dire aux arbres et aux rochers" ("Roman comique," chap. ix. ed. 1825).

"Je vous raconteray sincèrement et avec fidélité plusieurs historiettes et galanteries arrivées entre des personnes qui ne seront ny héros ny héroïnes, qui ne dresseront point d'armées, ny ne renverseront point de royaumes, mais qui seront de ces bonnes gens de médiocre condition, qui vont tout doucement leur grand chemin, dont les uns seront beaux et les autres laids, les uns sages et les autres sots; et ceux-cy ont bien la mine de composer le plus grand nombre" ("Roman bourgeois," ed. Janet, p. 6).

[2] Rabelais by Urquhart, London, 1653, 8vo; Cervantes in 1612; and again by T. Shelton in 1620 and by J. Philips, 1687.

it is and ever will be."[1] "Among all the books that ever were thought on," writes another, who curiously enough had about the same opinion of the favourite novels of his time as Sidney had had of the drama a century earlier, "those of knight errantry and shepherdry have been so excellently trivial and naughty, that it would amuse a good judgment to consider into what strange and vast absurdities some imaginations have straggled ... the Knight constantly killing the gyant, or it may be whole squadrons ; the Damosel certainly to be relieved just upon the point of ravishing ; a little childe carried away out of his cradle after some twenty years discovered to be the sone of some great prince ; a girl after seven years wandring and cohabiting and being stole, confirmed to be a virgin, either by a panterh, fire or a fountain, and lastly all ending in marriage. . . These are the noble entertainments of books of this kinde, which how profitable they are, you may judge ; how pernicious 'tis easily

[1] Scarron's "Comical romance : or a facetious history of a company of strowling stage-players," London, 1676, fol. Preface to the continuation. The translator is at some pains to anglicize his original ; when Scarron speaks of Paris, the translator puts London ; Ragotin is heard defending Spenser (chapter xv.). The poet in Scarron brags of his acquaintance with Corneille and Rotrou, and in the English text, with Shakespeare, Fletcher, and Jonson (chap. viii.). There were other translations of Scarron : "The whole comical works of M. Scarron," translated by Mr. T. Brown, Mr. Savage, and others, London, 1700, 8vo ; " The comic romance," translated by O. Goldsmith, Dublin, 1780 (?) 2 vol. 12mo. His shorter novels or stories were separately translated by John Davies, who states in the preface of "The unexpected Choice," London, 1670, that he did so at the suggestion of the late Catherine Philips, the matchless Orinda.

A POET'S DREAM REALIZED, FROM "THE EXTRAVAGANT SHEPHERD," 1653.

[p. 401.

seen, if they meet but with an intentive melancholy and a spirit apt to be overborn by such follies;"[1] a spirit, in fact, such as Lady Lurewell's, whose reading of "Cassandra" had, as we have seen, such remarkable consequences.[2]

Efforts made in England to imitate this style and to lead, by means of the romance itself, a reaction against the false heroism that the romance had introduced, proved sadly abortive. These attempts have fallen into a still more profound oblivion than those of the story-tellers of Shakespeare's time. The English were not yet masters of the supple, crisp and animated language which suited that kind of tale, and which the French possessed from the thirteenth century. A few original minds like Sidney in his "Apologie" had employed it; but they formed rare exceptions, and in the seventeenth century most men continued to like either the pompous prose with its Latin periods, held in highest honour by Bacon, or the various kinds of flowery prose used by Lodge, Greene, Shakespeare and Sidney. So the romance writers who attempted to bring about a reaction received no encouragement and were forgotten

[1] "The extravagant Shepherd, the anti-romance, or the history of the shepherd Lysis," London, 1653, another edition 1660. Strange to say, besides some adaptations from Spanish authors ("La Picara," 1665; "Donna Rosina," 1700?), a translation of Voiture's Letters, 1657, the same John Davies of Kidwelly, who had written this eloquent appeal against heroical romances, translated "Clelia," 1656, and part of "Cleopatra" in conjunction with Loveday.

[2] See also in Furetière's "Roman bourgeois" how the reading of "Astrée" made of Javotte "la plus grande causeuse et la plus coquette fille du quartier" (Ed. Janet, i. p. 173).

less from want of merit than because even their contemporaries paid no attention to them. Thinking to open up a new path, they got entangled in a blind alley where they were left. The ground was to be broken anew by more robust hands than theirs, the hands of Defoe.

Some of these attempts however are worthy of attention, notably one in which imitation of Scarron and Furetière is to be found, entitled "The Adventures of Covent Garden."[1] The scene is laid in London among the cultivated upper middle class : life is so realistically represented, that this work, now entirely unknown, is one of those that best aid us to re-constitute that society in which Dryden, Wycherley and Otway lived.

Peregrine, the hero of the tale, spends his evenings at the "Rose" or at "Will's," Dryden's favourite coffee-house, or at the theatre, where the "Indian Emperor," one of Dryden's heroic dramas, was being played. With the Lady Selinda, in whose box he sits, he discusses the merits of the play, the value of the French rules and the license of Shakespeare and Ben Jonson. Many interesting remarks occur in these conversations which seem put in writing after nature, and are very curious in the history of literature. If they do not exactly recall the Molière of the "Critique de l'Ecole

---

[1] "The Adventures of Covent Garden, in imitation of Scarron's city romance," London, 1699, 16mo. "Scarron" is here evidently for "Furetière." This work, the author of which is unknown, has long been forgotten, though deserving a better fate. It is dedicated "to all my ingenious acquaintance at Will's coffee-house."

des Femmes," they will recall Furetière, no insignificant praise. It is, besides, a compliment difficult to apply to any other English novelist of the period. Here is a specimen of literary criticism if not deep, at least lively, such as was going on at the play, or in the drawing-rooms at the time of the Restoration :

" You criticks, said Selinda, make a mighty sputter about exactness of plot, unity of time, place and I know not what, which I can never find do any play the least good (Peregrine smiled at her female ignorance). But, she continued, I have one thing to offer in this dispute, which I think sufficient to convince you. I suppose the chief design of plays is to please the people,[1] and get the playhouse and poet a livelihood ?

" You must pardon me, madam, replyed Peregrine, Instruction is the business of plays.

" Sir, said the lady, make it the business of the audience first to be pleased with instruction, and then I shall allow you it to be the chief end of plays.

" But, suppose, madam, said he, that I grant what you lay down.

" Then sir, answered she, you must allow that whatever plays most exactly answer this aforesaid end are most exact plays. Now I can instance you many plays, as all those by Shakespeare and Johnson, and the most of Mr. Dryden's which you criticks quarrel at as

---

[1] *Cf.* Molière : " Je voudrais bien savoir si la grande règle de toutes les règles n'est pas de plaire, et si une pièce de théâtre qui a attrapé son but n'a pas suivi un bon chemin. . . . Laissons nous aller de bonne foi aux choses qui nous prennent par les entrailles et ne cherchons point de raisonnements pour nous empêcher d'avoir du plaisir " (" Critique de l'Ecole des Femmes," sc. 7).

irregular, which nevertheless still continue to please the audience and are a continual support to the Theatre. There is very little of your unity of time in any of them, yet they never fail to answer the proposed end very successfully. . . . Certainly, these rules are ill understood, or our nature has changed since they were made, for we find they have no such effects now as they had formerly. For instance, I am told the 'Double Dealer' and 'Plot and no Plot' are two very exact plays, as you call them, yet all their unity of time, place and action neither pleased the audience nor got the poets money. A late play called 'Beauty in distress,'[1] in which the author no doubt sweat as much in confining the whole play to one scene, as the scene-drawers should, were it to be changed a hundred times, this play had indeed a commendatory copy from Mr. Dryden, but I think he had better have altered the scene and pleased the audience; in short, had these plays been a little more exact as you call it, they had all been exactly damn'd."

Further, some traits of character almost worthy of Fielding are to be remarked in the course of the tale, though, it is true, it grows confused towards the end, and touches the melodramatic in the same way as Nash's novel. Thus the above conversation is interrupted by the entrance of the coquette Emilia, long before loved by Peregrine who had vainly asked for her hand. "Peregrine would have answered, but a pluck by the sleeve obliged him to turn from Selinda to entertain a lady mask'd who had given him the nudg. He

[1] "Double Dealer," by Congreve; "Plot and no Plot," by Dennis; "Beauty in distress," by Motteux.

presently knew her to be Emilia, who whispered him in the ear : I find sir, what Guyomar said just now is very true :

> That love which first took root will first decay;
> That of a fresher date will longer stay.

Peregrine tho surprised was pleased with her pretty reprimand, being delivered without any anger, *but in murmuring, complaining accents, which never fail to move. . ."*

Thus again, Peregrine goes to the famous St. Bartholomew fair, which was still, as in Ben Jonson's time, a place of general meeting. " Lord C." is there discovered, who had a masked lady with him ; she pulls off her mask and smiles at Peregrine, who again recognizes Emilia. The mixed impressions that this sight makes on the hero are analysed in these terms :

" He took a secret pride in rivalling so great a man, and it confirmed his great opinion of Emilia's beauty to see her admir'd by so accomplish't a person and absolute a courtier as my lord C. These considerations augmenting his love increased his jealousy also, and every little familiarity that my Lord us'd, heightened his love to her and hatred to his Lordship ; he lov'd her for being admir'd by my Lord, yet hated my Lord for loving her."

The vain woman for her part is sufficiently interested in Peregrine to put a stop to a dawning passion which she discovers in him for another woman, and which might have ended in a marriage ; but not at any rate enough to repay his sacrifice by true love. Emilia's artifices are studied with much skill, and the author seems, here too, to be imitating nature, and recounting personal experiences : "*Quorum pars magna fui*," as he says on the title-page of his book. At one time Emilia feels that Peregrine is escaping her ; what does she conceive will keep him attached to her ? At such a crisis she is shrewd enough not to resort to vulgar coquetries, feeling that they are no longer in season. With excellent instinct she guesses that the only means of recovering possession of honest Peregrine is to appeal to his good heart : instead of promising him her favours, she asks of him a service. Peregrine would have despised himself had he not rendered it, and it is only afterwards that he perceives his chain is by this means newly forged. Emilia has fixed ideas on the usefulness of men of this sort, and puts them very clearly before Lord C. Only unsubstantial favours must ever be granted them, in order that the favours by which they see their rivals profit, may not give them too gloomy suspicions. They are very useful for defending publicly their mistress' honour ; they must if possible be men of a lofty and refined mind, for only such persons are simple enough to feed their passions on nothing.

The direct satire and caricature of heroical novels in the style of Scudéry and La Calprenède, which had been also practised in France, is to be found in a few English tales, of which the best, as entirely forgotten as the worst, is entitled "Zelinda, an excellent new romance, translated from the French of Monsieur de Scudéry."[1] With an amusing unconcern, and a

[1] By T. D., perhaps T. Duffet (Bullen), London, Bentley, 1676, 12mo.

very lively pen, the author hastens, on the first page, to give the lie to his title, and to inveigh against the impertinences of publishers in general. " Book-sellers too are grown such saucy masterly companions, they do even what they please ; my friend Mr. Bentley calls this piece an excellent romance ; there I confess his justice and ingenuity. But then he stiles it a translation, when (as Sancho Panca said in another case) 'tis no more so then the mother that bore me. Ingrateful to envy his friend's fame. . . . But I write not for glory, nor self-interest, nor to gratifie kindness nor revenge. Now the impertinent critical reader will be ready to ask, for what then? For that and all other questions to my prejudice, I will borrow Mr. Bays's answer and say, Because—I gad sir, I will not tell you—I desire to please but one person in the world, and, as one dedicates his labours and heroes to Calista, another to Urania, &c., at the feet of her my adored Celia, I lay all my giants and monsters."

There follows a story in the manner of Scudéry, the plot of which, however, is drawn not from Scudéry, but from Voiture,[1] and which is treated in a playful accent, and with an air of persiflage that reminds us of Byron's tone when relating the adventures of Don Juan. It is Voiture indeed, but Voiture turned inside-out. As with Byron, the raillery is from time to time inter-

---

[1] From his "Histoire d'Alcidalis et Zélide." Voiture had begun it in 1633 in the style fashionable at the Hôtel de Rambouillet, and even, as he pretends, with the help of Mdlle. de Rambouillet, to whom it is dedicated. It was left unfinished and was published after his death, being completed by Desbarres. A regular translation of it was published in English in 1678.

rupted by poetical flights, and, as with him, licentious scenes abound and are described with peculiar complacency.

Alcidalis and Zelinda, both pursued by a contrary fate, adore one another, but at a distance: for tempests, pirates, family feuds separate them, according to the classical standard of the grave romances of the day. They mutually seek one another; Alcidalis, who only dreams of Zelinda, has every good fortune he does not want. He believes his *fiancée* has been married to an elderly Italian duke distractedly in love with the young princess: "As we are never so fond of flowers, as in the beginning of spring, or towards the end of autumne; the first for their novelty, and the others because we think we shall see them no more: so the pleasures of love are at no time so dear to us as in the beginning of our youth and the approaches of our age." Alcidalis, deceiving the jealous vigilance of the duke, makes the tour of a promontory in a boat by night, climbs to a window by means of a rope-ladder, and in the second visit gains the favour of the duchess, who was not at all the lady whom he thought to find. "Ye gods! do I again behold the fair Zelinda? cries Alcidalis in his joy (a very pertinent question, for it is to be remembred there was no light)."

Very unseasonably the husband arrives; Alcidalis has as much difficulty in escaping as Don Juan; and the duchess, just like the first mistress of Byron's hero, bursts out into reproaches against her bewildered husband, who has much trouble to obtain her pardon. "O woman! woman!" continues the author in an apostrophe Byron would not have disowned; "thou dark abysse of subtility; 'tis easier to trace a wandring swallow through the pathless air, then to explicate the crafty wyndings of thy love or malice."

During this time, Alcidalis in flight, comes "to the sea side, where a ship being just ready to leave the port (for that must never be wanting to a hero upon a ramble)," he gets on board and resumes his search for the true Zelinda. He encounters many new adventures, and in a battle dangerously wounds a warrior. This warrior is a woman, Zelinda herself. The lovers recognize one another, embrace, and relate their adventures. Alcidalis omits nothing except the episode of the duchess, and shows himself as fond a lover as at starting: "Were I racked to ten thousand pieces, as every part of a broken mirrour presents an entire face, in every part of Alcidalis would appear the bright image of my adored Zelinda." At length they are married; the couple recline at their banquet of love, "and if no other pen raises them, they shall lye there till Doomsday."

V.

Thus in two different ways a reaction showed itself against the literature in fashion, and the merits of those who attempted it only made its failure the more felt. The caricature of the heroic romance and the attempt at the novel of common life were without effect. Their authors had come too soon, and remained isolated; the false heroism now scoffed at in France continued in England until the eighteenth century. The writers under Queen Anne, in order to destroy it, were obliged to recommence the whole campaign. Addison, as we have seen, found heroism still in fashion, and the great romances in their places in ladies' libraries. They were still being reprinted. There is, for example, an English edition of "Cassandra" dated 1725, and one of "Cleopatra" dated 1731. Fielding saw heroism still in possession of the stage, and he satirized it in his amusing "Tom Thumb." Carey attacked it in his "Chrononotontologos."[1]

The hundred years which follow Shakespeare's death are, therefore, taken altogether, a period of little invention and progress for romance literature. The only new development it takes, consists in the exaggeration of the heroic element, of which there was enough already in many an Elizabethan novel; it consists, in fact, in the magnifying of a defect. The imitation of France only resulted in absurd productions which were so successful and filled the literary stage so entirely that they left no space for other kinds of romances. In vain did a few intelligent persons, such as the authors of "The Adventures of Covent Garden" and of "Zelinda," attempt to bring about a reaction; their words found no echo. The other kinds of novels started in Shakespearean times continued to be cultivated, but were not improved. The picaresque romance as Nash had understood it, includes in the seventeenth century no original specimen but Richard

---

[1] These two pieces which appeared in 1730 and 1734 are not, as is often stated, caricatures of classical tragedy. In the same way as the Duke of Buckingham in his "Rehearsal" (1671), Fielding and Carey ridicule heroic drama, born of romance à la Scudéry, as Dryden and his followers had understood it.

Head's "English Rogue,"[1] one of the worst compositions in this style to be found in any literature. The allegorical, social, and political novel, as inaugurated by Sir Thomas More, continued by Bacon, by Joseph Hall, Bishop of Norwich, and by Godwin,[2] that novel which was to gain new life in the hands of Swift and Johnson, is, if we except Bunyan's eloquent manual of devotion, mainly represented in the second half of the century by barren allegories, such as Harrington's "Oceana," 1656, and Ingelow's "Bentivolio and Urania," 1660 ; or by short stories like "The perplex'd Prince," "The Court Secret," &c.[3] When we have read

---

[1] "The English Rogue described in the life of Meriton Latroon," London, 1665, 8vo, continued by F. Kirkman, 1661, *et seq.*, 4 vols. (reprinted by Pearson).

[2] The "Mundus alter et idem," by Hall, was written about 1600, and appeared some years later on the continent, without date. "The Man in the Moon or a discourse of a voyage thither," by F. Godwin, appeared in 1638, and was translated into French, which allowed Cyrano de Bergerac to become acquainted with it : "L'Homme dans la Lune ou le voyage chimérique fait au monde de la Lune" . . . by Dominique Gonzalès (pseud.), Paris, 1648, 8vo. The translation is by that same Baudoin who had already turned Sidney's "Arcadia" into French. Barclay's "Argenis" belongs to European rather than to English literature.

[3] "The perplex'd Prince," by T. S. In this romance Westenia is Wales; Otenia, England ; Bogland, Scotland ; the amours of Charles II. and those of the Duke of York (the Prince of Purdino) are related in it under fictitious names. "The Court Secret," 1689 ; Selim I. and Selim II. represent Charles I. and Charles II. ; Cha-abas, Louis XIV., &c. In "Oceana," Parthenia is Queen Elizabeth ; Morpheus, James I. ; in Ingelow's work, Bentivolio represents "Good will," and Urania "Heavenly light." "Oceana" and "Bentivolio" are didactic treatises rather than romances ; the first is a political treatise, and the second a religious treatise,

ten pages of these it is difficult to speak of them with coolness and without an aggressive animosity towards their authors.

Persistent and close analysis of human emotion and of the passion of love in the way in which Sir Philip Sidney had caught sight of it, disappeared from the novel until the day when a second "Pamela" was to figure on the literary stage, and to fill with emotion all London and Paris, down even to Crébillon fils, who was to write to Lord Chesterfield : " Without ' Pamela ' we should not know what to read or to say." And at reading it, the author of " The Sopha" was " moved to tears."

One work alone was published towards the end of the century in which an original thought is to be found, the " Oroonoko "[1] of Mrs. Behn. The sentiment that animates it is of another epoch, and belongs to a quite peculiar class of novel ; with her begins the philosophical novel, crowded with dissertations on the world and humanity, on the vanity of religions, the innocence of negroes, and the purity of savages. These are the ideas of Rousseau before Rousseau : other ideas of Rousseau had been, as we

---

an enormous morality in prose. "The Pilgrim's Progress" must be placed among religious literature properly so-called, as being its master-work in England.

[1] "The plays histories and novels of the ingenious Mrs. Aphra Behn," London (Pearson's reprint), 1871, 6 vols., 8vo, vol. i. "Oroonoko or the royal slave," first printed, 1698. The adventures and virtues of Oroonoko made him very popular ; his story was transferred to the stage by Th. Southern ; his life was translated into German, and into French (by La Place, 1745). Mrs. Behn's other novels show much less originality. She died in 1689.

have seen, anticipated, in the history of the novel, by Lyly.

Remains of the ordinary heroic style are of course not wanting. Being love-struck Oroonoko, an African negro, well read in the classics, refuses to fight, and following Achilles' example, retires to his tent. "For the world, said he, it was a trifle not worth his care. Go, continued he, sighing, and divide it amongst you, and reap with joy what you so vainly prize!" In trying to carry out this advice his companions are utterly routed, until after two days Oroonoko consents to take up his arms again, and the victors are at once all put to flight. Oroonoko's death is also in the heroical style, but a peculiar sort of heroism which recalls Scudéry, and at the same time Fenimore Cooper.

But more striking are the parts in which the manners of the savages are compared to those of civilized nations. "Everything is well," Rousseau was to say later, "when it comes fresh from the hands of the Maker of things; everything degenerates in the hands of man."[1] Mrs. Behn expressed many years before the very same ideas; her Oroonoko has been educated by a Frenchman who "was a man of very little religion, yet he had admirable morals and a brave soul," an ancestor obviously of Rousseau himself, and a fit tutor for this black "Emile." The aborigines of Surinam live in a state of perfection which reminds Mrs. Behn of Adam and Eve before the fall: "These people represented to me an absolute idea of the first state of innocence, before man knew how to sin: and 'tis

[1] Beginning of "Emile."

most evident and plain that single nature is the most harmless, inoffensive and virtuous mistress. 'Tis she alone, if she were permitted, that better instructs the world than all the inventions of man. Religion would here but destroy that tranquillity they possess by ignorance, and laws would but teach 'em to know offences of which now they have no notion. They made once mourning and fasting for the death of the English governor who had given his hand to come on such a day to 'em and neither came nor sent; believing when a man's word is past, nothing but death could or should prevent his keeping it."

The words "humanity," "mankind," are repeated also with a frequency worthy of Rousseau, and the religion of humanity is set in opposition to the religion of God with a clearness foreshadowing the theories of Auguste Comte. When the sea captain refuses to take the word of Oroonoko as a pledge equivalent to his own, "which if he should violate,. he must expect eternal torments in the world to come,"—" Is that all the obligations he has to be just to his oath? replyed Oroonoko. Let him know, I swear by my honour; which to violate, would not only render me contemptible and despised by all brave and honest men, and so give me perpetual pain, but it would be eternally offending and displeasing to all mankind, harming, betraying, circumventing and outraging all men." [1]

Most of these ideas, including an embryo-taste for landscape painting, were to be cherished and eloquently defended by Rousseau. Mrs. Behn, as a novelist, can

[1] "Oroonoko," *ibid.*, pp. 121, 79, 135.

only be studied with the authors of the middle of the eighteenth century ; she carries us at once beyond the times of Defoe, Richardson, and Fielding, and takes us among the precursors of the French Revolution. With the change she foreshadows, philosophy and social science are perhaps more concerned than the novel proper.

It can, all things considered, be stated with truth that, between the age of Elizabeth, and the age of Anne and the Georges, there is in the history of the novel a long period of semi-stagnation. The seventeenth century, which furnishes hardly any important name, added very little, apart from an exaggerated heroism, to the art of the novel. Defoe, Richardson and Fielding are, as novelists, more nearly related to the men of the time of Shakespeare than to the men of the time of Dryden. They have been thus so completely separated from their literary ancestors that the connection has been usually forgotten. It cannot, however, be doubted.

Now that we have carried so far this sketch of the history of the early English novel, as far indeed as the time of writers whose works are still our daily reading, we have to take leave of our heroes, picaroons, and monsters, of Arthur and Lancelot, Euphues and Menaphon, Pyrocles and Rosalind, Jack Wilton and Peregrine, Oroontades and Parthenissa ; nor let us forget to include in this farewell our Lamias, Mantichoras, dragons, and all the menagerie of Topsell and of Lyly. Mummified, buried and forgotten as most of these romances have long been, they managed somehow not to die childless, but left behind them the seed of better things. "No, those days are gone away," says Keats, thinking of the legends of early times,

> "And their hours are old and grey,
> And their minutes buried all
> Under the down trodden pall
> Of the leaves of many years. . . .
> Gone, the merry morris din;
> Gone, the song of Gamelyn;
> Gone, the tough-belted outlaw;
> All are gone away and past."

With them many reputations are gone. White fingers circled with gold no longer turn over the pages of "Euphues" or "Arcadia." But the writings of the descendants of Greene and Nash and Sidney afford endless delight to-day. And that is why these old authors deserve not the lip-tribute of cold respect, but the heart's offering of warmest gratitude; for they have had the most numerous and the most brilliant posterity, perhaps the most loved, that literary initiators have ever had in any time or country.

AQUARIUS.

INDEX.

INDEX.

A.

Acolastus, 316
Actors, Nash on, 316; as playwrights, 156-158
Addison, 25, 381, 396. 412
"Adventures of Covent Garden," 404-408; 412
"Alcida," Greene's, 112, 155
Alexander, poem imitated from the French romance, 39
Alfarache, Guzman d', 292, 293, 294
Alfred, literature under, 33
"Almahide," 370
"Almanzor and Almahide," 392
Amadis of Gaul, Munday's translation of, 349
Amourists, The, 245
"Anatomie of Absurditie," Nash's, 169 *note*, 279
Andrews, Dr., Sermons by, 382
"Andromaque," Racine's, English translation of, 395, 396
Angennes, Julie d', 352
Anglo-Saxons, songs and legends of the, 32; gloom of the literature of the, 33, 34

"Apologie for Poetrie," Sidney's, 229-233; 235, 254, 255, 301
Apulæus, 86
"Arbasto," 155; 175-178
"Arcadia," Sidney's, 226, 229; account and criticism of, 234-262; popularity, imitations and translations of, 262-283; criticised in the eighteenth century by Addison, Cowper and Young, 270-272; Milton's and Horace Walpole's criticism of, 272; Niceron on, 283; drawings from editions of, 16, 17, 273, 275, 277
"Arcadianism," Dekker and Ben Jonson on, 261
Arcady, land of, 218, 219
Architecture, Elizabethan, 12, 99, 100, 101, 102
Aretino, 298, 348
"Argalus and Parthenia," Quarles', 16, 264, 267; as a chap-book, 271-275
D'Argenson's opinion of England, 24
"Ariosto," 43, 173, 237, 363; Ha-

rington's translation of, 13, 76, 77, 79, 80, 366
"Arisbas," Dickenson's, 146
Arthur, the Celtic hero, 39; and his knights, 35
Arundel, Earl of, 159
Ascham, Roger, denounces foreign travel and literature, 71, 72, 73, 74, 75, 79 *note*, 85, 318; condemns Morte d'Arthur, 63, 74; on the study of Greek and Latin, 87, 88; his views on the old romances endorsed by Nash, 307, 308
"Astrée," d'Urfé's, 205, 247, 364, 365
"Astrophel and Stella," 229, 233, 234
D'Aubigné, 398
"Aucassin and Nicolete," 36, 37, 59, 60, 353

B.

Bacon, Francis, 24, 43; "New Atlantis," 50; and English prose, 52; essay on Gardens, 241; 300, 403, 413
Bacon, Friar, stories about, 28
Bandello, 81 *note*, 86, 147
"Baron de Foeneste," 398
Baudoin, translation of Sidney's "Arcadia" into French, 276-280
Baxter's "Sir Philip Sidney's Ourania," 262
Beattie, 26
Beckett, engraver, 19
Behn, Mrs., 414-417
Bell's "Theatre," engraving from, 14, 97

Belleforest's tales translated and imitated by Paynter, 86; "Histoires tragiques," 147
"Bentivolio and Urania," Ingelow's, 413
"Beowulf," the oldest English romance, 11; facsimile of the beginning of the MS., 31; 33, 34; want of tenderness in, 35
"Bérénice," Racine's, translated by Otway, 397
"Berger extravagant," 21, 280, 398, 401
Bergerac, Cyrano de, his "Etats et empires de la lune et du soleil," 50; his "Pédant joué," 128 *note*; style of, 258; humour of, 289, 290
Berners, Lord, 106-107
Bestiaries, 108, 111, 112, 115, 116, 119
Blount, Charles, Lord Mountjoy, Earl of Devonshire, 227
Blount, Edward, publisher of Lyly's comedies, 137, 138
Boccaccio, 43; "Filocopo," "Amorous Fiammetta," "Decameron," English translations of, 75, 76; 86
Boileau, 258, 356 *note*, 363, 390
Borde, Dr. Andrew, 288, 289, 326
Bossuet, 387
Bovon of Hanstone, poem imitated from a French romance, 39
Boyle, Roger, Lord Broghill, 384-389
Bozon, Nicole, 111
Breton, Nicholas, 192, 198-202
Brunne, Robert Manning de, 38, 39

INDEX. 423

Bullen, 22
Bunyan, John, 159, 413
Burghley House, 12, 101, 102
Byron's " Don Juan," 409, 410

C.

Cæsarius, 48, 49
Callot, 317, 337
Camden Society, 18
" Campaspe," Lyly's, 138
Carey, 412
"Carte du Tendre," 19, 359, 361
" Cassandra," 396, 403, 412 ;
" Cassandre," 362, 364, 382, 383
Castiglione's " Courtier," 76
Caxton's woodcut of Chaucer's pilgrims, 12, 45 ; his editions of Chaucer and work as a printer, 52–55 ; 60
" Cent Nouvelles," 47, 48
Cervantes, 43, 88, 399
Chappelain, Mdlle. G., translator of Sidney's "Arcadia," 277–280
Chapelain, Jean, author of " La Pucelle," 294, 350, 357
Characters, books of, 201-2 note
Charlemagne, poem imitated from French romance of, 39
Charles I., 84 ; 250, 252 ; 366, 382
Charles II., 381
Charles IX., 220
Chartley, 223
Chateaubriand, 231, 283
Chateaumorand, Diane de, 276
Chatterton, 26
Chaucer, Caxton's engraving of his pilgrims, 12, 45 ; a story-teller, but with small influence on the Elizabethan novel, 43, 44 ; homage of Pope and Dryden to, 44 ; faculty of observation in, 49 ; and mediæval story - tellers, 89 ; " Cooke's Tale," 204 ; read by Nash, 296
Chesterfield, Lord, 414
Chettle's edition of " Groatsworth of Wit," 165 note, 321 ;
" Piers Plain," 328, 330, 331
" Chrononotontologos," 412
Cibber, Theophilus, 381
" Civile Conversation," Guazzo's, 72, 73, 76
" Clarissa Harlowe," 25, 26, 31
" Clélie," 361, 364, 370 ; frontispiece of " La Fausse," 20, 375
" Cleopatra," 412 ; Queen, as represented on the English stage, 14, 97 ; "Cléopatre," 364, 369 ; frontispiece of, 20, 371
Clovis, 354
Colet, Dean of St. Paul's, 87
Comte, Auguste, 416
Condé, 352, 357
" Contes Moralisés " Bozon's, 111
Cooper, Fenimore, 415
Copland, 12
Corneille, 278, 282, 343, 355, 363, 373
Coryat, 302 note
Cotterel, Sir Charles, translator of " Cassandre," 373
" Cour Bergère," play derived by Mareschal from Sidney's " Arcadia," 282

"Court Secret," 413
Cowper, on Sidney's "Arcadia," 271
Coxon (or Cockson), Thomas, engraver, portraits by, 13
Crébillon *fils*, 414
Cromwell, 84, 363, 381
Crowne's "Pandion and Amphigenia," 19, 389-391; 392, 395

D.

Davenport, 173
Davies, John, drawing from his translation of Sorel's "Berger extravagant," 21
Day, John, "Ile of Guls," 263; collaborator of Dekker, 331
"Débat de folie et d'amour," 173
Dedekind, 339
Defoe, 25, 26; protest against the abbreviation of "Robinson Crusoe," 123, 124; 199, 260, 270, 294, 313, 320, 335, 345, 348, 390, 404, 417
Dekker, portrait of, 19; on *Arcadianism* and *Euphuism*, 261; on Nash in the Elysian fields, 327; plays and pamphlets by, 330-346; love of literature, 332; gaiety, 333; Lamb on, 332; Nash and, 334; "Wonderfull Yeare," 335-338; advice on behaviour at a play-house, 340-343
Desperriers, Bonaventure, 86
Devereux, Penelope, afterwards Lady Rich, Sidney's "Stella," 223, 224, 225, 227, 228
Dickens, Charles, 124

Dickenson, imitator of Lyly, 145, 146, 161 *note*
Disguises, fondness for, in Elizabethan times, 237-239
"Don Simonides," Rich's, 146, 147
Drayton, 331
Dryden, 354, 363, 389, 392, 396, 404, 417
Du Bartas, 271
Du Bellay, 70
Dupleix, Scipion, historiographer royal, 354
Dyce, reprint by, 18

E.

"Ecclesiastical Polity," Hooker's, 382
Eliot, George, 36, 124
Elizabeth, Queen, portrait by Rogers, 11, 96, 256; by Zucchero, 14; in pastoral romance, 218; manners of, 91-96; learning of, 92; toilettes of, 92; Hentzner on, 96
Elizabethan houses, 101, 102; dress, 128; literary men, 161; amusements, 18, 287, 298
"Emile," Rousseau's, 415
"Empress of Morocco," Settle's, 393, 395
"Endimion," Lyly's, 138, 139; Gombauld's, 19, 367, 369
English, ancestry of the, 40, 41, 42; effect of the French conquest on the literature of the, 43
"English Adventures," Boyle's, 388, 389
"English Rogue," Head's, 413

INDEX.

Erasmus, 51, 87, 88, 348
Essex, Earl of, 159
"Euphues," Lyly's, 103–142; written for women, 104, 105; on women in, 127–130, 133; natural history in, 107, 108–120; moral teaching in, 123, 124, 127; bringing up of children in, 130–132; popularity of, 137–142; Nash on, 139, 140; abbreviation of, 141
"Euphues his censure to Philautus," Greene's, 146, 168
Euphuism, Lyly and, 105; acclimatization of, in England, 106, 107; Shakespeare on, 140; Dekker and, 261
Exeter, Joseph of, 38
Exeter, Marquis of, seat of the, 12

F.

Fayette, Mme. de la, 397
Fénélon's, "Télémaque," 50; "Lettre à l'Académie," 229
Fenton's, "Tragicall Discourses," 80, 81
Fielding, 25, 124, 270, 313, 317, 406, 412, 417
Floire and Blanchefleur, 36
Florio's Montaigne, 227
Ford, Emanuel, disciple of Lyly, 192; "Parismus," 193–198; collaborator of Dekker, 331
Fortescue's, "Foreste," 81
Fouquet, 281
Fournival, Richard de, 107, 108
Fox, George, the Quaker, 158
"Francesco's Fortunes," drawings from, 11

"Francion," 293, 398
French, gaiety of the literature of the, 33, 34
Froissart, 43, 47, 86
Furetière, 398, 399, 404, 405
Furnivall, F. J., 39, 90, 102, 140, 162, 223

G.

Gaedertz, of Berlin, 17
"Gallathea," Lyly's, 139
"Gamelyne," tale of, 204
Gargantua and Pantagruel, story of, 50
Gascoigne, "Adventures passed by Master F. T.," 81
Gawain, a metrical romance imitated from the French, 89
"Généreuse Allemande," Mareschal's, 282
Gheeraedts, 16
Gil Blas, 24
Godwin, F., 413
"Golden boke of Marcus Aurelius," translated by Lord Berners and Sir Thomas North, 106, 107
Gomberville, 356
Gosse, 373
Gower, 296
"Grand Cyrus," romance of, 364, 383, 396
Green Knight, metrical romance from the French, 39
Greene, Robert, illustrations to his work, 11, 15; stories of, translated into French, 27; denounces foreign travel, 73 *note*; natural history of, 112;

imitator of Lyly, 145, 146, 170, 171 *note;* Warner on, 149, 150; character, birth, and education, 152, 153, 154; travels, 74, 154; writings, 151, 155; "Groats-worth of Wit," 156, 157, 158; "Repentances," 158, 159, 162; marriage, 159, 160, 166, 167; Nash on, 160, 161; complaint against plagiarists, 163; abuse of Shakespeare, 164, 165; illness and death, 162, 163, 165, 166, 167; Ben Jonson on, 166; contributions to the novel literature of Elizabethan times, 167-192; *Euphuism* of, 170-173; "Penelope," 174; imitated by Breton, 198, 199, 201; by Lodge, 202; style of his novels, 290; 295, 296, 300, 418

Greville Fulke, Lord Brooke, 220, 226, 245

Grimestone's translation of tales by Goulart, 81

"Groats-worth of Wit," 156, 157, 165 *note,* 328

Grobianism, 339, 344, 345, 346

"Grobianus," 338, 339

Guazzo's "Civile Conversation," translation of, 76

Guevara, 86, 106

"Gulliver's Travels," 50, 51

"Guls Horne-booke," Dekker's, 28, 261, 339, 340, 341, 342, 343

"Gwydonius," Greene's, 155

H.

Hall, Joseph, bishop of Norwich, 73 *note,* 413

Hampole, Rolle de, story of a scholar of Paris, 48, 49

Harington's translation of "Ariosto," 13, 76, 77, 79, 80, 366

Harrington's "Oceana," 413

Harrison's "Description of Britaine," 101

Hartley, Mrs., as Cleopatra, 14, 97

Harvey, Gabriel, Nash and, 297, 298

Hastings, battle of, results of, 33

Hathaway, 331

Haughton, 331

Havelock the Dane, a metrical romance, 39

Head, Richard, writer of a picaresque novel, 294, 412, 413

Henri IV., 352

Henrietta of England, Duchess of Orleans, 386, 387

Henry VIII., learning of, 87

Henslowe, 328, 331

Hentzner on Elizabeth, 96

"Heptameron," Reine de Navarre's, 398

Herbert, William, Shakespeare's friend, 234

"Hercules of Greece," romance, 349

Heroical novels and plays in England and France, 347-397; reaction against, 397-412

Heywood, T., 331

"History of the Ladye Lucres,"

81; drawing from German edition of, 14, 82
Hood, Robin, stories about, 28
Hooker, Richard, 382
Hurst, Richard, drawing from his version of Gombauld's "Endimion," 19
"Hystorie of Hamblet," 81

I.

"Ibrahim ou l'illustre Bassa," 364
"Ile of Guls," Day's, 263
Ingelow's "Bentivolio and Urania," 413
"Isle of Dogs," Nash's, 297, 298 *note*

J.

"Jack Wilton," Nash's novel of, 297; account of, 308–321
Jessopp, Dr., 218
Johnson, Dr., 151, 413
Jones, Inigo, sketches by, 14, 100; architecture of, 100, 101
Jonson, Ben, 151, 261, 270, 331, 341 *note*, 348, 404, 407

K.

Keats, 418
Kemp, the actor, 18, 287, 298
Kenilworth, festivities at, 223; park of, 241, 242
King Horn, a metrical romance, 39
"Knight of the Swanne," frontispiece of, 12, 61, 64

L

Labé, Louise, "Debat de Folie et d'Amour," 173

La Calprenède, 356, 369, 384, 398, 408; Mme. de Sévigné on, 353
"Lady of May," Sidney's masque of, 229, 289
La Fontaine, 232
Landmann, Dr., 106, 123 *note*
Laneham, Robert, account of the Kenilworth Festivities, 85
Languet, Hubert, the French Huguenot and friend of Sidney, on English manners, 136, 137; correspondence with Sidney, 221, 223, 288; poem on, in the "Arcadia," 222
"La Pucelle," 294, 350
Layamon, 39, 40
Lee, 392, 397
Leicester, Earl of, 91, 96, 159, 223
"Lenten Stuff," Nash's, 324, 325
Le Sage, style of, 47; "Gil Blas," 294
"Le Sopha," 24
"Lettre à l'Académie," Fénélon's, 229
"Life and Death of Ned Browne," Greene's, 187, 188
Lindsey, Earl of, 382
Lodge, Thomas, imitator of Lyly, 145, 150, 151; birth, education, travels, 202; novels, 203; "Rosalynde," 144, 204, 205, 206, 207–215; 290, 403
Longueville, Mme. de, 352, 357
"Looking Glasse for London and England," by Greene and Lodge, 215
Louis. XIII., 354

INDEX.

Louis XIV., 352
Loveday, Robert, translator of La Calprenède's "Cléopatre," 369; frontispiece of, 20, 369, 371
Ludlow Castle, 219, 220
Lyly, John, editions of "Euphues," 27; denounces foreign travel, 73 *note*; writes for women, 104, 105; his style, 107; knowledge of plants and animals, 119, 120; the moral teaching of Lyly's "Euphues," 126–135; comedies by, 137–139; imitators of, 145–215; Sidney's style compared with, 255; kind of novel, 290; and the Martin Marprelate Controversy, 297; an ancestor of Richardson, 317; anticipates Rousseau, 131, 415

M.

Malory's "Morte d'Arthur," 54–57, 60–63
"Mamillia," Greene's, 154, 155, 168
Mandeville, 296
Map, Walter, 38; his faculty of observation, 49
Mareschal, Antoine, 282
"Margarite of America," Lodge's, 202, 203
"Marianne," 24
Marlowe, heroes and heroines of, 247, 249; dies young, 295; Nash's criticisms of, 299, 306, 307
Mary, Queen of Scots, 92
Massinger, 331

Master Reynard, 292
"Matchless Orinda," The, 384, 391
Medicis, Marie de, 276
Melbancke, imitator of Lyly, 145
Melville, Sir James, ambassador of Mary Queen of Scots to the English court, on the manners of the English, 91–95; on the liking of the Elizabethans for disguises, 239
"Menaphon," Greene's, 146, 155, 160, 185–187
Meres, Francis, 198 *note*, 254 *note*, 300
Mérimée's style, 305
"Midas" comedy by Lyly, 139
Middleton, 331
Milton's "Comus," 220, 221; opinion of Sidney's "Arcadia," 250, 251
Molière, his love for old songs, 232; his denunciation of the behaviour of gallants at the playhouse, 343, 344; the "Précieuses ridicules," 373; English translations of, 397; the "Critique de l'Ecole des Femmes," 405
Monmouth, Geoffrey of, 38, 41
Montaigne, 43
Montausier, 352, 388, 391
Montchrestien, Antoine de, 354, 355
Montemayor's "Diane," 76; translation of, 227; style of, 229; imitated by Sidney, 236
Montesquieu's "Lettres persanes," 132

More, Sir Thomas, writes in Latin; the "Utopia," 50, 51; Erasmus' opinion of, 87; hero in Nash's novel, 348; his "Utopia," a political novel, 413
Morris, William, 63
"Morte d'Arthur," Malory's, 54-59; Ascham on, 63
Munday, Anthony, imitator of Lyly, 145, 193, 331, 349
Mürger's "Scènes de la vie de Bohème," 150, 151
"Myrrour of Modesty," Greene's, 155, 168, 349

N.

Nash, Thomas, portrait of, 18; his stories translated into French, 27; initiator of the *picaresque* novel, 294; birth, education, studies, and travels, 295, 296; works of, 297; love of poetry, 299, 300; style and vocabulary of, 302-307; Dekker on, 327, 334; begins the novel of real life, 347, 348; 406, 412, 418
Navarre, Queen of, 86
Newcastle, Duchess of, drawing from "Nature's Pictures," 20, 379; literary works of the, 374-381
Newton, 24
North, Sir Thomas, 106, 107
Novels, in Tudor times, 80-102; as sermons, 123, 124, 127; pastoral, 235-283; picaresque, 291-346; heroical, 348-414; philosophical, 414-416

Nucius, Nicander, on the study of Italian and French in England, 87; on the manners of English women, 91

O.

"Oceana," Harrington's, 413
Octavian, romance imitated from the French, 39
Oliver, Isaac, miniature of Sir Philip Sidney, 15, 221, 243; drawing by, 69
"Oroonoko," Mrs. Behn's, 414-417
"Orlando Furioso," Ariosto's, 76, 77, 79, 80
Osborne, Dorothy, letters to Sir William Temple, 382-384, 387, 388
Otway, 389 *note*, 397, 404
Owen, Miss, 373

P.

Padua, John of, architect, 12, 101
"Pamela," Richardson's, 127, 249, 250, 414
"Pandion and Amphigenia," Crowne's heroical novel of, 389, 390, 391
"Pandosto," Greene's, 155, 168, 169, 175, 178-185
"Parismus," Ford's, 193; compared with "Romeo and Juliet," 194-198
"Parthenissa," Lord Broghill's, 384, 385; Dorothy Osborne on, 386, 387
Pas, C. de, drawings by, 19, 369
Paynter, translations of tales by,

28 ; " Palace of Pleasure," 80;
  tales by, 86
Peele, 295
" Penelopes Web," Greene's, 155
Penshurst, Sidney's birthplace,
  Ben Jonson's description of,
  16 ; drawing of, 217
Pepys, Mr., 383
Percival, romance imitated from
  the French, 39
Percy, 26
" Perimedes," Greene's, 155
" Perplexed Prince," 413
" Petit Jehan de Saintré," 47
Petrarca, 43
Pettie, George, on English prose,
  72, 73 ; " Pettie Pallace," 81
Philips, Catherine, " matchless
  Orinda," 19 ; 370-373
Philips, Mr., husband of "match-
  less Orinda," 373
" Philomela," Greene's, 171-173
" Philotimus," Melbancke's, 148
" Pierce Penilesse," Nash's, 322-
  324
"Piers Plain," Chettle's, 328-330
" Pilgrimage to Parnassus," 140
Pinturicchio, 174
Pius II., 83
" Planetomachia," Greene's, 155
" Polexandre," 364
Pope, Alexander, 218, 237, 381
Porro, Girolamo, engraver, 13
Poussin, Gaspard, 237
" Princesse de Clèves," 24, 397
Prose, little cultivated in Eng-
  land, 50
Prynne, 382
Puritans, and Charles I., 250;
  manners of, 364, 366 ; and
  Cromwell, 381
Pytheas, an old traveller, 33

Q.

Quarles, Francis, drawings from
  his " Argalus and Parthenia,"
  16 ; " Emblemes," 264, 267
" Quinze joyes de Mariage," 338,
  345, 346
" Quip for an upstart Courtier,"
  Greene's, frontispiece of, 15,
  265 ; description of, 189-192

R.

Rabelais, 43 ; and the " Utopia,"
  51, 52 ; 88, 128, 289, 297, 304,
  305, 399
Racine, 355, 363, 395, 396, 397
Racine, Louis, 123
" Railleur ou la Satyre du Temps,"
  Mareschal's, 282
Raleigh, 218
Rambouillet, Hôtel de, 352, 356,
  357, 370-373 ; Mme. de, 381
Renaissance, tentative, of the
  fourteenth century, 43 ; short
  stories, outcome of, 47 ; period
  of the, 60, 68 ; effects of the,
  69, 70; art of the, 79 ; women
  at the time of the, 133 ; costumes and furniture in Sidney's
  " Arcadia " pure, 244 ; characteristics of, 303
" Returne from Parnassus," 140
  note, 316 *note*, 326
Rich, " Farewell to militarie profession," 81 ; imitator of Lyly,
  145 ; works of, 146, 147

INDEX.

Rich, Lord, husband of Sidney's "Stella," 223, 227
Richardson, 25, 26, 123, 124, 127, 131 ; " Pamela " and " Clarissa Harlowe," 169, 202 ; borrows from Sidney, 249, 250 ; 270, 317, 378, 417
Richelieu, 352
Rivers, Lord, 134
Robert the Devil, drawing of, 57
"Robinson Crusoe," 123, 124, 159
Robinson, Ralph, translator of More's " Utopia," 50, 51
Rogers, William, engraving by, 11, 256
"Roland," poem imitated from a French romance, 34, 39
" Roman bourgeois," 398
" Roman comique," 398
Romances, end of chivalrous, 25 ; pastoral, 217-283 ; heroical, reaction against, 397, 398, 411 ; French, translated and read in England, 363-384
Ronsard, 43, 88
" Rosalynde," Lodge's, compared with " As you like it," 202-213
Rousseau's " Emile," 130, 131 ; " Social contract," 221 ; and Mrs. Behn, 414-416
Rowley, 331

S.

Sainte More, Benoit de, poems by, 34, 35
Saint Dunstan, literature under, 33
Salisbury, John of, 38

"Sapho and Phao," Lyly's, 138
Sarasin, 350
Scarron, 398, 400 *note*, 404
" Scipion," 365
Scott, Sir Walter, 26, 36
Scudéry, George de, 278, 348, 355, 356 ; preface to " Ibrahim," 358, 408, 409, 415 ; Madeleine de, " Clélie," 20 ; 355-357 ; 361, 384, 388, 396
Settle's " Empress of Morocco," 20, 21, 293 ; 392-395
Sévigné, Mme. de, admirer of heroism in romances and plays, 352, 353, 357, 381
Shakespeare, interior view of a theatre in time of, 17, 18, 286 ; 24 ; glory of, 26 ; editions of the plays of, 27 ; 43 ; his daily reading, 85 ; outcome of his age, 88 ; Cleopatra, 97, 99, 156 ; source of " Twelfth Night," 147 ; of " Winter's Tale," 155, 178-185 ; " Parismus " compared with " Romeo and Juliet," 194-198 ; of " As you like it," 202-213 ; source of part of " Lear," 262 ; source of " Two Gentlemen of Verona," 149, 150, 236 *note;* little known in France, 279 ; a copy of, in Louis XIV.'s library, 281 ; earliest French criticism on, 282 ; humour of, 289 ; beginning of career of, 299, 300 ; on music, 300, 301 ; interposes himself in his plays, 314, 315 ; and Molière, 343 ; style of, 403, 404

Shirley, 288
Sidney, Mary, Countess of Pembroke, portrait of, 16; fame of, 234, 235; works dedicated to, 263
Sidney, Sir Philip, 217-283; miniature and portraits of, 221, 222; "Arcadia," 16, 17, 226, 229, 234-283; stories of, translated, 27; birth, 219; education and travels, 74, 220, 221; love for "Stella," 222-225; "Shepheardes Calender," dedicated to, 225; at Wilton, 226; Marriage and death, 226, 227; literary work and style, 228-263; "Apologie," 229-233, 235, 254, 255, 301; Du Bartas on, 274; known to Florian, 283; humour of, 288-290; Nash on, 299; ancestor of Richardson, 317; prose of, 403; analysis of feeling by, 414
"Sir Charles Grandison," 31
Smith, Wentworth, 331
Smollett, 294
Smyth's "Straunge and tragicall historics," 81
"Sociable letters," Duchess of Newcastle's, 378
"Sopha," 414
Sorel, Charles, 280, 298
Spenser, Edmund, 43; Nash on, 298, 299, 300
Steele, Richard, 25, 381
"Stella," books dedicated to, 227, 228
Sterne, 313

"Strange Fortunes," Breton's, 199, 200
Suckling, Sir John, 388
Surrey, Earl of, 74, 245; Nash on, 300; 348
Swift, 345, 384, 413
Swinburne, 63
Sylvius, Æneas (Piccolomini), 81

T.

Tacitus' opinion of the English, 123
Tarleton, 298
Tasso, 43; translations in English of, 76
"Télémaque," 50
Temple, Sir William, 382, 384, 387, 388
"Tendre" country, Map of, 19, 20, 359, 361
Teniers, 317
Tennyson, 63
Thackeray, 124; "Vanity Fair," 291
Thorpe, John, architect, 12, 101
"Til Eulenspiegel," 292
Tintoretto, 244
Titian, 244
"Tom Thumb," Fielding's, 412
Tom-a-Lincoln, stories of, 28
"Tom Jones," 26
Topsell's Natural History, 14, 15, 103, 109, 111-113; 115-117; 119, 121, 125, 145, 171, 417
Tormes, Lazarillo de, 292-294
"Tragicall Discourses," 80, 81
Tristan, tales of, 25
"Trojan War," romance imitated from the French, 39

INDEX.

Turberville, drawings from his "Booke of Faulconrie," and "Noble Art of Venerie," 15
Turenne, 352

U.

Universities, Lyly's experience of, 153
D'Urfé, 247
"Utopia," More's, 50, 51

V.

Villemain's lectures on the eighteenth century, 31, 32
Vinci, 231
Virgil, 363, 398
Voiture, 409
Voltaire's prose tales, 47, 51

W.

Wace, 39
Walpole, Horace, 272
Walsingham, Sir Francis, 220, 226
Warner, imitator of Lyly, 145; "Pan his Syrinx," and "Albion's England," 148, 149
Warwick, Guy of, metrical romance from the French, 19, 39, 67, 349–351
Watson, Thomas, 139, 245
Webster, heroines of, 249; 331
Wentworth, 331
Whetstone, collections of tales translated by, 28; "Heptameron," 81
William the Silent, 226
Wilson, 331
Wilt, John O., drawing by, 17
Wireker, Nigel, 38, 49
Women, their learning and manners in Tudor times, 89, 90, 91; Ascham and Harrison on, 90, 91; Caxton on, 133, 134; English and Italian compared, 133, 134; Rich's stories for, 147; excluded from the stage, 301, 302
"Wonderfull Yeare," 335–338
Worde, Wynkyn de, 12, 64
Wroth, Lady Mary, "Urania," 268–270; Ben Jonson on, 270
Wyatt, Sir Thomas, 74, 245
Wycherley, 404
Wyle, Nicolaus von, 82

X.

Xenophon, 86

Y.

Young, on the "Arcadia," 271, 272

Z.

"Zelauto, the Fountain of Fame," Munday's, 146, 147, 148
"Zelinda," adaptation of Voiture's, 408–412
Zucchero's portrait of Elizabeth, 14, 329

UNWIN BROTHERS, THE GRESHAM PRESS, CHILWORTH AND LONDON.

BOOKS FOR RECREATION AND STUDY

T. FISHER UNWIN, Publisher,

SIX-SHILLING NOVELS

In uniform green cloth, large crown 8vo., gilt tops, **6s,**

Effie Hetherington. By ROBERT BUCHANAN. Second Edition.
An Outcast of the Islands. By JOSEPH CONRAD. Second Edition
Almayer's Folly. By JOSEPH CONRAD. Second Edition.
The Ebbing of the Tide. By LOUIS BECKE. Second Edition.
A First Fleet Family. By LOUIS BECKE and WALTER JEFFERY.
Paddy's Woman, and Other Stories. By HUMPHREY JAMES.
Clara Hopgood. By MARK RUTHERFORD. Second Edition.
The Tales of John Oliver Hobbes. Portrait of the Author. Second Edition.
The Stickit Minister. By S. R. CROCKETT. Eleventh Edition.
The Lilac Sunbonnet. By S. R. CROCKETT. Sixth Edition.
The Raiders. By S. R. CROCKETT. Eighth Edition.
The Grey Man. By S. R. CROCKETT.
In a Man's Mind. By J. R. WATSON.
A Daughter of the Fen. By J. T. BEALBY. Second Edition.
The Herb-Moon. By JOHN OLIVER HOBBES. Third Edition.
Nancy Noon. By BENJAMIN SWIFT. Second Edition. With New Preface.
Mr. Magnus. By F. REGINALD STATHAM. Second Edition.
Trooper Peter Halket of Mashonaland. By OLIVE SCHREINER. Frontispiece.
Pacific Tales. By LOUIS BECKE. With Frontispiece Portrait of the Author. Second Edition.
Mrs. Keith's Crime. By Mrs. W. K. CLIFFORD. Sixth Edition. With Portrait of Mrs. Keith by the Hon. JOHN COLLIER, and a New Preface by the Author.
Hugh Wynne. By Dr. S. WEIR MITCHELL. With Frontispiece Illustration.
The Tormentor. By BENJAMIN SWIFT, Author of " Nancy Noon."
Prisoners of Conscience. By AMELIA E. BARR, Author of " Jan Vedder's Wife." With 12 Illustrations.
The Gods, some Mortals and Lord Wickenham. New Edition. By JOHN OLIVER HOBBES.
The Outlaws of the Marches. By Lord ERNEST HAMILTON. Fully illustrated.
The School for Saints : Part of the History of the Right Honourable Robert Orange, M.P. By JOHN OLIVER HOBBES, Author of "Sinner's Comedy,' "Some Emotions and a Moral," "The Herb Moon," &c.
The People of Clopton. By GEORGE BARTRAM.

11, Paternoster Buildings, London, E.C.

T. FISHER UNWIN, Publisher,

WORKS BY JOSEPH CONRAD

I.

AN OUTCAST OF THE ISLANDS

Crown 8vo., cloth, **6s.**

"Subject to the qualifications thus disposed of (*vide* first part of notice), 'An Outcast of the Islands' is perhaps the finest piece of fiction that has been published this year, as 'Almayer's Folly' was one of the finest that was published in 1895 . . . Surely this is real romance—the romance that is real. Space forbids anything but the merest recapitulation of the other living realities of Mr. Conrad's invention—of Lingard, of the inimitable Almayer, the one-eyed Babalatchi, the Naturalist, of the pious Abdulla—all novel, all authentic. Enough has been written to show Mr. Conrad's quality. He imagines his scenes and their sequence like a master; he knows his individualities and their hearts; he has a new and wonderful field in this East Indian Novel of his. . . . Greatness is deliberately written; the present writer has read and re-read his two books, and after putting this review aside for some days to consider the discretion of it, the word still stands."—*Saturday Review*

II.

ALMAYER'S FOLLY

Second Edition. Crown 8vo., cloth, **6s.**

"This startling, unique, splendid book."
Mr. T. P. O'CONNOR, M.P.

"This is a decidedly powerful story of an uncommon type, and breaks fresh ground in fiction. . . . All the leading characters in the book—Almayer, his wife, his daughter, and Dain, the daughter's native lover—are well drawn, and the parting between father and daughter has a pathetic naturalness about it, unspoiled by straining after effect. There are, too, some admirably graphic passages in the book. The approach of a monsoon is most effectively described. . . . The name of Mr. Joseph Conrad is new to us, but it appears to us as if he might become the Kipling of the Malay Archipelago."—*Spectator*

11, Paternoster Buildings, London, E.C.

T. FISHER UNWIN, Publisher,

THE EBBING OF THE TIDE

BY

LOUIS BECKE

Author of " By Reef and Palm "

Second Edition. Crown 8vo., cloth, **6s.**

" Mr. Louis Becke wields a powerful pen, with the additional advantage that he waves it in unfrequented places, and summons up with it the elemental passions of human nature. . . . It will be seen that Mr. Becke is somewhat of the fleshly school, but with a pathos and power not given to the ordinary professors of that school. . . Altogether for those who like stirring stories cast in strange scenes, this is a book to be read."—*National Observer*.

PACIFIC TALES

BY

LOUIS BECKE

With a Portrait of the Author

Second Edition. Crown 8vo., cloth, **6s.**

" The appearance of a new book by Mr. Becke has become an event of note —and very justly. No living author, if we except Mr. Kipling, has so amazing a command of that unhackneyed vitality of phrase that most people call by the name of realism. Whether it is scenery or character or incident that he wishes to depict, the touch is ever so dramatic and vivid that the reader is conscious of a picture and impression that has no parallel save in the records of actual sight and memory."—*Westminster Gazette*.

" Another series of sketches of island life in the South Seas, not inferior to those contained in ' By Reef and Palm.' "—*Speaker*.

" The book is well worth reading. The author knows what he is talking about and has a keen eye for the picturesque."—G. B. BURGIN in *To-day*.

" A notable contribution to the romance of the South Seas."
T. P. O'CONNOR, M.P., in *The Graphic*.

11, Paternoster Buildings, London, E.C.   *d*

T. FISHER UNWIN, Publisher,

CLARA HOPGOOD

BY

MARK RUTHERFORD

EDITED BY

REUBEN SHAPCOTT

Second Edition. *Crown 8vo., cloth,* **6s.**
(*The Third and Cheaper Edition is now ready, Crown 8vo., cloth,* **3s. 6d.**)

"The writer who goes by the name of Mark Rutherford is not the most popular novelist of his time by any means. There are writers with names which that recluse genius has never heard of, probably, whose stories give palpitations to thousands of gentle souls, while his own are quietly read by no more than as many hundreds. Yet his publisher never announces a new story by the Author of 'Mark Rutherford's Autobiography,' and 'The Revolution in Tanner's Lane,'—which we believe to be one of the most remarkable bits of writing that these times can boast of—without strongly exciting the interest of many who know books as precious stones are known in Hatton Garden. . . . . . 'Clara Hopgood' is entirely out of the way of all existing schools of novel-writing. . . . . . Had we to select a good illustration of 'Mark's way' as distinguished from the way of modern storytellers in general, we should point to the chapter in which Baruch visits his son Benjamin in this narration. Nothing could be more simple, nothing more perfect."—*Pall Mall Gazette.*

11, Paternoster Buildings, London, E.C.

T. FISHER UNWIN, Publisher,

A FIRST FLEET FAMILY: BEING A HITHERTO UNPUBLISHED NARRATIVE OF CERTAIN REMARKABLE ADVENTURES COMPILED FROM THE PAPERS OF SERGEANT WILLIAM DEW, OF THE MARINES

BY
LOUIS BECKE and WALTER JEFFERY

Second Edition. Crown 8vo., cloth, **6s.**

"As convincingly real and vivid as a narrative can be."—*Sketch*.

"No maker of plots could work out a better story of its kind, nor balance it more neatly."—*Daily Chronicle*.

"A book which describes a set of characters varied and so attractive as the more prominent figures in this romance, and a book so full of life, vicissitude, and peril, should be welcomed by every discreet novel reader."—*Yorkshire Post*.

"A very interesting tale, written in clear and vigorous English."—*Globe*.

"The novel is a happy blend of truth and fiction, with a purpose that will be appreciated by many readers; it has also the most exciting elements of the tale of adventure."
Morning Post.

CUBA AND PORTO RICO
WITH THE OTHER ISLANDS OF
THE WEST INDIES,
BY ROBERT T. HILL,
Of the United States Geological Survey.

BAHAMAS,	A valuable Work of Reference.
JAMAICA,	A Scientific Presentation.
HAITI,	An indispensable Guide.
SAN DOMINGO,	A readable Narrative.
ST. THOMAS,	500 Pages.
ST. KITTS,	160 Illustrations.
ANTIGUA,	Price 16s.
MONTSERRAT,	
GUADELOUPE,	
MARTINIQUE,	
ST. LUCIA,	
BARBADOS,	
ST. VINCENT,	
GRENADA,	
TRINIDAD.	

Flora,
Climate,
Soil,
Products,
Minerals,
Agriculture,
Scenery,
Topography,
Sanitation,
People,
Transportation,
Statistics,
History,
Routes of travel,
Administration,
Accessibility,
Possibilities.

"His book is a very good example of its kind, carefully written, full of the information that is required."—*The Times.*

"He has written the most important book that has been published on the subject."—*Chicago Tribune.*

"His volume of 429 pages, with profuse Illustrations and an index, forms a little condensed library of reference."—*N. Y. Times.*

"The book is well and ably written ... is brightened by a truly magnificent series of photographs ... beautifully reproduced on fine paper."—*Edinburgh Scotsman.*

Tourists to Cuba, Porto Rico and the West Indies will find this a most reliable and the only General Handbook.

T. FISHER UNWIN, PATERNOSTER SQUARE, LONDON.

3 GREAT ART BOOKS EDITED BY JOSEPH PENNELL.

Lithography and Lithographers:
SOME CHAPTERS IN THE HISTORY OF THE ART.

With Technical Remarks and Suggestions by JOSEPH and ELIZABETH ROBINS PENNELL. Together with 154 Illustrations, besides a Frontispiece Portrait of Joseph Pennell by JAMES MCNEILL WHISTLER, and other original lithographs by A. Legros, W. Strang, C. H. Shannon, A. Lunois, J. McLure Hamilton and T. R. Way. (13½ × 10½ inches, xiii + 279 pp.) £3 13s. 6d. net. Also, a Fine Edition signed by JOSEPH PENNELL; on Japan paper, £15 15s. net.

"The selection is done as admirably as the reproduction, which is saying much.... The authors.... present, in fact, the first complete and intelligent historical survey of the art in the different countries of the world."—*St. James's Gazette.*
"The present volume contains a great number of admirably-reproduced examples by many artists, and these illustrate in a very complete manner, not only the growth of ideas in regard to lithography, but also the varied possibilities of the stone in different hands."—*Morning Post.*

"The Greatest English Artist since Hogarth."
The Work of Charles Keene.
With Introduction and Comments by JOSEPH PENNELL, and numerous Pictures illustrative of the artist's method and vein of humour; to which is added a Bibliography of Selected Works and Notes by W. H. CHESSON. The Edition is limited to 750 copies (250 of these for America), an Ordinary Edition at £3 13s. 6d. net., and 15 copies of a Fine Edition at £15 15s. net.

"This work.... will be a revelation even to those who are beginning to estimate this consummate artist at his true merit."—*Literature.*
"Mr. Pennell's is the fullest critical appreciation of Keene we have yet had."—*Daily News.*
"Extraordinarily good and well worth having...., we thank Mr. Pennell very warmly for the thorough performance of a task that called out to be accomplished."—*Daily Chronicle.*
"The bibliography by Mr. W. H. Chesson.... is a labour of real merit and value, carried out in a thorough and workmanlike manner."—*Graphic.*

"The Masterpiece of a Great Spanish Artist."
PABLO DE SEGOVIA:
The Adventures of a Spanish Sharper.
BY FRANCISCO DE QUEVEDO.
Illustrated with over 100 Drawings by DANIEL VIERGE. With an Introduction on "Vierge and his Art," by JOSEPH PENNELL; and "A Critical Essay on Quevedo, and his Writings," by H. E. WATTS. Super royal 4to, parchment, old style (limited edition), £3 13s. 6d. net.

London: T. FISHER UNWIN, PATERNOSTER SQUARE.

www.ingramcontent.com/pod-product-compliance
Lightning Source LLC
Chambersburg PA
CBHW032131010526
44111CB00034B/583